Afrikology: Deconstructing and Reconstructing Knowledge and Value In Africa

Insights in Semiotic Economics

Series Editors: Tony Bradley & Ronnie Lessem

Insights in Semiotic Economics

Semiotic Economics is a new sub-discipline. It relates to the current ferment about the teaching of economics and its connection to real-world events. Since the global financial crash (2007–09), groups such as Post-Crash Economics, Rethinking Economics, and Alternative Economics have formed, led by students and many young, radical academics. They have questioned why so little conventional textbook and taught economics explains real-world experience and phenomena, especially at a macro-level. As such, a range of models have been dusted off, fashioned and re-emphasised, many of which are centuries old, to challenge the dominance of neoliberal, market-based, capitalist economics.

At the same time, there has been a surge in the development of heterodox approaches to economics, which reflect many contemporary concerns. These include ecological, feminist, indigenous, well-being, core/non-monetary, social-solidarity, Islamic, spiritual, love and mutualist economics—to name but a few perspectives—each of which contests the idea of TINA (there is no alternative to neoliberalism). In consequence, there is an urgent need to examine the ways in which economic meaning is reflected in each of these alternative perspectives, alongside the assumptions of more conventional approaches. This is the primary purpose of Semiotic Economics.

Even so, beyond the narrow academic objective of examining the meanings of alternative economic models, there is a deeper requirement, which is to document and develop cases that reflect the distinctive cultural genius of particular societies, out of which these approaches are emerging. In this respect, our perspective on Semiotic Economics is an evolution of the work of leading theorists and commentators in integral economics over several decades, notably Professor Ronnie Lessem and his co-workers (1). One of these co-workers, Tony Bradley, has taken a pioneering role in developing this new perspective of Semiotic Economics. Together they are the editors of this series for Beacon Academic, reflective of the need for a Northern world Research Academy, as part of the global movement for communiversities (2).

Insights in Semiotic Economics will address four specific aspects of this community-based and academic movement. Firstly, the meaning-systems that are used to define alternative economics; secondly, the questions, theories and models generated within these approaches; thirdly, empirical and philosophical studies of culturally located cases, considered through the lens of semiotics, or the study of meaning-systems, signs and significance; fourthly, we will directly address the lacuna in classical semiotics which neglects the deep structures and archetypes that shape meaning, and which are so important in interpreting the significance of economic models.

But, we describe the development of Semiotic Economics as urgent for more than academic reasons. As leading economist Professor Neva Goodwin (3) has commented:

> The neoliberal experiment… contributes to poverty and inequality, while gravely damaging communities, natural resources, democratic processes and human well-being. In the new economy the reorganisation of important aspects of work and ownership will make it possible for people to be happier and more fulfilled, while extracting a lower level of resources. The transition to a new economy needs to be as inclusive and inviting as possible. There is great urgency to making the transition before we cross socio-political as well as ecological tipping points.

Yet this doesn't go far enough in focusing on what we mean by Semiotic Economics. In the summer of 2019 (when we are writing), it appears that many of these tipping-points are already being crossed. As such, the need for dissemination of alternative economics is vital. This is already beginning to happen. However, few people are systematically presenting the alternative meaning-systems (semiosis) that lie behind these alternatives. This edited book series will do just that. And in doing so, it will empower academics, students and educated lay-people alike, who are making these meanings, to pursue their activities and studies, in alternative economics more fully. Additionally, it will offer an opportunity for those researching and teaching—through the lens of Semiotic Economics—to bring the fruit of their work to a wider audience. This is the first book series on Semiotic Economics. Its appearance could hardly be more timely for the challenges we face, as the crises of the 21st century deepen, threatening cultures and the very sustainability of human life on earth, because of our conventional economic system.

1   **Lessem** R and **Schieffer** A (2010) *Integral Economics: Releasing the Economic Genius of your Society*. Abingdon. Routledge

2   **Lessem**, R, **Adodo**, A and **Bradley**, T (2019) *The Idea of the Communiversity: Releasing the natural, cultural, technological and economic GENE-ius of societies.* Manchester. Beacon Academic

3   **Goodwin**, N (2014) Rethinking Economics Conference Address, New York

ABOUT THE AUTHORS

Anselm Adodo is the Director of Africa Centre for Integral Research and Development, Nigeria and founder of Arica's foremost herbal research Institute, the Pax Herbal Clinic and Research Laboratories (Paxherbals). His research interest is Phytomedicine, Taxonomy of African medicinal plants, indigenous knowledge systems, rural community development, Africanized economic models, health policy reform, and education transformation in Africa. Apart from publications in journals, magazines, national dailies and peer-reviewed journals, Anselm has written more than ten books. He is an adjunct visiting lecturer at the Institute of African Studies, University of Ibadan, Nigeria, an Adjunct Research Fellow of the Nigerian Institute of Medical Research, a Fellow of the Nigerian Society of Botanists, a Research Associate at the University of Johannesburg, South Africa, and an adjunct professor at Morehouse School of Medicine, Atlanta, Georgia, USA.

Ronnie Lessem, born in Zimbabwe and now based in the UK, was co-Founder of TRANS4M (France) which has since evolved, together with Dr Anselm Adodo and Aneeqa Malik, into Trans4m Communiversity Associates (TCA) in the UK, which focuses on the regeneration of particular societies. It is currently mainly active, through its emerging Communiversities—promoting Communal learning, a Regenerative Pilgrimium, Research academy and integral Laboratory—in Southern Africa (South Africa, Zimbabwe), West Africa (Nigeria), the Middle East (Egypt, Jordan), the Near East (Pakistan), and Europe (UK). Hitherto Ronnie Lessem has launched projects on European management, with IMD in Switzerland, European-ness and Innovation, with Roland Berger Foundation in Germany, African management, with Wits Graduate Business School in South Africa, and Arab as well as Islamic Management, with TEAM International in Cairo and Jordan.

He studied economics at the University of Zimbabwe, the economics of industry at the London School of Economics, Corporate Planning at Harvard Business School, and has since written some 50 books, the most recent, with Anselm Adodo and Tony Bradley, on *The Idea of the Communiversity* (Beacon Academic, 2019), and, with Munya Mawere and Daud Taranhike, *Nhakanomics: Harvesting Knowledge and Value for Regeneration Through Social Innovation* (African Talent Publishers, 2019).

Afrikology: Deconstructing and Reconstructing Knowledge and Value In Africa

Anselm Adodo & Ronnie Lessem

Foreword by Dr Douglas Mboweni

Insights in Semiotic Economics, Volume 2

Series Editors: Tony Bradley & Ronnie Lessem

BEACON ACADEMIC

First published in the UK by Beacon Academic, Earl Business Centre, Dowry Street, Oldham, OL8 2PF

First paperback edition published in 2021

www.beaconacademic.net

ISBN: 978-1-912356-43-0 Paperback
ISBN: 978-1-912356-44-7 Ebook

Cataloging-in-Publication record for this book is available from the British Library

Cover design by Joel José

CONTENTS

FOREWORD

Dr Douglas Mboweni CEO, Econet Wireless Zimbabwe Ltd

Fr. Dr. Anselm Adodo and Prof. Ronnie Lessem address, in this powerful work, a central question. What is the kind of framework that will work to establish sustainable balance in our frightfully fragmented world? Adodo and Lessem proffer an answer with their worlds-wide dimensional framework with a focus on Afrikology.

I have known Fr. Dr. Anselm Adodo and Prof. Ronnie Lessem for more than three years and have been exposed to their tremendously encouraging worlds-wide dimensional thinking and work. Their perspective on the transformation of individuals, entities and societies has had a huge impact on my own perspective and work at individual, village and corporate levels. I am a citizen of Joseph village under Chief Negari in the Mwenezi District of Masvingo Province, Zimbabwe.

At village level, I am using the worlds-wide dimensional perspective to *Afrikologically* uplift Joseph village, to be a local and global player without losing its local grounding. Currently I serve as the Chief Executive Officer of Econet Wireless Zimbabwe Limited, Zimbabwe's largest telecommunications company, listed on the Zimbabwe Stock Exchange. Even at this corporate level, I am finding the worlds-wide dimensional view to be a very empowering framework of conducting business in a multi-cultural world.

We live in a world which is desperate for impactful and sustainable solutions, a world that has been let down by so many man-made systems, a world that has suffered immensely from the irresponsible actions of mankind. It is not a surprise therefore that there are loud cries emanating from all the four ends of the globe, for an inspired way of thinking and doing things, for actionable thinking that functions in harmony with nature as well as culture whilst riding on the appropriate technologies to establish sustainable enterprises. The future has to be completely re-imagined and innovated in a holistic manner that embraces the dignity of every individual as a human being, the preservation of every square inch of the globe and the equitable stewardship of every resource placed before mankind by the creator.

In their work, Adodo and Lessem, emphasise the need to consciously and actively recognise that communities, organisations and societies grow and evolve interdependently, thereby releasing their GEN*E*-ius. What is this GEN*E*-ius? The Gen*e*-ius approach, as they articulate it, necessitates the need to be locally Grounded whilst Emerging both locally and globally so as to newly globally Navigate and ultimately globally-locally *E*ffect both the local and global environment in a sustainable way. Therefore, as it tries to understand and create knowledge epistemologically, the Afrikology GEN*E*-ius is found by being Grounded in the African South, Emerging both locally and globally, thereby drawing also on the East, North and West to Navigate and ultimately *E*ffect the local and global environments.

Such a process, Adodo and Lessem argue, is very important for global integrity which can only be reached when all the four worlds engage effectively whilst remaining anchored on their respective grounds. This is very important in a multicultural environment as the dominance of one culture, or the "One world fits all" approach, creates an imbalanced world, to the detriment of the peoples of the world. Lessem in theory, and Adodo via Pax Herbals in Nigeria - also with Abou El Eisch-Boes citing the renowned case of the Sekem Group restoring the Earth in Egypt - in practice, remind us that complementarism and integration are fundamental aspects to holistic living. In so doing the best aspects of the different worlds are integrated, without the loss of the local grounding of each world. This is why the *Afrikology* work by Adodo and Lessem is critical in a world where the African voice has been drowned by the voices from other worlds. I am already participating in initiatives so that the African voice is heard *Afrikologically*.

Lessem and Adodo's work provides a valuable contribution to the sustainable balanced future of our world. The serious inequalities created by the individualism of the North and West can be solved by picking and integrating lessons from the *Ubuntu* (brotherhood) of the South. This recognises that each individual's humanity and welfare is ideally expressed in relationship to that of others. Every person depends on other people to be a person. It is my hope that you will be encouraged and challenged to think and act outside the box, as you thoughtfully go through and reflect on this important work.

Douglas Mboweni (PhD)
Citizen of Joseph Village
Current CEO of Econet Wireless Zimbabwe Limited

Preface
Hearing the Wild Drumbeat

*Tony Bradley, Series Editor and Centre Director, SEARCH –
Social and Economic Action Research Centre at Hope,
Liverpool Hope University, UK*

We live in an age of increasingly violent culture wars. Some of these involve extremes of physical violence. Whilst others stem from the violent use of language, symbols and meanings, to impose the hegemony of cultural and political ideologies. Perhaps, the most tragic situations are those that oscillate between violence that is both physical and significant, in the sense of pointing to signs of the times. As I write this Foreword, we are in an important liminal moment, between the election of Joe Biden, as President-Elect of the United States of America, and the admission, by President Donald Trump, of his defeat in that election.

How long this threshold time is, you will know, as a reader, but I cannot guess. What is evident, once again, is that the culture wars divide, in that nation, is immensely deep, of chasm proportions, exposing the many rift valleys of identity across the world, not least affecting those of African origin and citizenship. The tribes are disunited. Consequently, I can think of no more important time, than the current one, in which to welcome this *significant* book on the study of African identity, culture, research and enterprise.

Positioning *Afrikology* within *Insights in Semiotic Economics*

This book series—*Insights in Semiotic Economics*—seeks to shed a direct light on the ways in which alternative economic models emerge from the ground of particular communities and cultures, with their distinctive meaning-systems. The first volume (Bradley et al, 2020) drew attention to the correspondence that exists between Islamic philosophy and culture, and what many of the authors in this Series refer to as an Integral worldview. This perspective identifies the multi-faceted ways in which a cycle of development, from grounding in communities, through cultural emergence and knowledge-based navigation, effects new and more holistic economic practices.

This GEN*E*tic process—grounding, emergence, navigation and *effect-ing*—is able to address imbalances in the dominant economics of neoliberal-ism, by GEN*E*rating alternative systems. In the previous case—from Volume 1—the authors revealed ways in which the Integral-Islamic has produced a system of finance that challenges debt and interest-based monetary policy and practice. Equally, in doing so, they lit up a path towards examining econom-ics semiotically; that is to say, addressing methods for uncovering the mean-ing-systems within economic models.

In this second volume of the Series, Ronnie Lessem and Anselm Adodo (as-sisted by some of their colleagues in the Trans4m Communiversity Associates community, TCA, most specifically P. Maximilian Abou El Eisch-Boes, from the renowned Sekem [see Chapter 8] in Egypt) turn their attention to the cul-tures of Africa, and the economics which that culture has, in the past, and is, in the present, distinctively generating. This exercise could not be more timely.

The current culture wars—which have sparked an acute phase of violence in the United States and is threatening to spill-over into other parts of the world, not least the UK, where I live and work—has focused on the simple, irreducible fact that Black Lives Matter. And, of course, all black lives, as all human cultures, have their origins *Out of Africa* (Blixen, 1937/1954), as Karen Blixen, the Danish anthropologist and agriculturalist, famously wrote.

Not that establishing the nature of African heritage is easy. The case of Professor Jessica Krug, a white Jewish woman from Kansas, who posed as a black person of African diaspora heritage, and who taught on race and iden-tity, brought questions of cultural appropriation into sharp relief, earlier in 2020. Her popular book, *Fugitive Modernities* (Krug, 2018), which sought to explore the history of "those fleeing expanding states and the violence of the transatlantic slave trade", proved to have a more significant title than even she had admitted. As a child of the port city of Liverpool, which was at the very dark heart of the evil triangular slave trade, and became prosperous through its market in black flesh, I wince at the ways in which African culture can be so misused, even in the 21st century.

Less acutely, but, also, reflecting the nature of sensitivities surrounding African culture, have been the cases of British music stars Adele and Rita Ora, who have been accused of cultural appropriation. These issues are of far less seriousness than the brutality and violence surrounding the injuries to Jacob Blake and the killings of George Floyd and Breonna Taylor. If, as you are read-ing this, you don't recognise their names, please search them out. What their tragedies reveal, as we enter the third decade of the 21st century, is that the world has yet to wake up to the profound debt which all civilizations owe to Africa, its heritage and, equally, our need to consider and respect its destiny.

It is in this light—and, of course, for those of us who know and have lived in Africa, it is the antithesis of a dark continent—that this book will illuminate the distinctive cultural contribution of Africa, through what the authors, white and black, European and African residents but, each born from African soil, refer to as *Afrikology*. Nor is it a single cultural or philosophical thought-form. Africa is not a country, of course, it is a continent. It encompasses such diversity as Morocco and Mozambique, Sudan and South Africa, Angola and Algeria.

Equally, whilst Africa has contributed so much to human thought, culture and economy, it has, also, been the recipient of global movements, from the ancient civilizations of Greece and Rome, to modern Europe, the Americas and, latterly, but not in*significantly*, China. But, it is the hegemonic influence of the Northern and Western worlds over Africa's Southern and Eastern soul that is the starting-point for this book. *Afrikology* is born out of the interplay between the communities of its continent, with their unique values and spirituality, and the reasoning and enterprise of its multitudinous peoples. Europe does not have a monopoly in thinking and research. America is not the only source of business, economics and markets.

Indeed, the drumbeat, the music and the dance of Africa, quite frequently, expresses the meaning of the continent as eloquently as does its words. And, as part of our Series on *Insights in Semiotic Economics*, it is meaning which is at the core of this book. Semiotics is the science of meaningful signs. In our Series we are concerned to demonstrate the relationships between economic objects, their subterranean significance—what I call their 'archetypes of signification' (see Bradley, 2020)—the pointers that they make towards processes of transformation and the interpretations which work out in new innovations, enterprises and fresh economic objects. Herein, Ronnie Lessem and Anselm Adodo address each of these, as they orientate their way around the re-GEN-Erative cycle.

The themes of the book

They begin, as does all meaningful business and economics, with examining value, especially the value of the land, in both the ancient and modern settings of Egyptian culture. This is so much a part of the origination of *Afrikology*. From there they take us into an examination of African cosmology, especially through the lens of the Dogon people, revealing that this represents the centrepiece of African culture and wisdom.

In the second major part of the book the authors turn from local Grounding to the emergence of *Afrikology* onto a global stage. Firstly, this is through African Creation Energy, with its 'squaring of the circle', through which we see the cyclical GENE and its four poles in fresh light. Secondly, they unveil the distinctive African ethno-philosophy, on the shoulders of such as Placide Tempels (1945/2010), *Bantu Philosophy*, and the political programmes of Nkrumah and Senghor. Each, in their own way, reflect the traditionalist grounding of *Afrikology* in their tribal homelands, whilst, at the same time, indicating the direction of Africa's unique cultural modernity.

Through the third part of the book Lessem and Adodo take us to one of the most significant aspects of *Afrikology*, so far as they are concerned, as scholars, namely that of the distinctive research philosophies and epistemic roots of African learning. For too long the Northern and Western worlds have claimed a global domination of epistemology and an interpretation of what it is 'to know', all too frequently through a secularised version of rationalist science and method. But, as these authors ably demonstrate, Afrikological science and research is deeply integral, intertwining process and substance, so that the Western fetishizing of the subject-object dichotomy is dissolved.

Indeed, the rediscovery, in recent decades, by European and American social science, of emic anthropology, phenomenology, action research, the range of ethno-methodologies, and semiotics itself—the meaningful heart of this Series—each can be traced back to an *Afrikology* of methodology. Thence, in the second chapter of Part Three, we are taken to a contemporary example of *Afrikological* research-in-practice, through the work of CIRD-A (Centre for Integral Research and Development out of Africa).

The fourth and final Part of the book completes the GEN*E*tic cycle by revealing the Nature-grounding to science-based innovation, of two of Africa's most remarkable and transformative communal businesses. First, we see the fusion of European associative thinking and African rootedness, through the biodynamic agricultural pioneer-enterprise of Sekem (with its learning centre at Heliopolis University), in the Egyptian desert, as it was, before Sekem turned it green. This is courtesy of one of Sekem's principals: P. Maximilian Abou El Eisch-Boes.

Second, we are taken into the communitalist world of Anselm Adodo's own plant and Nature-power-based herbal medicine centre, of Pax Herbals. Therein we see a different fusion of Roman Catholic spirituality and traditional African knowledge, where the life of plants is understood more as co-creators of the world than as crops to be harvested. The significance of Pax Herbals through the Covid-19 pandemic has been a remarkable example of how a distinctive indigenous approach to medicine has attracted the eyes of the world, away from vaccines and global Pharma, onto the life of African soil and plants. This is a fitting final chapter, before the authors conclude, as we see through their eyes, the work that they have pioneered, both, in theoretical practice (Lessem) and practical theory (Adodo), as *integral advantage* and *transformation management*.

What we hear as well as see through the encircling of African philosophy and praxis, in this book on *Afrikology*, is the wild drumbeat of Africa, which needs to be recognised for what it is, in the world's destiny of the 21st century. This is not a continent of poverty, malnutrition, disease and economic inequality. Of course, there are some pockets of each of these phenomena in Africa, as there are in Europe, North America, Asia and Latin America. But, the heart and drumbeat of Africa is to reflect its role as the origination and the end-steward of civilization. Through *Afrikology* we see beyond the superficial Western concerns of cancel culture and appropriation, to dig deep into the soil of human society and unearth the African universe of solidarity and relationship. "Ubuntu: I am because we are". It is a wild drumbeat that the world desperately needs to hear. And thanks to Lessem and Adodo its persistent rhythm is able to be more acutely heard.

November, 2020

References

1 **Blixen**, K (1937/1954) *Out of Africa*. London: Penguin Books.
2 **Bradley**, T (2020) Semiotic Economics: the fourth way beyond neoliberalism: North, Chapter 7, in Bradley, T, Lessem, R, Malik, A and Oshodi, B, *Integral to Islamic Finance: a semiotic approach, Insights in Semiotic Economics, Volume 1*. Manchester: Beacon Academic.
3 **Bradley**, T, **Lessem**, R, **Malik**, A and **Oshodi**, B (2020) *Integral to Islamic Finance: a semiotic approach, Insights in Semiotic Economics, Volume 1*. Manchester: Beacon Academic.
4 **Krug**, J A (2018) *Fugitive Modernities: Kisama and the politics of freedom*. Durham: Duke University Press.
5 **Tempels**, P (1945/2010) *Bantu Philosophy*. Orlando: HBC Publishing.

PART ONE

Centering and Integration

CHAPTER 1

Local Identity to Global Integrity

European man walked into Africa by and large totally incapable of understanding the continent, let alone of appreciating the raw material of mind and spirit with which this granary of fate, this ancient treasure house of the lost original way of life, was so richly filled. He had, it is true, an insatiable appetite for the riches in the rocks, diamonds and gold… but not for the precious metal ringing true in the deep toned laughter of the indigenous people around him.

Laurens Van der Post (1) *The Dark Eye of Africa*

COMMUNIVERSITY DNA: LOCAL IDENTITY TO GLOBAL INTEGRITY

- *Worldliness* thereby accommodating all worlds, makes for 'global integrity' in a *trans-modern* world, whereby
- *Each world is incomplete and imbalanced* in individual self and needs the other three, complementary-wise, to become fully and thereby integrally operational.
- *Each world has its underdeveloped or dysfunctional manifestation,* and its developed, or functional, one, the latter applying as one world becomes integrated with the other.
- *Global Integrity* is reached when one world is able to engage with the other three worlds, *inter-culturally* (south, east, north, west, centre), and with its own depths, *intra-culturally* (grounding, emerging, navigating, effecting, integrating).

1.1. Introduction

1.1.1. What Gave Rise to our Imbalanced World?

The worlds of political economics and enterprise, on the one hand for us (2), scientific research and learning on the other, are dominated by one cultural frame of reference—"north-western"—to the point that the hidden strengths of other cultures, even those of China and India which are being ignored by individuals, organisations and societies, alike. Arguably this is a reason why many are pursuing a strongly "westernised" technological and economic course today for the global spread of the coronavirus, which, though heralding geographically from China, is a symptom, more generically, of our distance from and domination of nature, as original "southern" grounds of our being.

Before the demise of that communism that only nominally prevails in China today, there was at least an alternative political and economic approach, albeit one in opposition. Now, the post-modern age of the information society is almost universally capitalist and even in its latest manifestation, that of globalisation, with Donald Trump and Boris Johnson ruling the "north-western" roost (at the time of writing in May, 2020) it exploits difference (market and consumer segmentation) rather than differentiating and integrating between and within cultures and economies, academies and societies. No ecology, including the modern economy, polity or university, can thrive for long when one element is rampant. Perhaps that is what the coronavirus today is telling us!

For us, one of the most striking aspects of the COVID-19 pandemic is how the most important and powerful symbol of life, the air we breathe has also become a suspicious carrier of the deadly virus. We now wear face masks to protect us from an enemy that we think may enter into our body system through the very symbol of life itself, the air.

And yet, one of the most glaring signs of our disconnect from nature is our neglect of that very air. In the world of modernity, such has become a forgotten dump site for a host of gaseous effluents, radiations, and industrial pollutants. We have totally ignored the importance of air quality and its significance to life. Instead, our fascination is elsewhere: television, mobile phones, iPod, iPad, computers, atomic bombs, social media, newspapers, all of which so readily grab our senses and mould our participation with the world. The ability of, now especially, social media to shape our worldview, reasoning and sense of judgment is amazing, for good and evil.

COVID-19 is calling our attention to the changes happening in the air itself. The changing atmosphere, global warming and climate change, deforestation, destruction of our ecosystems, human encroachment into animal habitats, genetic modification of food, gas flaring, etc. reflect our massive dissociation from our integral world. The air is the element that keeps us alive, and without which, nothing happens. By denying that birds and animals have their own form of language, we cut ourselves off from the deep meanings of our words, severing language from that which supports it. We inhabit a world where everyone is talking, and no one is listening. Communication then becomes a shouting game rather than a listening interaction. No wonder we find it so hard to communicate even amongst ourselves!

Our health, our life, our future, depends on the quality of the air around us. It is, as we shall later see in chapter 7, our very life capital. The rich, the poor, the sick, the healthy, black people, white people, we all breathe the same air. There is no separate air for different categories of people. At the end of the day, what we put into the air will come back to us, either to purify us or poison us. It is the air that most directly envelops us. The air is the element we are most directly in touch with. Without air, none of us can survive more than a few minutes. As we busy ourselves rushing to meet the next appointments and prepare to attend the following meetings or plan for a future wedding or anniversary, we must not forget that we do all these because the air is there. Without air, we are nothing. Everything else is illusory. The air is the real deal. And now we turn from our very such nature to our polity and economy, and thereafter to culture, and then back to nature.

1.1.2. From Left and Right Towards Stasis and Disintegration

For the past 250 years then, and most particularly during the course of the twentieth century, global politics and economics has been marked by two sets of politically and economically—as well as intellectually—divisive, rather than culturally and psychologically integrative, forces. This has been reflected in the "East/West" mutually antagonistic divide of communism/capitalism, and the North/South chasm of wealth and poverty. The result, worldwide, has been, to a considerable degree, stasis and disintegration. We see this vividly illustrated by the Brexit divide in Great Britain specifically, in recent years, and by the rise of populism in the world at large, as Left and Right suffer their mutual demise. In fact, and moreover, the so-called economic success stories today, most notably China now in the so-called "east", feed off America's excesses in the proverbial "west", as per its hyper-consumption and militarily oriented, thereby grossly indebted, society, and indeed brings with it a virus in its wake.

The collapse of the Berlin wall within the Germanic heartland of Europe seemingly heralded, four decades ago, the re-birth of a continent, if not of the whole of the world. The sudden demise of communism called for—in prospect but not yet in current reality—newly variegated technological

5

and economic, integral and dynamic, worldviews, born out of variety rather than duality. For both capitalism and communism were born out of partial, monolithic views of our humanity. Each being European, and respectively Scottish and German in origin, neither doctrine, despite the seminal nature and scope of each, attempted to capture the cultural richness of the European continent (see opening quotation to this chapter from *Afrikaaner*, Laurens Van der Post), not to mention the whole of the globe, an endeavour taken up by artists (Van der Post was a novelist) rather than political economists, scientists or technologists.

Whereas Adam Smith, by implication, called upon the merchants of the world to unite, Karl Marx invited the workers to do the same. Sad to say, never the twain really met. Ironically in fact, Smith promoted the cause of labour (labour theory of value), and Marx promoted capital (*Das Kapital*). Each, moreover, appealed to one class of society rather than to another—Smith to the merchants, Marx to the proletariat—while neither appealed explicitly to Scottish-ness, to English-ness, or to German-ness, not to mention African-ness or Asian-ness, or indeed Zimbabwean-ness. Yet Smith, little recognised today in each case, was an embodiment of the Scottish Protestant enlightenment, while Marx was a messianic (albeit non-confessing) Jew. In the same way as European cultural variety was explicitly ignored by both of the great modern ideologies, so was the variety of "trans modern" cultures, and indeed integral worldviews, both in Europe and worlds-wide, in communities and societies at large. Capitalism or communism was assumed to be of unilateral appeal, north of the equator or south, eastern hemisphere or west.

1.1.3. The Ever-Present North-South Divide

On the one hand, then, the supposed dissolution of the East/West divide, after the fall of the Berlin wall, has never materialised, with America, and now China as well as Russia, continuing to ride roughshod across an ever more polarised world (witness the tragedy in Syria today). On the other hand, the ever present, indeed today growing, North/South divide between the rich nations and the poor represents an ever more repressive and destabilising, chasm, rather than a dynamically integral growing, reciprocally together. This is seen most acutely in the many crises in the "southern" world, e.g. the land rights issue in Zimbabwe and South Africa or the collapse hitherto of Greece and the Euro/zone. For poverty and ignorance, on the one hand, inevitably breeds social, political and economic instability. Rampant materialism, on the other, feeds into personal and national debt, aided and abetted by banks eager to lend.

Such a "North/South" divide, moreover, accentuates "global terrorism", on the one hand, and the current crisis in Europe, on the other, if not in the world at large, with the *Middle East* occupying centre-stage, as our global horror story unfolds, because indeed it is the missing centre, at least in our integral terms. The two way, polarised state of Europe, north-south meanwhile, or indeed of the UK (Scotland versus England) or in fact Spain (Catalonia versus Madrid) is therefore a shadow of the divide across the world stage, just like the East-West divide in NATO (Turkey versus Western Europe) in the same way as "the power of the markets" is an economic projection of our own cultural and spiritual, if not also political, repression. How more specifically so?

1.1.4. Divided Inner and Outer Worlds

From Two to Four Worlds: Unity-in-Variety

While the reality of "communist" East and "capitalist" West, if not also "rich" North and "poor" South, in political and ideological terms, have proved altogether divisive rather than mutually supportive, their symbolical importance in cultural and psychological terms is what is key to our *Four Worlds*. Essentially, as we move from the politics of division to the psychology of integration, contradiction between opposing forces is replaced by complementarity between opposites, rivalry between factions is transformed into unity through variety, disintegration within and between worlds, and indeed growing inertia, is turned into duly integral realities. How might this come about, both internally (inner worlds)—through learning and research, as well as externally (outer worlds)—economically and enterprise-wise, with an integral communiversity-and-polity, in our terms, in between? We start with the outer worlds.

Inhibited Outer Worlds: The Outer Calling

Politics, economics and enterprise, through the ages, have been characteristically outgoing activities. For unlike philosophical, spiritual, artistic or even profound scientific activity it has involved extroverted rather than introverted attitudes and behaviours. The aggressive, individualistic, and competitive "north-western" (Anglo-Saxon) nature of polity, economy and indeed military activity, today heralded via *knowledge management*, has in fact dominated man's consciousness in the modern era to the exclusion of more spiritual and artistic activities, more like *knowledge creation*, even though, in Europe at least, an artistic Renaissance and spiritual Reformation had to precede a scientific Enlightenment and Industrial Revolution. Consequently, as technological and economic adaptation has raced ahead of psychological and cultural transformation, natural and cultural diversity have fallen by the wayside, rather than serving to evoke integral realities, that is for us across east and west, north and south.

Economies at large, as well as business enterprises around the globe then, if they and their societies are to prosper *together* over the long term, need to draw more purposefully and creatively on their indigenous *communal*, alongside their exogenous *worldly-wise*, cultural and philosophical soils. While the business and economic ethos in America is superficially ("topsoil"-wise) different from that in China—and these two countries combined have recently dominated the business world—further variants, including those within Europe, Africa and much of Asia today, and in Japan hitherto, remain now substantially hidden. It is as if a business and economic geologist has been unable to differentiate, at least in any fundamental way, granite economic and enterprise formations in the Pyrenees from limestone business cliffs in Wales! The implication is, as it were, that volcanic rock in Japan (ever less so today), limestone formations (only superficially visible) in China, and coal shale in America are the only identifiable formations in the "econosphere". Now, moreover, it seems that even the volcanic rock is being eroded, leaving us, if we're not careful, with only "world class" coal shale, or upcoming limestone formations, with which to do business!

The old ideological divide in fact, whereby either the free marketplace (capitalism) or state (communism) reigned supreme, served to hide such worldly variations, whether Van der Post's cultural-psychological terms or our technological-economic ones, even distorting, along the way as we have noted, the original ideas of Adam Smith (3) and Karl Marx (4). Perceived business and economic differences were restricted to easily visible surface phenomena, what may be termed "topsoil" or "surface" attributes, such as culinary preferences, susceptibility to corruption, social habits, flexible labour practices and time keeping orientations of different cultures. Substantive "bedrock" or "mainstem" differences were, by implication then, lumped together under the respective guises of misconstrued "capitalism" or "socialism", with a so-called mixed economy being seen to lie somewhere in the nondescript in between.

For all the core or "root" natural and cultural differences, such as in the arts and in depth religion, differences between, for example, the French and the English, the American and the European, the Brazilian and the Chinese, the Shona and the Ndebele in Zimbabwe, none of these entered into the forefront of our cultural-and-economic awareness. It was as if political and economic ideology concealed cultural and psychological, if not also natural, variety. Why then should this have been so?

Hidden Inner Worlds: Our Inner Calling

Until comparatively recently, that is within the last thirty years or so, culture and psychology were considered to be entirely peripheral to business and economics. Ronnie Samanyanga Lessem can well remember, in seeking his future vocation in the late fifties, being told by the then Minister of Finance, in colonial Rhodesia, that psychology (he wanted to pursue industrial psychology at the time) was for "backroom boys". Still to this day, business in its raw and primal context, and "the economics of the euro-zone", for example, is much more about buying and selling, or indeed in today's terms, "e-commerce" or "financial bailouts", "competitiveness" or "export markets" than it is about personal development and the purposeful natural as well as cultural co-evolution, of, for instance, a pre-modern into a trans-modern Greece or Germany, Zimbabwe or Zambia, in its nature and spirit, its technology and economics.

Economics then, as a rationally based science underpinning business activity, has been hitherto more concerned with "culture free" notions of "monetarism" or "scientific socialism", or indeed now financial derivatives, comparative interest rates and the monolithic and overbearing "view of the markets", than with culturally comparative philosophies, or naturally based ecosystems. In fact, whereas at least since the nineteen sixties, industrial and organisational psychology, if not also anthropology, has entered into mainstream MBA curricula, that same MBA remains an extraverted "western" import, wherever in the world you go, while economic policy at large has remained dominated by the capitalism–socialism divide, without due consideration, as Unger has pointed out, of innumerable, imagined alternatives. Even today, the Anglo-Saxon world is arguing for "flexible labour" if not also "flexible pound" (capitalist) policies, against its more "social welfare" (socialist) Euro oriented continental European counterparts, while the rest of the world, China if not Japan, Korea and India apart, stand watching from the side-lines. Old habits, our "two-world" heritage, die hard!

To that extent such evolved philosophies as, for example, the rationalism of the Enlightenment, Renaissance based Italian humanism and Taoist based Chinese holism, and the naturalism of indigenous peoples, have remained on the periphery watching their worlds literally catch fire, economically eclipsed by the narrowly misconceived pragmatist Adam Smith and the equally misinterpreted "scientific socialist" Karl Marx. Moreover, economic dynamics, in its capitalist dispensation, is restricted to "wilful entrepreneurs", on the one hand, and depersonalised "markets", on the other, so that social and cultural, not to mention ecological and spiritual, for example Taoist (Chinese) or Ntu-ist (African "vital force"), dynamics, are left out in the cold, while "westernised" leadership and entrepreneurship rule, ever more, the roost. Even "management", which at least at the end of the last century, was differentiated between American and Japanese, if not also European, approaches, has been eclipsed

9

by the one size, invariably "western" leadership and entrepreneurship, that allegedly fits all.

Indeed the altogether restrictive, and allegedly "culture-free" capitalist-communist duopoly, had been recently—in the nineteen seventies and eighties—partially broken by the Japanese, and their hitherto successful brand of communitarianism, which seemed to transcend the conventionally polarised economic debate. In the nineties, though, the Japanese communitarian miracle, came to an end, to be replaced, more recently, by a Chinese if not also an Indian form of materialism, that is only differentiated from "western" capitalism through, at least in the Chinese case, the material political, governmental influence on the economy. If we're not careful we could be back to square one, or even square zero, with "north-western" capitalism, or what Thomas Piketty (5) has recently called all-pervasive, and for him regressive, "proprietarianism", of a kind that would even lead Adam Smith —imbued with his moral sentiments—to turn in his grave, becoming the only available horse in town!

Indeed, this is why we have "anti-capitalist" and "emergency extinction" protestors on the streets today! In fact, from our "four world" view of Integral Realities, the most viable alternative to the ideological duopoly, as opposed to Integral Dynamic, of Smith and Marx, has originally come not from "culture free" politics and economics, but from the culturally sensitised depth psychologist and integral philosopher Carl Jung (5). That said, and anecdotally, when Samanyanga, then serving in the 1990s as adjunct faculty at the renowned IMD (Institute for Management Development) in Lausanne, proposed that Jung's work served as the key to open the "European Management" door, as opposed to the typically "westernised" approach that business school was then following, he was literally thrown out the institute's door, duly relegated to a portacabin outside!

In fact, while Jung himself might be seen to be totally disconnected from the world of business and economics, the Myers Briggs inventory based on Jung's work, is one of the most prolifically used "management tools" in contemporary enterprise. Needless to say, this pragmatic tool for assessing managerial style has been totally disconnected from the dynamic and integral pursuit of individuation, or self-actualisation—and the overall psycho-dynamic philosophy and archetypal imagery of Jung. So why has Jung been such a seminal influence on the birth and evolution of our Four Worlds?

1.2. The Dynamics of Individuation

1.2.1. The Transformation Journey

Jung (6) in fact, while of Swiss nationality, was particularly trans-cultural in orientation, as we are through our *integral worlds*. A student of the literature and mythologies of comparative cultures all around the world, he took a particular interest in China in the "east" and also spent a considerable amount of time in the depths of Africa in the "south". Most of his work of course was conducted in "northern" Europe and he made frequent lecture tours to the United States in the "west".

As an inter-disciplinary scientist he studied philosophy and theology, biology and medicine, as well as mythology and psychology. As a psycho-dynamic as well as integral psychologist, philosopher and human being, as we shall see, he also had a profoundly transformational orientation toward his work, also mediating between his so-called collective unconscious (including collective archetypes) and individual consciousness (individual deep self and surface persona). However, as a developmental psychologist, who has also, as we shall see below, informed the world of learning, he ignored the worlds of economics and enterprise, which is where we come in!

Jung's quaternity of psychological and managerial types, in fact, has formed not only the basis for the MBTI (7) but also a source of inspiration behind our work at TCA, albeit that Jung restricted his dynamic (individuation as self realisation) as well as integral approach (four personality types) to the transformation of individuals, rather than also communities, organisations, economies and societies. His individual, psychological types, then, are mutually interdependent rather than mutually exclusive. In other words, following Jung, as an individual or community, organisation or society develops—individually over one life span or collectively over many—and spreads, across the globe, each will need to migrate across the quaternary.

That is what the process of *individuation*, or indeed transformation, is all about, bearing in mind that such progressive "individuation" is an idealised form, that all too seldom materialises as such. Indeed that de-formation, recently revealed in our colleague Tony Bradley's (8) BQA—Biblical Quaternity Archetype—whereby the "South" typically "Falls" to the material "West" rather than ascending first to the spiritual "East", for us is the key to so-called "under-development". Indeed it is for that very reason today that Zimbabwe, officially today, is "open for business" rather than "open for transformation".

To the extent that we do individuate or indeed engage in a *transformation* journey, individually or collectively, our particular, human grounding (local) in our childhood and youth, psychologically and culturally, emerges holistically (local-global) as self interacts with world, physically, emotionally, intellectually. Mid-life crisis moreover, ideally speaking (though all too seldom actually) heralds a further potential dynamic, now rational-holistic development (newly global), whereby you newly conceive of your integral self, individually and collectively, while ultimate maturity serves to effect (global-local) such, pragmatically and "for real".

TABLE 1.1. THE FOUR WORLDS

PRAGMATIC: Western: <u>Enterprise</u> Laboratory
The practical treatment of things, emphasising the application of ideas, whereby thought is a guide to action, and truth is empirically tested by the practical consequences of belief.

RATIONAL: Northern: <u>Research</u> Academy
The power to make logical inferences, whereby reason is a source of power independent of sense perceptions, based on deduction through a priori concepts, rather than via empiricism.

HOLISTIC: Eastern: <u>Transformation</u> Journey
The belief that the determining features in nature are wholes, that organisms progressively develop, are irreducible to the sums of their parts, but function in relationship to them.

HUMANISTIC: Southern: <u>Learning</u> Community
Asserts the dignity of (wo)man, promoting human and social welfare, incorporating the arts and humanities, fostering self-fulfilment/collective and community relations.

Unlike capitalism and communism, which, in effect (this was not Marx's intention who borrowed Smith's labour theory of value) shut each other out, the inner worlds of "southern" feeling (humanistic), "eastern" intuiting (holistic), "northern" thinking (rational) and "western" sensing (pragmatic)—see above—progressively, and indeed cyclically, welcome each other in, through psycho-dynamic individuation, that is for you as a person if not also for a community. Indeed for an enterprise or a community-and-society, such transformative "individuation" is inevitably a more complex, "trans-personal", "trans-cultural", "trans-disciplinary", and ultimately *trans4mational*.

Jung's four personality attributes then, potentially contained within the individual, are aligned, then, with our four ontological, economic and enterprise perspectives, potentially contained within an organisation, or a society, as well as with our integral Communiversity. Each individual, for Jung though, and each culture for us, has a predominating tendency. When fully functional, epitomised by an institutionalised *research academy*, as opposed to dysfunctional, for example, rationally based *thinking* firstly, is a predominant characteristic of the systematically oriented academies, enterprises and economies of the North, albeit that the European "north", also has its "south", "east" and "west". Each region, as such, has its own source of integrity, though, arguably, a "mini" version of such.

Humanistically oriented *feeling*, conversely, is a prevailing characteristic of the communally based "functional" individuals, enterprises and societies of the South, embodied for us here in *communal learning,* albeit that "northern" colonisation did its best to stamp such out! In fact for Zimbabwean anthropologist, Clapperton Mavhunga (9), now based at Massachusetts Institute of Technology, in America: *non-western parts of the globe such as Africa had their own unique ways of learning, improving existing knowledge and applying it to solving different problems at hand in a sustainable and integrated way.* Therefore, just as modern science and laboratories are suited to some modern contexts, African ways of knowing are and were suited to their own context, if only we invest more time in decolonizing and studying them. Such an approach to communal learning, all too seldom recognised and indeed codified today, as Mavhunga has indicated, is more African than European, more Irish than Scottish, more humanist than rationalist.

Holistically oriented *intuiting,* moreover, comes naturally to "just-in-time" Eastern managers—as in Japan, Singapore or elsewhere—though again these have been wilting, in the face of a resurgent market onslaught, of late. That said the Japanese economic *transformation journey* (the Japanese economic miracle) in the latter part of the last century, reflected in the all-pervasive approach to organisational *knowledge creation* heralded so clearly by organisational sociologists Nonaka and Takeuchi (10):

> ... a "western" or "northern" approach thereby emphasises the absolute, depersonalised, and non-human nature of knowledge. As such it is typically expressed in propositions and formal logic. In contrast "easterners", consider knowledge to be a dynamic human process of justifying personal belief with a view to finding the truth. Any organisation, for them, that dynamically deals with a changing environment ought not only to process information efficiently but also to creatively transform information into knowledge, in support of a profound purpose.

Sadly, such a seminal, "eastern" approach to enterprise development, albeit aligned with other worlds (see "knowledge spiral" below) was never aligned with such an integral, eastern approach to macro-economic development, in theory or practice.

Pragmatically based *sensing* is favoured finally by entrepreneurial Westerners, their competitive enterprises and financial markets, albeit today overdone, though currently ruling the roost, and "southern" Europe, if not the "Global South" as a whole, buckles before their weight. It is embodied, for us Communiversity-wise, in our integral enterprise, in the form of a *Socio-Economic Laboratory*. At the same time, and ironically speaking, it is the same such *experiential* approaches to learning in the evolved "west", as well as to enterprise, which transforms more restrictive orientations to "education and training", so commonplace in an imitative "south" into a more evolved approach to individual and communal learning.

1.2.2. The Shadow-side of Transformation

Just to make matters a little more complicated Jung argues that each of us carries around a shadow. That means there is a side (one of the four psychological or philosophical functions) to our individual, corporate or societal personality, which is hidden from us, that prevents us—individually and collectively—from becoming, in our terms, *integral*. In effect it is that "shadow" side, conventionally and societally repressed, which yearns for recognition, having been cast out for so many youthful and adult years, before we enter our proverbial mid-life crisis. It was indeed what drew Ronnie-becoming-Samanyanga back to Africa in the 1980s (when he was in his late thirties). To the extent that it is repressed it appears in dysfunctional guise, and duly inhibits integral development. This is a major feature of our world today, both due to internal and external sources of oppression (think of the Middle East today). This indeed is why the local, in order to evolve or emerge, needs to marry up one world with another, locally-globally, without allowing one to dominate over the other.

In fact, the craving that people in the "south" and "east" have for the "west" is a symptom of that ill-begotten "shadow" cause, which Bradley identified with their "Fall" (see above). More specifically, while the sense bound "west" has relegated the functioning of intuition to the "new age" shadow-lands, thought-bound "Brussels bureaucrats" have wittingly cast out feeling (one of the reasons for the advent of Brexit) to the extent that it surfaces, unwittingly, as rampantly depersonalised rules and procedures. While governments in Africa or Latin America might have dysfunctionally submitted to "scientific socialism", fully functioning "thoughtful" bureaucracies are few and far between there. Finally, farsighted Japanese or Korean corporate affiliates had lost conscious touch with, or sight of, in the 1990s, short term shareholder value, committing themselves to ruinous property speculation instead.

So the "northern" thinker, or technocrat, or indeed academic, as per our research academy, needs psycho-dynamically to consciously acknowledge the "southern" feeling, or community, vis à vis communal learning, that has been concealed inside (see Mavhunga above), and vice versa. In other words, unlike capitalism and communism which denied, if not killed off, each other, the "four worlds", as indeed per south-east-north-west, are mutually and integrally interdependent. Local identity (self-affirmation) to global integrity (societal integration) are indeed our dynamic watchwords as such.

Dynamic integration thereby needs to follow from clear-cut integral differentiation, and in our "one world fits all" brand of capitalism, and the now all pervasive, duly "westernised' approach to leadership and entrepreneurship, we have no such differentiation, if not also subsequent integration. This is why, for us, the world is on fire, while, for Unger an exclusive "vanguard of production" prevails over an inclusive one.

1.2.3. Rounding Out – Releasing Genius

There needs to be scope, then, for individuals and communities, organisations and societies to interdependently grow and evolve, and thereby release their GENE-ius. As such they need, on the one hand, to be encouraged, ID-wise for us, to integrally round out, communally, as feeling ("southern"), intuiting ("eastern"), thinking ("northern"), and sensing ("western"), over the course of their individual and communal lives, thereby encompassing integral realities. So the inherent "southerner", needs to also learn from the east, north and west, while not compromising, but rather co-evolving their southern communal selves. On the other hand, and dynamically, as we shall see, they need to be locally Grounded (origination), to Emerge locally-globally (foundation), to Navigate newly globally (emancipation), and ultimately *E*ffect (transformation) globally-locally.

This is indeed what happened economically in the Japanese glory days, in the 1970s and 1980s, when Japanese Spirit and Western technique were in fully dynamic flow. Grounded locally in their own *Zen* Buddhist and Shinto heritage, naturally and culturally, the Japanese fused together culture and enterprise, locally-globally emerging as *kaizen*, thereafter navigating their way to the future, newly globally, in the well-known form of their *Lean Production,* at one time effectively leading the world in process-based, large scale manufacturing, as is still the case for Toyota, if not also Toshiba and Canon, today. This was then prolifically adopted, now globally-locally, in Europe and America, if not also the rest of Asia and Africa. The corresponding release of GENE-ius (Grounding, Emergence, Navigation, Effect), worlds-wide, as we see in Part 2, is of course easier said than done, but it remains a *transformational* "stretch target".

1.2.4. Four Worlds in Dynamic Balance

Through our Four Worlds, structurally then, we are establishing an initial basis for individual and communal learning, whereby via our transformation journey, the politics and economics of capitalist-communist division, characterising modernity, might be replaced by the nature and culture of integration and unity. As such, as we shall see in Part 3, an economy needs to be not only communally self-sufficient, but also culturally developmental, knowledgeably social, and "oikonomically" alive. Similarly, enterprise-wise (PHD), marketing turns to community building (as per community), human resources to conscious evolution (as per pilgrimium), operations to knowledge creation (as per academy) and finance to sustainable development (as per laboratory).

However, first we need to pursue the *outer-directed* "four world" argument, most specifically in relation to enterprise and economy, before we turn to the *inner directed* learning and regeneration, more purposefully, altogether in extraverted-introverted integral "four world" guise. Indeed for Jung himself, as cited in Laurens van der Post's other seminal work (11) of non-fiction, on *Jung and the Story of our Time*, Jung's book on psychological types, furthermore, is a turning point in the art of human communications about which Van der Post says we hear so much and do so little these days. It is a discovery, as it were, of a foolproof technology of mind for making communication between men, no matter what their differences. It is deliverance at last from the confusion of tongues which made the building of the tower of Babel impossible, the ancient story which all of us can take to our twenty first century hearts with profit.

We start then, in outer directed enterprise and economy guise with the proverbial "west", which altogether, in duly dis-integrated guise, underpinned, whether at the UCRN (University College of Rhodesia and Nyasaland) in the then Rhodesia, the LSE (London School of Economics) in the UK, and Harvard Business School in the USA, Samanyanga's economic and managerial education.

1.3. The Micro Transcultural Perspective: Competitive to Co-operative

1.3.1. Pragmatic – Competitive: Individual Freedom – Westerness

Every firm competing in an industry has a competitive strategy, whether explicit or implicit. The goal of such a strategy is to find a position in the industry where the company can best defend itself against environmental forces or else influence them in its favour.

Michael Porter, *Competitive Strategy*

WESTERNESS, as our most apparently familiar economic and enterprise territory then, emerges out of a so-called "spirit of freedom"; that is the free spirited individualism. Pragmatism, as its philosophical mainstem, is linked to both individualism and empiricism. Cultures that have emerged in this pragmatic world, generally characterised as Anglo-Saxon, have always shown a need to be practically oriented, seeking to understand and control, and to secure COMPETITIVE advantage, through exploiting resources and opportunities. The dysfunctional expression of such "western-ness" is in outright materialism, its positive manifestation is in free enterprise. From a strategic perspective in effect, the champion of such an approach to *competitive strategy* is Michael Porter (12), with his pre-emphasis on competitive rivalry between firms.

For the Dutch cross-cultural management theorist, Fons Trompenaars', "Riding the Waves of Cultures" (13), such "westerness" is *achievement* oriented and *inner directed*. Moreover, and especially in U.S. terms, it is important to distinguish the "ready-fire-aim" Tom Peters' (14) approach of such "western" culture from its more rational "northern" overtones. In fact their integration provides the key to the success of, for example, America's Microsoft—as in Bill Gates' "Business at the Speed of Thought" (15).

We then need to turn, with a view to becoming integral, from pragmatic "west" to the rational "north", from Michael Porter's Competitive Strategy to Peter Drucker's "Management" (16). Specifically, in turning from the pragmatic to the rational, we change emphasis from an individual like Richard Branson to the organisational, and from personalised competition, embodied for example in Britain's Virgin, to institutionalised competence, exemplified, for instance, by the French utilities.

1.3.2. Rational – Coordinated: Functional Organisational Systems – Northerness

> All *businesses depend on three factors of production*—human, capital and physical resources. There must be objectives for their supply, employment and development.
>
> Peter Drucker, *Management: Tasks, Responsibilities and Practices*

NORTHERNESS, as per Austro-American management guru Peter Drucker (17) provides us with internal networks and a configuration that conserves resources, so as to harness core competence and distribute resources evenly. Cultures in the northern quadrant have a need for effective systematisation, and thereby emphasise sustainability more than competitiveness. Most typically "northern" are the Scandinavian countries, though France and

Germany, Austria and Switzerland as well as the Benelux countries, and indeed parts of America, have strong elements of such. In these northern contexts the depersonalised organisation takes precedence over the needs of the individual personality. Whereas "northern-ness" is negatively manifested as unsustainable bureaucracy its positive expression is through effectively COORDINATED management and organisation. For example, ten million buildings in metropolitan France have long been heated by "chauffagistes", run privately as government controlled concessions.

For Fons Trompenaars, while rational management has *neutral* as opposed to emotional overtones, and is *sequential* rather than synchronous, on other dimensions such as achievement/ascription and individual/collective it is again generally somewhere in the middle. Ultimately moreover, Peter Drucker's approach to planning and to management epitomises this rational, principled and analytically based "micro" orientation. We now turn from the rational, institutional, and competent "north", epitomised by a company like say BMW, to the holistic, inter-organisationally oriented, co-operative "east", which is in fact where Dee Hock's original and thereby counter-cultural VISA (as we can see our "worlds" are not restricted by their geographical location) came to the fore, at its inception, before Hock gave in to the prevailing "western" powers that be.

1.3.3. Holistic — Chaordic: Business Ecosystems – Easterness

> No single bank could do it. No hierarchical stock corporation could do it. No nation-state could do it. In fact no existing organization as yet conceived of could do it. It required a transcendental organization, linking together in wholly new ways an unimaginable complex of diverse institutions and individuals.
>
> Dee Hock, *The Birth of the Chaordic Age*

Such was American executive Dee Hock's "counter-cultural" description of the birth of VISA, in the 1970s, a global banking venture which by the new millennium had sales of over 100 billion dollars. *EASTERNESS* then, as embodied in the early version of VISA, destroys the boundaries between us, individually, organisationally or societally, and the world in which we live. Cultures and philosophies of the East, duly espoused by businessman-philosopher Hock, promote a dissolution of the individual, corporate or national ego through transcendent processes, rather than material structures, deleting the boundaries between person-and-institution as well as self-and-other.

For Hock (18), then: "it's about connections, massive changes in interconnectivity. Deeper than that, it's about dissolution of the notion of boundaries between separate, connected things. It's about relationships and growth; about all things growing from one another and everything growing from some indefinable *essence that is;* about all things being inseparably interrelated". Interestingly enough, for him the *Chaordic Alliance* so-called, and thereafter *Chaordic Commons,* after he had retired from Visa, became the source of his ongoing *transformation journey,* in the mature phase of his life.

Holism then, on which such "easterness" is based, is rooted in the ancient Buddhist philosophies of China, India and Japan, in modern-day Germanic idealism and romanticism, in ecology (for Hock) and in the post-modern sciences of complexity. Dee Hock, as a student of all of these, defines his CHAORDIC approach as involving "any self-organising, self-governing, adaptive, non-linear, complex organism, organisation, community or system whether physical, biological or social which harmoniously combines characteristics of both chaos and order". Inter-organisationally based business clusters or business ecosystems, historically epitomised by the Japanese "kereitsu", therefore take pride of place here.

Trompenaars' gives us insight into such eastern distinctiveness. For him, an holistically oriented culture like that of Japan, and to some extent that of Korea, Singapore and Taiwan, is *particularist* as opposed to universalist, *outer* rather than inner *directed,* as well as *diffused* not specific in orientation, *synchronous* rather than sequential, *ascriptive* as opposed to achievement oriented, as well as being hierarchical, neutral and masculine. Overall, the whole before the part, the collective before the individual, as well as interdependence rather than independence, are all key. Once we move across to the Indian sub-continent and to such countries as Indonesia, Malaysia and even China, the southern familial element combines forces with the eastern. As such, and as we move into the "deep south" the distinctiveness of an "eastern" *kereitsu,* like Mitsubishi, gives way to a "southern" co-operative enterprise like the rural, building supplies retailer Cashbuild (19) in South Africa, which might be aligned, organisationally at least, with our *learning community.*

1.3.4. Humanistic – Co-operative: Business & Society – Southerness: Community

> We invest money to buy plants, put up buildings, purchase materials and pay running expenses. The wealth created, however, is not driven by self interest, but rather serves as a reward and vote of confidence in us by society, for the services we render to it.
>
> Albert Koopman, *Transcultural Management*

Albert Koopman was the founder of a highly successful—in social and economic terms—South African co-operative enterprise in the 1980s and 1990s, which was explicitly built upon what Koopman has termed "the divine will of Africa", that is its communal culture. SOUTHERNESS, then, allows us to retain a living record of our evolution through the stories we tell, as has been the case with Koopman and with Cashbuild. Cultures in indigenous southern worlds are based on shared values in which individual ownership and claims to land and capital do not traditionally exist. There is a saying in southern Africa, "I am because you are", which is identified as "Ubuntu", and has recently been brought into management circles, at least over there.

Focus at this point is on community specifically, and on society generally. In that context the Southern part of Europe (Greece and Ireland, Italy, Spain and Portugal), Latin America, Africa and, in part, and south-east Asia come into their own. The dysfunctional manifestations of "clan-ishness" though, often exacerbated through nepotism and corruption, serve to conceal the functional expression of the south through community oriented, or family based, COOPERATIVE enterprise. Such dysfunction is born out of a lack of clear differentiation from, and some degree of integration with, the other three worlds, as has recently been born out especially in the "Greek tragedy", economically speaking.

We now turn from our "four worlds", or integral realities, in outer direct-ed, economy and more specifically enterprise-guise, to their particular appli-cation to individual and organisational learning and development, in antici-pation of our focus on communal learning/learning community. As such we shall be bridging the divide between what was alluded to earlier in this chapter, the extraverted nature of economics and enterprise, also aligned with research, (wherein for Rhodesia's Minister of Finance, in response to the young Lessem's then desire, in the 1960s, to pursue industrial psychology, "psychology was for backroom boys"), and the more introverted nature of learning and develop-ment, or indeed transformation, also aligned with knowledge creation.

1.4. Individual/Organisational Learning Cycle

1.4.1. Outer Directed Becoming Inner Directed

Prior to even conceiving of "four worlds" in fact, in our pursuit of a then suitable approach to *Experiential Learning* in the UK, Ronnie Lessem came across, as a management educator based at City University Business School in London in the 1980s, the seminal work of American educationalist David Kolb (20), also a follower of Jung, who was based at M.I.T at the time. Interestingly enough, Ronnie-becoming-Samanyanga, being by nature introverted, was persuaded by his extraverted European family, and then Minister of Finance, in similarly extrovert Rhodesian guise, as we saw above, to divert his prior intentions from industrial psychology (inner directed) to the economics (outer directed) of industry.

As such his studies of enterprise and economics, in his twenties and early thirties, preceded those of learning and development, later on, in the same way as the exogenous British coloniser of Rhodesia, hitherto, had eclipsed the thereby colonised indigenous Zimbabwean. Subsequently though, in the 1980s, he, while Zimbabwe had become independent, began to retrace inner directed steps, discovering the likes of M.I.T's David Kolb and then Peter Senge along the learning-ful way.

1.4.2. West – Active Experimentation – Towards Self Mastery

In fact Kolb, whose model of individual, if not also communal, learning, is today followed by South African academic partner, Da Vinci Institute, was heavily influenced by the personality types of psychoanalyst Carl Jung. Moreover, Kolb in turn influenced the work of his fellow M.I.T. organisational theorist, Peter Senge (21), famed for his work on organisational learning that first came out in the 1990s. This encompassed in turn self mastery, mental models, team learning and shared values, as well as overall systems thinking, as we shall see. All of these psychologists were the "introverted" counterpart to the "extravert" economists and management academics.

An orientation towards what David Kolb has termed *"active experimentation"*, aligned with our *Laboratory* to begin with, in the pragmatic west, focuses on materially influencing people and practically changing situations. It emphasises actual applications as opposed to reflective understanding. A pragmatist, therefore, individually or communally, is concerned with what works as opposed to what is absolute truth, thereby emphasising doing as opposed to thinking per se. Such western managers, and learners, are then willing to take risks in order to achieve their objectives.

Kolb's active experimentation then, being closely aligned with individual achievement, blending also with self-actualisation, resonates with the first, above attribute of Peter Senge's learning organisation, whereby individuals pursue *self mastery*. Its downside, of course, is a seat of the pants, reactive and "leap before you look" approach to people and things. We now turn from "west" to "north".

1.4.3. North – Abstract Conceptualisation – Mental Models

An orientation towards *abstract conceptualisation*, in the rational north, focuses on using logic, and theory, aligned with our *Research Academy*. It thereby emphasises thinking as opposed to feeling; a concern with deductively building general theories as opposed to empirically apprehending specific events. The approach to problem solving, then, is more scientific than artistic, or practical, more "northern" than "western" or "southern". Such a learner or researcher, or indeed learning organisation or research academy, is good at systematic planning, and manipulation of abstract symbols. As such he or she, or it, values precision, the rigour and discipline of analysis. In recent guise, such capacity for abstraction has been reflected in an approach to "*mental modelling*", which Peter Senge associates with his learning organisation. Such a rational-hierarchical-administrative, if not also systemic, orientation can be associated with the Gallic and indeed Nordic worlds in general, and with large scale organisations in particular. The downside of this approach is its cold and calculating approach, degenerating into "paralysis through analysis".

We now turn from "north" to "east", though, less explicitly so than in the other worldly cases. After all Kolb and Senge are both "westerners", albeit with some "eastern" inclinations. However, and something we have noticed, ironically over the years, the most evolved, somewhat integral, models of learning, comes from the "west", rather than the "east" or "south", supposedly because of their modelling capacity.

1.4.4. East – Reflective Observation – Individual and Group Learning

An orientation towards *reflective observation*, in the holistic east, focuses on understanding the meaning of ideas and situations by profoundly observing and meaningfully developing them in context. It emphasises emergent activity, as UK based strategy guru, of South African origin, Ralph Stacey (21) has described, set within an evolving, and interdependent, business or innovation ecosystem, as opposed to an immediately practical or methodical application within a single organisation. The concern here is with what emerges as fitting and beautiful, whereby order is realised "far-from-equilibrium" through chaos. There is also an emphasis on long term evolution as opposed to immediate results, befitting our *transformation journey.*

Managers with a reflective orientation enjoy intuiting the meaning of situations and ideas and are good at seeing their overall pattern, or implications. They also, for Senge, favour *team learning*, insofar as dialogue and connectivity is preferred to discussion and individuality. The downside of this holistic approach can be a love of complexity in itself, or truth or beauty, without utility. We finally turn "south".

1.4.5. South – Concrete Experience – Shared Values

An orientation towards *concrete experience*, in the humanistic south, focuses on being involved in experiences and dealing with immediate human situations in a personal way. It emphasises feeling as opposed to thinking; a concern with the uniqueness and "storied" nature of present reality as opposed to theories and generalisations. It involves an emotionally oriented, "artistic" orientation as opposed to a systematic, scientific approach to problems. Managers with a concrete-experience orientation enjoy and are good at relating to others, for us set within a *Learning Community*. They are often instinctive decision makers and function well in unstructured situations. The highly developed visionary leader, in this "southern" respect, is the one who can uplift hearts more than minds, *developing a shared sense of vision and value.*

1.4.6. Individual and Communal Learning Integrally

For us, the overall, and integral learning cycle then, starts communally in the "south", emerges transformatively via the "east", navigates its research way through the "north", and enterprisingly culminates in the "west". The downside of a purely southern, *experiential* approach, in isolation from what integrally follows, is its immersion in the concrete here and now, without any subsequent regeneration, codification or institutionalisation. With a further view to such we now turn, four worlds-wise, from learning to knowledge creation, constituting now a bridge between inner directed learning and outer directed enterprise.

1.5. Individual and Organisational Learning to Knowledge Creation

1.5.1. In the Face of a Crisis Turning to Knowledge Creation

In the 1990s Ronnie was fortunate to be able to spend three years on a project, based in Munich sponsored by the Roland Berger Foundation (Germany's largest management consultancy), on European-ness and Innovation, together with Japan's Ikijiro Nonaka cited above. He was already then renowned for his (22) work on *The Knowledge Creating Company*, and his so-called SECI "knowledge spiral" resonated well with our four worlds. It was also Ronnie's exposure to such knowledge creation, and the so-called "hypertext organisation" that promoted it, that would set him on the road to the next stage in his journey, towards social, as opposed to purely technological, R & D and thereby innovation.

Specifically then, for the two Japanese organisational sociologists, Nonaka and Takeuchi, also based, in turn, at Berkeley in California and at Harvard Business School. Their SECI knowledge spiral, as such, analogous to our four worlds, characterising the "knowledge creating" organisation, now starting out for us in the communal "south", involved for Nonaka and Takeuchi:

Socialisation – "Southern" Knowledge Origination

In the first instance an informal community of social interaction, for Nonaka, provides an immediate forum for nurturing the emergent property of knowledge at each organisational level. This is the "southern" humanistic pole, incorporating altruism, empathy, and a sense of reciprocity. Such *tacit to tacit* socialisation, moreover, relies on shared experience that enables members to "indwell" into others and to grasp their world from "inside". This shared experience also facilitates contributing to the "common good".

Externalisation – "Eastern" Dialogue

Once mutual trust and a common implicit perspective has been formed through shared experience, the team needs to articulate the perspective through continuous dialogue. This process activates so-called "externalisation", from tacit to explicit, whereby participants engage in the mutual co-development of ideas. This constitutes a holistic "eastern" orientation. Such dialogue, moreover, should not be single faceted and deterministic but multifaceted, creating unity-in-variety. The emergent concepts, for Nonaka, then provide a basis of crystallisation, or knowledge combination.

Combination – "Northern" Knowledge Systematisation

The third mode of knowledge conversion involves the use of social processes to rationally combine different bodies of explicit knowledge held by individuals, through such exchange mechanisms as formal meetings, office memos and codes of conduct that, for example, are the stuff of traditionally oriented bureaucracies. The reconfiguring of existing information, that is the sorting, adding, re-categorising and re-contextualising of such explicit knowledge can, at the same time, lead to new combinations of knowledge. Modern computer based data processing systems, in fact, provide a graphic example of such knowledge "combination".

Internalisation – "Western" Knowledge Application

In the conversion of explicit into tacit knowledge, finally, that is "internalisation", action is important. We are now in the realm of "western" pragmatism. Individuals internalise knowledge, tacitly, through direct, hands on experience, thereby both reaching out for, and holding onto, what they have competed for, both internally and externally. Moreover, for explicit knowledge to become tacit it helps if the knowledge is verbalised or diagrammed into manuals, documents, or stories, as any good consultant knows.

We now turn from enterprise, learning and knowledge creation to research, still in such "four world" integral terms.

1.6. Learning/Knowledge Creation to Research/Cooperative Inquiry

1.6.1. Management and Mankind

For all this seminal work on learning and indeed knowledge creation, affecting and informing individual and communities, organisations if not also whole societies, what we have so far left out of account, crucially for us as our integral work unfolds—from learning and transformation to research and enterprise—is *integral* research. As such it was only in the new millennium that we came across so-called *Cooperative Inquiry* (CI), though Ronnie had already met its English founder, John Heron (23), in the 1980s, when he invited him to speak at a conference Ronnie organised on *Management and Mankind*. Interestingly enough at the time, having only just become part of the management faculty at City University Business School in London, he was already reaching out to wider society.

In fact, and remarkably enough already in the 1970s, Ronnie becoming Samanyanga (24) was to undertake a project, as Director of the recently formed Urban and Economic Development (URBED) Group, based in London, on *Linking the College and the Community: Centre of Knowledge and Economic Development* (the Communiversity emerging four decades later). At the time John Heron, while an educator and psychologist at the University of Surrey, together with his close colleague Peter Reason at the University of Bath, were the two leading co-creators of action research in Britain.

The emergent worldview that action research espouses can be described as systemic, holistic, relational, feminine, and experiential, but *its defining characteristic is that it is participatory and developmental*; our world does not consist of separate things but of *relationships which we co-author*. Within the context of CI then, human persons are linked in a generative web of communion with other humans and the rest of creation. *Human persons do not stand separate from the cosmos; we evolved with it and are an expression of its intelligent and creative force.* As we are part of the whole we are necessarily actors within it, which leads us to consider the fundamental importance of the practical. All ways of knowing, then, support our skillful being-in-the-world from moment to moment, our ability to act intelligently in support of worthwhile purposes.

Such a participatory worldview is at the same time a political statement as well as a theory of knowledge. Just as the classical Cartesian worldview emerged out of the political situation of the time, and found its expression in science and technology, so a participatory worldview implies democratic, peer relationships as the political form of inquiry. The political dimension affirms people's right to have a say in decisions that affect them and which claim to generate knowledge about them. It asserts the importance of liberating the muted voices of those held down by class structure and neo-colonialism, by poverty, sexism, racism and homophobia. We now turn to Heron's specific "modes of knowing", again analogous to our "four worlds", to Kolb's "learning cycle", and to Nonaka and Takeuchi's "knowledge spiral".

As such Heron's work constitutes a bridge between learning and research.

1.6.2. Four Modes of Knowing: Experiential, Imaginal, Conceptual, Practical

The co-operative paradigm has two wings, that is political (value based and transformation oriented) and epistemic (knowledge based and informative). *Co-operative inquiry, distinctively speaking, does research with other people, who are invited to be full co-inquirers with the initiating researcher.* They become involved in operational decision-making, and are then committed to this kind of research design in principle, both politically and epistemologically.

Four ways of knowing are distinguished:

- Practical Knowledge: *evident in exercising skill, and closely aligned with the empirical, and with the path of realisation, builds upon the experimental, and the real*
- Conceptual Knowledge: *closely linked with theory, and closely aligned with critical rationalism, builds on hypothesis formation, and upon multiple discourses*
- Imaginal Knowledge: *which can be identified with interpretive approaches, evident in the intuitive grasp of the significance of patterns, builds on the narrative and dialectical*
- Experiential (empathetic) Knowledge: *closely aligned with phenomenology, and evident in meeting and feeling the presence of some energy, person, place, or process*

26

As a result, for Heron:

- *experiential* knowing lies at the base of a "knowledge pyramid", comprising the direct, lived "being-in-the-world", our "south"
- *imaginal* knowing, underlying your becoming as you *emerge,* constitutes our "east"
- supports propositional or *conceptual* knowledge, our "north"
- upholds *practical* knowing, the exercise of your practical research effect, our "west"

At the same time, what is above consummates what lies below. Practical knowing, know how, praxis, is the consummation of the knowledge quest. It is grounded in and empowered by all the prior forms of knowing, and is immediately supported by propositional knowing which it celebrates and affirms at a higher level in its own relatively autonomous way. It affirms what is intrinsically worthwhile, by manifesting it in action. It is characteristic, moreover, of a Communiversity laboratory, thereby aligned with a research academy, thereby linking learning and enterprise.

1.7. Conclusion

1.7.1. Communal Learning to Socio-economic Laboratory

Our ultimate port of call is Communiversity Development (see Table 1.2. below). Such is initiated, firstly *transculturally* via our integral realities (four worlds), by Individual and *Communal Learning.* Thereafter, we turn, *transformationally* through our integral rhythm, to individual and collective *Re-GENE-ration* via an individual *transformation Journey;* further to such, thirdly, we turn via our Integral Realms, in *transdisciplinary* guise, to *Research* and Innovation via a *Research Academy;* and fourthly turn *transpersonally* via what we have termed our Integral Rounds of self and communal, organisational and societal development, to *socio-economic Laboratory.* Finally, through our *Communiversity* as a whole, and thereby *Integral Polity,* we pull the integral threads together.

Such a Communiversity then, and as Jung and Van der Post have articulated above, serves to interlink the inner and outer directed forms and forces of our individual and communal learning and regeneration (inner words), and outer directed research and enterprise (outer worlds), healing the divide between Zimbabwe and Rhodesia.

TABLE 1.2. FOUR WORLDS TO COMMUNIVERSITY: OUR CD

FOUR WORLDS: TCA	EXPERIENTIAL LEARNING	KNOWLEDGE CREATION	COOPERATIVE INQUIRY/ ENTERPRISE
South/ Cooperative Community	Concrete *Experience*	Socialisation *Originate*	Experiential *Cooperative*
East/Chaordic *Journey*	Reflective *Observation*	Externalisation *Dialogue*	Imaginal *Chaordic*
North/Coordinated *Academy*	Abstract *Conceptualisation*	Combination *Systematisation*	Conceptual *Coordinated*
West/Competitive *Laboratory*	Active *Experimentation*	Internalisation *Application*	Practical *Competitive*

1.7.2. Local Identity to Global Integrity

Conventional wisdom tells us to "think global, act local". That is why our ultimate aspiration is to attend a "globally", renowned elite university, be it London School of Economics or Harvard Business School, as indeed Ronnie becoming Samanyanga did. However, in his case he started out supposedly locally, at UCRN, though, being an offshoot of colonised Rhodesia, it was not locally for real. In fact it was born out of that vacuous experience that he sought to turn the conventional wisdom around, at least in the fields of business and economics, to *feel local, intuit local-global, think newly global and act global-local.*

The shorthand for such, which is the title of this centering chapter, in the overall context of science (including social science) and technology is *local identity to global integrity.*

We now turn from Integral Centering, as such, to our first, local port of Afrikological call, which will take us, back and forward, to Ancient Egypt.

1.8. References

1 **Van der Post** L (1958) *The Dark Eye of Africa.* Cape Town. Lowery
2 **Lessem** R & **Palsule** S (1997) *Managing in Four Worlds.* Chichester. Wiley-Blackwell

3   **Smith** A and **Sutherland** K (2008) *The Wealth of Nations: Selected Edition.* Oxford. Oxford World Classics

4   **Marx** K (2008) *Capital: A New Abridgment.* Oxford. Oxford World Classics

5   **Piketty** T (2020) *Capital and Ideology.* Cambridge. Harvard Univ. Press

6   **Stevens** A (1994) *On Jung.* London. Penguin

7   **Briggs Myers**, I (1980) *Gifts Differing.* Palo Alto. Consulting Psychologists Press

8   **Lessem** R and **Bradley** T (2020) *Evolving Work.* Abingdon. Routledge

9   **Mavhunga** C (2017) *What Do Science, Technology and Innovation Mean for Africa.* Cambridge, MA. MIT Press

10   **Nonaka** I and **Takeuchi** H (1995) *The Knowledge Creating Company.* Oxford. Oxford University Press

11   **Van der Post** L (2002) *Jung and the Story of our Time.* New York. Vintage Classics.

12   **Porter**, M (1994) *The Competitive Advantage of Nations.* New York. Macmillan

13   **Trompenaars**, F (1994) *Riding the Waves of Cultures.* New York. Nicholas Brealey

14   **Peters, T & Waterman**, R (1982) *In Search of Excellence.* New York. Harper Row

15   **Gates**, W (1999) *Business at the Speed of Thought.* New York. Free Press

16   **Boisot**, M (1999) *Knowledge Assets.* Oxford. Oxford University Press

17   **Drucker** P (1999) *Management: Tasks, Responsibilities and Practices.* Abingdon. Routledge

18   **Hock**, D (1999) *The Chaordic Alliance.* San Francisco. Berrett Koehle

19   **Koopman**, A (1991) *Transcultural Management.* Oxford. Blackwell

20   **Kolb** D (1983) *Experiential Learning: Experience as the Source of Learning and Development.* New York. Prentice Hall

21   **Senge** P (2006) *The Fifth Discipline: The Art and Practice of the Learning Organisation. Second Edition.* New York. Random House

22   **Stacey** R (1994) *Strategic Management and Organisational Dynamics.* London. Pitman Publications

23   **Nonaka** I and **Takeuchi** H (1995) *op cit*

24   **Heron** J (1996) *Cooperative Inquiry: Research into the Human Condition.* London. Sage

25   **Lessem** R & **Tarran** H (1978) *Linking the College and the Community: Centres of Knowledge and Economic Development.* Journal for Further and Higher Education, Volume 2, Issue 3, pages 27–42

PART TWO

Local Grounding and Origination

CHAPTER 2

Kemet

GROUNDING AND ORIGINATION: COMMUNAL LEARNING

- Value provides the communal ground, identity and purpose, the *raison d'être for everything* that is produced or offered, building on everyday social reality.
- Value gives a *sense of purpose* to communal structures, systems and processes.
- Value is the *source of being* in a community for those within and without.
- *Value preserves* the organisational and community culture through consensus.
- At their best, value-based communities are *infused with vision*, embodying a unique contribution to their society; at their worst rigid dogma prevails.

2.1. Introduction

2.1.1. Worlds-Wide Academies

Our *centering*, "newly global focus" is on our *Anthroposophical* Research Academy, evolved out of the ancient Egyptian cross-roads of civilization. Thereafter, as we turn *south* we enter our "newly global" *Afrikological* Academy. Turning *east* we enter our *Soulidarity* Academy. Then in turning to the "newly global" *north* we enter our *Integral* Academy. Finally, as we turn to the already globalised *west* so we enter our *Technological* Academy.

FIGURE 2.1. WORLDS-WIDE ACADEMIES

Integrality
Europe
North

Technology   Anthroposophy   Soulidarity
America   Civilizational Cross-Roads   Asia
West   Centre   East

Afrikology
Africa
South

We then turn to civilization's ancient cross-roads.

2.1.2. Kemet to Sekem: South to West

Specifically then and firstly, in the Egyptian case, we start out locally, originally grounded, naturally and communally, in *Kemet*. Secondly, now locally-globally, as our emergent foundation, culturally and spiritually, we turn to *Maat*. Thirdly moreover, for our emancipatory navigation, scientifically and artistically, "newly global" *Anthroposophy* is established. Finally, and now globally-locally, technologically and economically, is *Sekem* as an enterprise.

FIGURE 2.2. INTEGRAL EGYPT

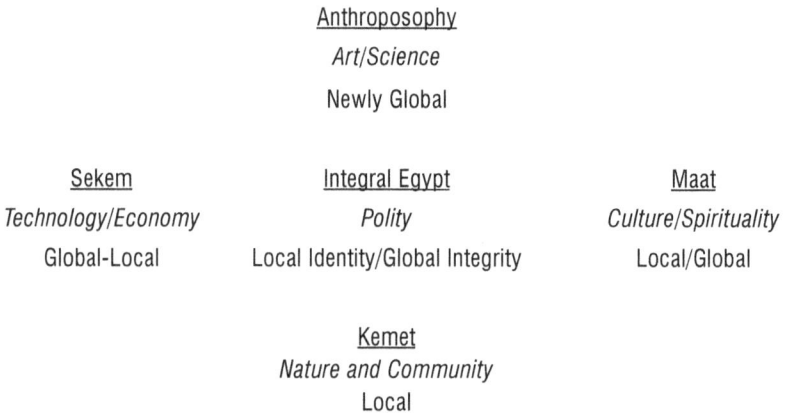

Anthroposophy
Art/Science
Newly Global

Sekem   Integral Egypt   Maat
Technology/Economy   *Polity*   *Culture/Spirituality*
Global-Local   Local Identity/Global Integrity   Local/Global

Kemet
Nature and Community
Local

2.1.3. Kemet: Archetypal Product of the Land

For our local Grounding in Egypt, we firstly turn to the late British Arabist and museum designer, Michael Rice, for a localized perspective on that ancient land. We begin there, naturally and communally, and end by previewing the Sekem Group, an integral enterprise in modern Egypt, together with their Heliopolis University for Sustainable Development, with which we were originally closely connected. This provides then for our African nature-and-community of origin, on the one hand, and grounds for such value based communal learning, on the other, in this case in the context of Egypt, ancient cross-roads of civilizations.

To begin with then, tapping into natural and communal value grounds, according to Rice (1), *the economy of Egypt was rooted in the rich alluvial soil which the Nile river deposited along its banks when it flooded every year*. From south to north the people of the Valley were peasants tilling the soil, either as small farmers or as the retainers of a noble or official. That constituted the grounds for their ancient learning, rather than any university or school.

The essential agrarian nature of Egypt, moreover, was reflected in much of the symbolism which was so powerfully an expression of the Egyptian psyche. Its ancient name, "Kemet" meant "Black" and supposedly acknowledged the debt people owed to the land that served them, if not also to the black, African people from whence it originally came.

The unifying factor as such was the bountiful nature of the Nile river. *Egypt was then the product of, indeed grounded in, the land.*

2.1.4. Preoccupied with Order and Balance

Furthermore, the ancient Egyptian was preoccupied with the idea of order and balance which ensured the life of Egypt, and indeed the cosmos, was aligned with the return of the seasons and the cycle of the farmer's year. The constant interplay of sunlight, shadow, moonlight, haze or the dawn inspired numberless generations of artists to capture the essence of Egypt in whatever medium they might employ.

For a thousand years, moreover, Egypt was in truth "the Peaceable Kingdom". Secure from external threat, prosperous by the beneficence of the Gods expressed in the gift of the Nile, the Egyptians were free to give rein to their prodigious creative energies. Of course it could not last forever, at least naturally and materially, but psychologically and spiritually (psychically) the story goes on, and for Sekem, as we shall see, the role of consciously taking such further on, awaits it.

2.2. The Old and New Kingdoms

A Time of Formation

The high point of ancient Egypt's contribution to the civilization of the world, Rice goes on to say, and one of the highest points of human experience thus far achieved by our peculiar species, is to be found in the period known as "the Old Kingdom", which lasted from 2650 to 2130 BC. This was a time of almost unremitting achievement, in the arts, in architecture, in the management of society, in the definition and promotion of religious belief, in the formulation and conduct of elaborate rituals and state ceremonies.

The New Kingdom and the Rise of the Feminine

It might not be fanciful, moreover, to suggest that the New Kingdom (1570–1070 BCE), for Rice, was more feminine in character than its predecessors. Not only do women appear in much more significant roles in society than *hitherto, but even the art is softer, lighter, more delicate than had been the case before.* In fact their influence can be seen strikingly over the next 500 years.

After the end of the 20th Dynasty (cc 1000 BC) the cancer which had been gnawing at the body of Egypt at least since the beginning of the 18th Dynasty finally triumphed. The power which destroyed Egypt was, ironically, what might be termed "organised religion", represented by the temple bureaucracies which had been accumulating power and wealth until they rivaled, if they did not exceed, the power and wealth of the Kingship. Before that came about, though, one of the most creative periods in Ancient Egypt occurred.

A Veritable Learning Community: Koptos, Gebtu and Kemet

In fact, the name *Egypt* was coined by Greek colonists in the 4th century CE, and it is a corruption of the name *Koptos,* itself a corruption of *Gebtu.* This was the name of the ancient area in the south of the country, probably existing as long ago as 3000 BCE. The name that was most commonly used by the ancient Egyptians themselves, however, was *Kemet,* whereby *the name, meaning "Blackness", stems from the inhabitants themselves, from the color of their skin.*

Thanks then to the precious cargo of knowledge *these Black settlers brought with them into the Nile Valley around 5000 BCE—astronomy, timekeeping, husbandry and perhaps even stone building—*within a few centuries of their arrival, the place began to develop and flourish and eventually became a country with the most enlightened and creative civilization the world had ever known: the country we now call Egypt. As such the grounds of their learning were as much communal as they were individual, whether in relation to science, agriculture or construction.

2.3. Gods as Energy Patterns

One Becomes Four

In fact rather than "polytheism" the religious outlook of the ancient world, according to Oxford philosopher and cultural historian Jeremy Nadler (2), is better described as *henotheism*, "heno" meaning one in Greek. The henotheistic orientation is one in which the divine is conceived of as being fundamentally a unity, but a unity that reveals itself in a multiplicity of forms. *In the Heliopolitan creation myth,* upon which we shall elaborate below, *the original divine unity is referred to as Nun, visualised as a vast and infinite ocean within which every possibility of existence is contained, but in a state of potentiality.*

As such then, as the life-potential of Nun (One) is activated, something solid appears in the midst of the ocean of potentiality, and this is Atum (Two). Atum then comes into being out of the non-being of Nun and, in the very act of Atum's becoming, a third principle arises—Kheprer, the Becoming one. The completion of this first phase of Nun's self-manifestation is the unfolding of the light in the darkness of the infinite waters, imaged as the appearance of a "light-bird", which symbolises the fourth aspect of Nun's self-unfoldment: Ra (Four). In this manner the *One "becomes" Four,* that is *Nun-Atum-Kheprer-Ra,* also reflected, as we shall see, in our integral enterprise.

Gods, Nature and the Psyche

The gods moreover were experienced in and through nature this way: not as identified with natural phenomena but rather as underlying energy-patterns that a range of natural phenomena might express through their characteristic forms of modes of behavior. Instead of regarding these inner experiences as belonging to oneself, the ancient attitude was that each human soul participated in a "psychic world" common to all. This indeed resonates with Swiss psychoanalyst Carl Jung's (3) notion of a collective unconscious. We now turn, more concertedly, to the ancient Egyptian metaphysical, alongside its physical, landscape.

2.4. The Ancient Egyptian Metaphysical Landscape

2.4.1. Revisiting the Integral Egyptian Worlds: *East and West, North and South*

In ancient Egypt one is constantly impressed by the balance and interplay of the opposites: life and death, abundance and barrenness, light and dark, day and night, silence and solitude. Their landscape teaches the metaphysics of the equilibrium of the opposing principles. As such, the directions of east and west, north and south are never in doubt. Through the whole span of the Nile valley there is *an almost unbroken constancy in the northward flow of the river.*

This physical division of the country by the Great River is given symbolic meaning by the cosmic and divine event of *the daily birth of Ra in the east,* his journey across the heavenly Nile (of which the earthly Nile is but an image), *and his senescence and descent into the realm of the dead beyond the desert cliffs of the west.* East and west are therefore not just physical directions but also mythical and metaphysical orientations. The east has to be the side of rebirth, of new life, for every morning the whole country turns east as it awakens to the enlivening rays of the newborn sun.

But just as the country is divided into easterly and westerly realms, as much mythological and geographical, so it is also divided between the *northern,* low-lying expanse of the Delta, and the narrow Nile valley to the *south.* Looking *southward,* one can have the sense of g*azing into another mysterious, metaphysical zone,* where geography again blends into mythography.

The Egyptians, and the sacred river, then, came to the earth from the Underworld or Dwat, the source of life, health and fertility for the physical realm. If in looking south one gazes at Dwat, one sees what was termed the "face" of Egypt, the "Beloved Land", whereas *the north symbolised the "back of the head".* The word for "east", moreover, symbolises "Left", and for "west", symbolizes "right". *In no other country,* for Nadler, *are directions in space so clearly defined in the landscape.* Physical then, as opposed to metaphysically, in the north, Egypt is bounded by the Mediterranean Sea in the east and in the west by the deserts. In the south the river runs its course from its distant origins in the mountains of Ethiopia to its outpourings in the Delta, 4000 miles away. *This quadrilateral containment of the land of Egypt had a considerable and lasting influence on the Egyptian personality, giving people a deep sense of security.*

Sadly, and altogether in Egypt today, this quality is largely lost, as the country has failed to continually re-GENE-rate itself over time, and today, arguably inhibited by the country's higher education authorities, and conventional academic establishment. Heliopolis University (HU) also struggles to rise to that regenerative occasion, which is why we have been evolving our Communiversity in place of a standard University.

2.4.2. Standing At the Centre of a Cross

No matter where a person stands, therefore, in the Nile valley, he or she is *at the centre of a cross whose axes are described by the Nile and its embankments on the one hand, and by the sun's course on the other.* It is an interesting fact, moreover, that the Egyptians-as-*Kemet* not only felt themselves to be well grounded in the "black" earth, but regarded their land not only as being at the centre of the world, but also being in a sense the *whole* world. This was not through ignorance of other parts of the world, but due to a feeling that characterises the relationship of ancient people to the earth: the feeling that in the part of the earth they inhabited, the *whole* was present.

We now turn to the three myths of cosmogenesis, starting out from that of Heliopolis.

2.4.3. Myths of Cosmogenesis

Heliopolis – Fourfold Move from Potentiality toward Actuality

The cosmogony that evolved at Heliopolis, where indeed HU today is based, firstly then and of most significance for us, focused on the creation of the universe from the specific perspective of the priesthood Ra. The Greek Heliopolis means "City of Helios", the sun god Helios being the Greek equivalent to Ra, as per Sekem in Egypt, via the vitality of the sun. In this Heliopolitan cosmology the description of the outpouring of the eternal world of pure spirit into materiality begins with Nun. *Nun* (for us Grounding) *is the whole diverse and varied universe existing in a state of natural and communal potentiality.* Within the waters of Nun resides a creative principle that is the spark of life, which the Egyptians referred to as Atum, which means "to complete". *Atum* (for us Emergence) *is the principle which initiates the movement from potentiality to actuality.*

Atum's act of self-generation is simultaneously an act of world generation. In this act the principle of Becoming is born Kheprer, "the Becoming One" (for us Navigating). It is at this moment that process and change begins. There are ultimately *two epiphanies* (for us Effecting) *to Atum:* first *solidity within fluidity, from out of the Primordial Ocean;* secondly *the light (Ra) that shines into the darkness of non-being.*

Hermeopolis: Ordering of the Universe

Hermeopolis, on the other hand, was the chief centre of the cult of Thoth, whose relationship with the moon is comparable to that of Ra with the sun. As moon god, Thoth was particularly concerned with the regulation and ordering of the universe. It is likely that the Egyptian name Thoth has the connotation of "measurer". Thoth's feminine counterpart, as we shall see, is Maat, principle of order, truth and justice.

Memphis: Shaper of the Material World

In, thirdly, the Memphite cosmogony, the emphasis is shifted toward the active involvement in the creation of the universe, whereby Ptah (see also chapter 4, *Africa Creation Engineering*) is personally engaged in creation right down to the emergence of all that life. Ptah then is the godhead that is conceived as form-giver and shaper of the material world. For this reason he was the chief god of craftsmen and all workers in metal and stone. *The name Ptah probably means "sculptor" or "engraver" and so we may conceive Ptah at work in the world giving to all creatures their forms.*

Viewed in this light, the *cosmogonies of Heliopolis, Hermeopolis and Memphis do not appear as rivals as much as complementary aspects* of a greater cosmogonic scheme in which different phases of the emanation of the divine into material manifestation are given emphasis. In fact there is an uncanny resemblance between the three ancient Egyptian cosmologies, and the Christian Holy Trinity, which arguably, for us, underlie what we term our gene-IUS. Thereby moral Inspiration stems from Heliopolis, Universal order from Memphis, and Synergy between the two from Hermeopolis, via Thoth and Maat. We now turn more specifically, more sociologically so to speak, to the peoples of Ancient Egypt.

2.5. The Peoples of Egypt

Ancient Egypt as Matriarchal

For Moustafa Gadalla (5), an independent Egyptologist and founder of the Tehuti Research Foundation, based in the USA, the ancient Egyptians were, controversially in fact, matrilineal or matrifocal. On earth the female was the source of energy—the sun. In fact the matrilineal/matriarchal system followed the planetary laws. *Throughout Egyptian history as such, it was the queen who transmitted the solar blood.* Egyptian kings claimed a right to the throne through marriage to the eldest Egyptian princess. The relationship between husband and wife, moreover, is shown symbolically in the Ancient Egyptian symbol for the wife (*Auset*) being the throne—the source of legitimacy. The husband (*Ausar*) is the overseer (eye) that sits below the throne. The eye (male) is located below the eyebrow (female).

This brings us to matrilocal communities.

Matrilocal Communities: Towards a Commonwealth

The rights of a group, in Ancient Egypt, were linked to a particular place. The matrilineal system, then, was the basis of the social/political organisation in ancient Egypt. However, the Egyptians recognised that the needs of each matrilocal community could not be fully satisfied with just local production. *In order to protect the individuality of the polity and its sociopolitical coherence, a co-operative system between several polities was needed—a kind of commonwealth.* This was organised into three basic levels—matrilocal community, district jurisdiction, and province, as non/coercive political organisations. Such served to reinforce communal learning.

Government, according to Gadalla, was therefore not from the top (pharaoh) to the bottom (local community). It was from the bottom to the top — from local matrilocal community to districts to regional and "national"— each under a governor: government from the people, by the people, and for the people. This Egyptian system, for Gadalla, in direct contrast against the conventionally "pharaonic" view of ancient Egypt, was the true form of a grassroots republican democracy. In fact, and more generally, Nigerian American anthropologist Imi Amadiume (6) maintains, in her seminal work on *The Reinventing of Africa,* alluding to the Senegalese macro-historian *Cheikh Anta Diop,* that matriarchy, nature and community were homegrown in Africa—despite many historians' arguments to the contrary, and indeed the subsequent colonial manipulation of that historical, African position. Thereby the community, rather than the individual, held pride of place.

The Dual Overseeing/Administrative System

On every level of government, as such, from the smallest matrilocal community all the way to Egypt at large—there was a dual governing system. At the head of ancient Egypt was the pharaoh, who represented the cosmic link between the natural (earthly) and supernatural (divine) powers. His role was not to rule, Gadalla maintains, but to perform rituals to maintain the welfare of the society. The pharaoh then deputed his authority to the supreme/chief judge/governor to run the daily affairs.

This dual system was tailored after the Ancient Egyptian cosmic allegorical prototype system of government, between *Amen-Ra* (King of the Universe) and the government—*Tehuti-Thoth* (god of wisdom).

2.6. As Above So Below

Heru (Horus) and Tehuti (Thoth)

Every action, no matter how mundane, has in ancient Egypt in some sense a cosmic corresponding act: *ploughing, sowing, reaping, brewing, building ships, playing games—all were viewed as earthly symbols of divine activities.* In other words, for the *Baladi* (ancient Egyptians), every "physical" aspect of life had a symbolic (metaphysical) meaning. But also, every symbolic act of expression had a "material" background.

Both *Heru* (Horus) and *Tehuti* (Thoth) for example are shown in numerous illustrations in the ancient Egyptian temples performing the symbolic *Uniting of the Two Lands. Heri* represents conscience, mind, intellect, and is identified with the heart. *Tehuti* represents manifestation and deliverance, and is identified with the tongue. One thinks with the communal heart and acts with the effective individual tongue.

The Cyclical Renewal Festivals

The main theme of the ancient Egyptian texts, for Gadalla, *is the cyclical nature of the universe and the constant need for the renewal of such cycles, through well-designated festivals.* The Egyptians viewed these as part of human existence, which constitutes the rhythm of the life of the community and of the individual. This rhythm results from the order of cosmic life.

The renewal and rejuvenation of the life of the cosmos then, of the community, and of the individual are affected by rites. These rites had/have the power to bring about the rejuvenation and rebirth of divine life. The official annual number of festivals—*mouleds*—in present-day Egypt, although controversial in Islam, is estimated at more than 3000. For example, the three main festivals of Sidi Ahmed el-Badawi, in honor of the 13th century Moroccan Sufi mystic who then settled in Egypt, at the city of Tanta, attracts almost as many visitors as Mecca does pilgrims from the whole of the Islamicized world.

Egyptian Pharaohs Expected to Secure Rich Harvests

Contrary then to the Bible and Hollywood's distorted image of the pharaoh, according to Gadalla, as a harsh tyrant, living a luxurious, useless and easy life, the pharaoh had no political power. He lived in a mud-brick dwelling, and spent his time performing his duty to act as an intermediary between the natural and supernatural worlds, by conducting rites and sacrifices.

The Egyptian pharaohs were not expected to be leaders of victorious armies, but were expected to secure a regular succession of rich harvests. In the first place then, the pharaoh's main function was religious. He was a representative of the people to the powers and energies of the universe. He was the conduit, the go-between. *He was the source of prosperity and well-being of the state, to his people. He was their servant, not their tyrant. The normal flow of events and all phenomena of life, were intimately linked to the ruler's vital force.* It was therefore considered that the Egyptian king was not supposed (or even able) to reign unless he was in good health and spirit. Accordingly, he was obliged to revitalise his vital force, by regularly attending physical and metaphysical practices, which were known as *Heb-Sed* rituals.

Indeed, much of the above could equally have applied to Ibrahim Abouleish, the founder of Sekem in Egypt, though once we enter Egyptian academe, the Professor, sad to say, assumes more conventionally masculine and authoritarian proportions. Sadly, and historically as such, the "great man", or indeed the rich man—usually a man—has taken over from the richness of the community, and individual learning, albeit amongst masses of students, has taken over in the modern Egyptian university from the learning community of old.

2.7. The Cosmic Land of Egypt: Rise, Fall and Rise Again

The Commandments of Maat: Truth, Justice and Balance

Yet in his renowned if controversial book, *The Egypt Code*, Egyptian born Belgian engineer and prolific author Robert Bauval (7) proposed that the whole of Egypt has been developed as a kind of "kingdom of heaven" that was meant to function in harmony with the cycles and changes in the sky, including the four seasons and the four winds, like our "four worlds". Egypt thus became a cosmic land governed by cosmic law—a sort of astrological ten commandments—inscribed not on stone tablets but in the sky, as *maat*.

Interestingly, moreover, "maat" was personified as a woman, a goddess with wings outstretched, wearing on her head "the feather of truth". *Egyptologists thereby define maat as being "truth, justice and balance"*. Bauval and his co-author, Egyptian born engineer author and politician Ahmed Osman (8), in a subsequent book on *The Soul of Egypt* would also add that "maat" was the cosmic instrument by which all things serving the well-being of Egypt were regulated and maintained as they had been at the moment of creation.

Maat Long Forgotten

Fast forward to the 20th century to modern Egypt, *Maat*, Bauval and Osman claim, had been long forgotten, as much in the academic as in the political realm. *New laws, new religions, and new social systems had dislocated and confused the Egyptians for the last two millennia.* Immense problems of ecology and urban development and terrible social and cultural upheavals were just around the corner. The ancient Gods, once so protective and benevolent to Egypt, had long abandoned her; foreign masters had ruled Egypt for the past two thousand years. And now the unthinkable was about to happen: the killing of the Nile flood. The first dam on the Nile to control the annual flood was built in 1910 by the British at Aswan in Upper Egypt. Half a century later, in 1965, a much larger dam, the Aswan dam, was built by the Russians.

No more did the Nubians enjoy their peaceful and prosperous ways on the banks of the Nile; the rising level of the artificial lake drowned their villages and settlements, forcing 15,000 to resettle in the desert in houses that quickly turned into slums. Ironically, too, the very rich soil of the Nile valley was almost ruined; no longer washed and cleansed by the yearly floodwaters,

43

its salinity increased to levels detrimental to crops and husbandry. Last but not least, many ancient temples were lost. In fact, the 20th century in that particular force-fitted and alien British "colonial" and Nasserite "socialist", Aswan guise, represented a repeat of history, for Bauval and Osman, in hitherto Roman guise.

2.8. Finding Maat Again

Egypt's Ancestral Origins Rooted in its Black and Fertile Soil

The objective for Bauval and Osman today, in rediscovering the *Soul of Ancient Egypt,* and Restoring the Spiritual Engine of the World in the process, is to seek out the true natural and cultural grounding of Egypt in its soul—so that it can be grafted onto the two present-day religions of Egypt: Coptic Christianity and Islam. For they firmly believe that only then can the true identity, the true "grounds" of all Egyptians be re-established. Indeed, for Ibrahim Abouleish himself Heliopolis University was to be established in that rooted guise, but the academic powers that be, in the country, had other ideas!

For Bauval and Osman then, as for Aboulcish, Egypt today has a second chance to fulfill its destiny and hopefully find *maat* again: that balance between order and justice, for us the local and the global. As such, *Egyptians need to be reminded of their ancestral origins rooted in its black and fertile "Kemet" soil,* for us its natural and communal "grounds" for learning and development, as is also the case for us in other parts of Africa. *Only once this fundamental truth is recognised and regarded with pride, will Egypt rise again* as the place where the world's soul manifested itself in a golden civilization that still awes and inspires us today. In Hermes' words (8):

> ... And this will be the geniture of the world: a reformation of all good things and a restitution, most holy and most reverent, of nature itself, recorded in the course of time.

We now return to Heliopolis.

2.9. Reconstituting Heliopolis

The Culture Growing in Egypt Was Essentially African

Let us first remind ourselves where Michael Rice, from the psychological and mythological outset, was coming from. For him the psychological principles related to the individual can, with some qualifications as to scale and the influences of the social environment, be applied also to those groups that make up societies themselves, in this case that of Egypt. It must not be forgotten, as such, that *the culture growing in Egypt was essentially African. At the same time the Egyptians seemed to have retained a distant memory of a mystical land far away to the "east", on "the edge of the world".*

For us, altogether, this represents first Egypt's grounding, as *Kemet,* in the natural-communal "south" and emergence, as *Koptos,* in cultural-spiritual "east", from our integral perspective. Furthermore, and geographically as well as integrally as we have seen, in the north, Egypt is bounded by the Mediterranean Sea, in the east and west by the deserts. In the south the river runs its course from its distant origins in the mountains of Ethiopia to its outpourings in the Delta. *This quadrilateral—*for us integral—*containment of the land of Egypt had a considerable and lasting influence on the Egyptian personality, giving people a deep sense of communal security.*

Sekem-Heliopolis as the Epicenter of Creation

For Bauval and Osman then, the objective today, in rediscovering the soul of Ancient Egypt, and restoring the "Spiritual Engine of the World", for us Afrikologically so to speak, is to seek out the true natural and cultural roots, the grounding, of Egypt in its African soul as *kemet.* As such, Egyptians need to be reminded of their ancestral origins rooted in its black and fertile soil.

The "vitality of the sun", in contemporary guise, is now provided by the Sekem Group in Egypt, a combination of agricultural economic, social and cultural enterprises, born out of the desert ground. For its founder, the recently late Ibrahim Abouleish (10), in Egypt as such:

> SEKEM is starting to have a place in a worldwide association of people and initiatives who are concerned with a healthier more humane future on earth. The net of life created by SEKEM and its initiatives is becoming connected to a larger, worldwide net. In this new phase our achievements are multiplied and perceived globally through international forums. My vision now has a new, further level; to found a "council of the future of the world" together with other institutions striving towards developing a better world. This council would not be an abstract term, but carry a concrete message into the world: there is nothing more powerful than the invisible net of life, which connects people with their hearts. Its fabric is woven deeper than our understanding, and long before we first shake a hand we have moved along its threads. The nest of life is more real than the most dangerous weapon, and unattainable for all outer violence. Only from it can real peace radiate. He who counts on its effectiveness is practicing the most effective form of social art, because without using power or thoughts for advantage, he can trust he

45

will be carried by his energy and endurance. To learn to see the threads and to be able to form them determines the art of social networking.

Such a vision is consistent with Egypt as a matrix of civilizations, but how specifically does Sekem today, and indeed Heliopolis University (HU), economically as well as ecologically, academically as well as epistemologically, draw on its ancient Egyptian heritage?

2.10. The Vibrant Economy

2.10.1. The Cultivating Culture

Dry-Weather Farming

Egypt is (and was) one of the most arid areas in the world. The River Nile in Egypt received 90% of its water during a 100-day flood period every year. The Ancient Egyptians then managed their limited water supply efficiently, and became, according to Gadalla (11), the best dry-weather agrarians in the world. Diodourus, the formidable ancient Greek historian as cited by Gadalla, spoke of the efficient Egyptian farming system:

> ... being from their infancy brought up to agricultural pursuits, they far excelled the husband-men of other countries, and had become ac quainted with the capabilities of the land, the mode of irrigation, the exact season for sowing and reaping, as well as the most useful secrets connected with the harvest, which they had derived from the ancestors, and had improved by their own experience.

Not only did the Ancient Egyptians provide water to the lowlands, but they were able to irrigate the lands, in their local communities, that were too far from the river to be directly flooded by it. To reach all the way to the sands of the desert, they utilised a system of canals and water elevating devices. Sekem and HU then draw on fertile, ancient grounds in Egypt, as does our Communiversity, as we shall see, in Nigeria.

Division of Labour

Ancient Egypt did not have castes in the strictest sense of the word. But there was a general division of labour based on four main groups, from the communal ground up:

- the *farming community,* ranging form nobles to farmers (the bulk of the population) to stock breeders, gardeners and superintendents of waterways

- *people working outside the populated areas*, such as herdsman, shepherds, poulterers and fowlers
- specialised *professionals and artisans,* such as smiths, leatherworkers, boat builders, paper makers, scribes, weavers, masons, musicians and bards
- *intermediaries* consisting of clergy, judges and doctors.

In relation to the farming community, moreover, land for the Egyptians was not something that could be owned. People had the right to occupy land only if they worked it, and could only own the fruits of their labour. The Ancient Egyptians had no verb meaning to possess, to have or to belong to. This is indeed resonant with the *Commons* movement today, as recently depicted by German biologist Andreas Weber (12), in his book *Enlivenment: Towards a Poetics for the Anthropocene:*

> For millennia, human societies understood the biosphere as a commons based economy and treated their internal cultures, material resources, and immaterial exchange relations as part of a huge, all-encompassing commons. Modern industrial cultures typically condescended to such "primitive" economies by dismissing their "superstitions" extolling the virtues of objective science. Yet it is the moderns who have profoundly lost touch with insights into the principles underlying life. Enlightenment philosophers projected back the evil they experienced in their own highly hierarchic societies onto the picture they painted of the state of nature of early humans.

Such a commons based society, in ancient Egypt then in modern turn was eclipsed by the modern, Egyptian hierarchical society, in polity and economy, in religion and education. What was the nature and scope of the broader industrial base?

2.10.2. Manufacturing and Services

Metal Procurement, Mining and Manufacture in Communal Guilds

At an early period, the Egyptians learned how to work metals, and 5000 years ago the Ancient Egyptians had already developed the techniques of mining, refining and metalworking. Because of it being the largest and richest population in the ancient world, moreover, Egypt imported huge quantities of raw materials, and in return exported large quantities of finished goods. The Egyptians possessed considerable knowledge of chemistry and the use of metallic oxides, as manifested in their ability to produce glass and porcelain in a variety of natural colours.

The science and technology to manufacture metallic products and goods were known and perfected there by groups of craftsmen, as ancient communal guilds, so that metal alloys were produced in large quantities. As such, the Egyptians sought raw material from other countries as well as their own, used their home-grown expertise to explore, mine and transport raw materials from all over the inhabited world.

Economic and Social Exchange in Market and Community

In ancient Egypt an active exchange of goods and services took place between the different individuals and groups, either directly or via intermediate brokers and traders who were also able to expand activities between various communities. While farming proliferated in rural communities, the cities attracted industries such as textiles, glass, metals, wood, and leather making. Public marketplaces, which were also rich sources of social interchange, meanwhile provided the means to exchange and buy goods.

While Egypt exported glassware, for example, of the finest quality, to Greece and Rome, it imported timber from Phoenicia, animals from Africa, mineral ore from Iberia. The principal imports from Arabia and India were spices. The Ancient Egyptians also established various peaceful colonies in present day Syria, Yemen, the United Arab Emirates, and the Iberian peninsula. We now turn from the ancient Egyptian economy to the ancient priesthood that were, at least in part, responsible for such, what Anwar Sawaf has termed "sacred commerce".

2.11. Sacred Commerce

2.11.1. The Merchant Priesthood on A Spiritual Quest

Egypt's Ayman Sawaf (13), a business entrepreneur and social philosopher now based in the UK, spent the first ten years of his business career designing, manufacturing and selling lights, spearheading one of the largest lighting companies in the Middle East with assembly lines in Europe and the Far East. At that time, as he writes, he knew nothing of spirituality or emotions; life for him was all about maths, statistics, engineering and business. By his mid 30s he was in an early midlife crisis, challenged on both home and health fronts and fed up with life.

Revered as a spiritual path, for Sawaf now writing post-midlife crisis, commerce emerged long ago, he maintains, as a tool to advance mankind. Thereby, at least among the Merchant Priesthood of old Egypt it was viewed as a gift from god/goddess, sacred and balanced by its very nature. Commerce was seen as a solution or a map to deal with issues of social as well as economic survival, security and community, and as an ally in a process of conscious evolution whereby they were ready to take that ultimate spiritual adventure: coming home. *Historically, the role of the Merchant Priesthood had been to work behind the scenes, seeing what they could do to improve the human condition on their spiritual quest.* This was their service to local community and global humanity.

Their principal role and concern, as such, had been to protect the divine Gift by creating and protecting an environment conducive to democratic principles and to encourage and keep the balance between feminine and masculine energies, thus enhancing the sacred in everything and keeping chauvinism at bay. They knew that democracy with its promise of equality and freedom is a prerequisite for the tools of commerce, Sawaf maintains, not to be abused by one segment of society against another. As Gadalla also has pointed out, above, *the gift of Sacred Commerce would rise when feminine and sacred values arose within a culture and then go underground beneath the next wave of chauvinism.*

While the masculine was a penetrating energy that was interested in doing, acting, providing, reasoning things out, and manifesting, the feminine energy was more concerned with being, feeling, experiencing and intuiting as a means of knowing, and enjoying all that is made manifest in form. Trade existed then from the first day humans walked on earth, but it was in Ancient Egypt that it was first instituted, according to Sawaf, as a sacred communal practice. Since then, this sacred practice has re-emerged in many forms through every known civilization, he says, bringing about the empowerment needed to create and evolve human societies. Sadly though, this is a far cry from how such is seen today, with the advent of financial capitalism and the like, whereby we have lost sights of such a grounding in *sacred commerce.*

2.11.2. Goods Were Viewed as Vessels of Communal Energy

Merchant priests knew then that a healthy society must have a solid communal foundation, or indeed grounding. *Principles of flow, balance, and abundance were understood as essential, and commerce was a key means to that end. Goods were viewed as vessels of energy. They were also means to engage and connect on a personal level.* Trade then also functioned as a social discourse. Great value was placed on communal learning, and on cultivating empathy and friendly relationships, as the basis of commercial dealings. These qualities and a general sense of conviviality fostered a balanced psychic state in individuals and communities. Relationships were understood to be the means by which a harmonious psyche is established throughout a culture and society.

Once initiated on the path, *the Merchant Priest-in-training began to explore and develop the "hara"—the vital centre below the naval that,* for Sawaf, *is the seat of emotional power.* Both men and women took up this form of learning. They learned to recognise and "read' emotions in fine detail, attending to many layers and levels of expression. From physical manifestations such as facial expressions, muscle tension, skin tone, vocal quality, and even heart rate and blood pressure, the Merchant Priest learned to sense the texture and temperature of the emotional side of trade.

This would—in time—give them the ability *to equalise and balance the energy of emotions that swirled around the communal and economic marketplace. The marketplace was rife with envy, jealousy, anger and the Merchant Priest would minister to the collective psychic state.* In a sense they were the first diplomats; theirs was the work of negotiation, very different in nature and scope from that deployed today, say, by a Donald Trump! They could literally sculpt the emotional reality of the marketplace. It was this balance between the emphasis and value placed on psychic sensitivity and the grounded practical abilities that allowed the Merchant Priests to become one of the most respected priestly castes.

2.11.3. Queen Hatshepsut, and Akhenaten to Merchant Priest Joseph

Historically in fact we see the first real signs of the Merchant Priesthood during Queen Hatshepsut's reign in Ancient Egypt from 1479 to 1457 BC, known as the era of the "New Kingdom", as we saw above, a period during which Egypt developed a great empire as wealth and new ideas spread across the country. *The Merchant Priests served the benevolent queen well, and this new trade route allowed her subjects to enjoy prized imports—ivory, spices, gold and aromatic plants.* Simultaneously these activities began to bring different cultures and communities together to learn from each other. Again we see the power of the feminine at work.

Hatsheput's successor though, according to Sawaf, Thutmosis III, undid nearly all the progress his step-mother had made during her 20-year rule. He displaced the Merchant Priests and stripped them of almost all their authority so they were no longer influential. This is typical of *their history: it would rise when the feminine and sacred values rose within a culture and go underground beneath the next wave of chauvinism,* forming secret societies to conceal their activities from the ruling class.

With the reign of Akhenaten, the reach and influence of the Merchant Priests once again expanded. He fostered the vision of a non-violent, almost democratic society, and his reign saw the first flowing of a rational philosophy as well as the bare beginnings of a school of scientific thought. Akhenaten even dreamed of a single civilization throughout the Mediterranean, united by a complex web of trade routes and free trade among people as one of the first seeds of what we now talk of as a globalization movement albeit with a different, more "feminine" impulse from that which prevails today. Indeed some consider Akhenaten, who anticipated monotheism, to have foreshadowed feminism. He took his wife as an equal and ruled side by side with her rather than with her "at his side", as other sovereigns of the time. He was the last pharaoh, moreover, to revere Joseph, the Hebrew with the many-colored coat. An early Merchant Priest, Joseph had lived in Egypt hundreds of years before Akhenaten.

Visions played yet another role in Joseph's ascent to high office as the greatest Merchant Priest of the time. He championed the cause of the Nilometer, with which he was able to foresee whether the Nile flood would be high or low and could advise his people what to plant and where. In the ascent of the youngest brother in fact, Joseph, the story questions the traditional social hierarchy, showing also that nature and community have their own intelligent process and will gather whatever forces are needed to manifest its inherent patterns. These grounded patterns are seeds or archetypes that have been there from the beginning.

2.11.4. Akhenaten, Moses and Hermes

Before Akhenaten in effect disappeared, according to Sawaf, he initiated one of his advisors in the northern Egyptian city he built into the full mysteries of a monotheistic religion. Like the pharaoh's mother, that advisor was a Hebrew, the man we know as Moses. In addition to introducing him to the notion of one God, he shared the secrets of the merchant Priesthood with him. King Solomon in fact, with his principles of fairness and justice for all, not just the privileged, was the true inheritor of Moses, according to Sawaf, and the Merchant Priesthood lineage.

From the land of Israel this lineage then continued to spread across the eastern Mediterranean into Greece. Several hundred years later, when Alexander invaded Egypt, the Greeks built a completely new capital on the very site where Akhenaten's had stood. The Greeks named their new city Hermeopolis (later named Alexandria) in honour of the god Hermes. *Hermes was the messenger god, the god of commerce and writing, and the god of all forms of social and economic exchange,* equivalent to the god Bes (god of commerce) in Egypt. This brings us to our conclusion, as we revisit the phenomenon of Sekem in an ancient light.

2.12. Conclusion: Bringing the Ennead to New Light

2.12.1. Heliopolis as the Epicenter of Creation

It is a curious fact, for Bauval and Osman (14), that when one is exposed for a prolonged time to Egypt's natural topography—its mighty river, its lush and verdant Nile Valley, its arid but inspiring deserts, its fauna, and the seasonal changes observed in the sky—all tend to inspire *a profound sense of wonder and awe, a curious connection with eternity, which will gradually instigate a deep reverence for the invisible cosmic forces that seem to regulate earthly events.*

Moreover, on "the natural gift of the Nile", the yearly flood, totally determined the livelihood of Egyptians, and it was inevitable that from it would also develop a theology, which, for want of better words, might be called a natural religion. Egyptologists have reconstructed the cosmology of the ancient Egyptians:

Before anything existed there was a liquid nothingness or, as the case may be, the Primeval water called Nun—the primordial soup before creation. Out of Nun emerged the Primeval mound on which the first sunrise took place. The Primeval Mound was associated with the Creator God called Atum. The original Mound of Creation was at the most hallowed place in Lower Egypt, called Heliopolis by the Greeks (literally "City of the Sun"). The first consciousness thus emerges from the primordial *Nun;* it is the creator God, *Atum,* who is going to complete creation, creating four divine pairs, the *Ennad* of eight-plus-one, according to Heliopolitan cosmogony. The first two pairs correspond with the four elements in turn:

1. *Shu* and *Tefnut* = air (space) related to the sun, and humidity (water, moisture)
2. *Nut* and *Geb* = sky God and earth Goddess (fire and light)

These are followed by two more sets of pairs, the four children of Geb and Nut:

1. *Osiris* and *Isis* = maker of human laws and patroness of nature
2. *Seth* and *Nephthys* = combatant God and Goddess of protective guardianship

These Heliopolitan gods, albeit mythologically interrelated as per the overall so-called Ennead, each embody specific and complementary, masculine-feminine individualities, which serve to build on the prior, overall process of individuation to which we have alluded above. Even today, in spite of the extensive urban development of Greater Cairo, it is still possible to see the natural mounds that dominate the otherwise flat lands of the Nile Valley and adjacent desert. The most prominent of these was the one at Heliopolis, which represented the Mound of Creation. It was clear, then, that Heliopolis was seen as the epicenter of creation. Its time, as we shall see, after a longstanding demise, is coming again. Heliopolis University for Sustainable Development, in fact, is physically based on that very site.

2.12.2. Grounded in the Ennead – Emerging through the Integrators

In building on Rice's *Egyptian Legacy* as well as on Bauval and Osman's *Soul of Egypt*, not to mention also Sawaf's *Sacred Commerce*—moving now in conclusion from grounding to emergence—we revisited and renewed the original Heliopolitan Ennead. Indeed, while the contemporary *Enneagram,* originally developed by two Latin American psychiatrists in the 1960s, Bolivia's Oscar Ichazo and the better known Chilean, Claudio Naranjo (15), has since proliferated, worldwide, its ancient Egyptian grounds have been totally lost. While its developers refer to esoteric Christianity, traditionally, and to the occult orientations Russia's Ouspensky, in modern times, they seem oblivious to its Heliopolitan origins. Moreover, disconnected from such a dynamic, mythological and dynamic source, it has become overwhelmingly *typological.*

So for example, one of the contemporary American proponents of the enneagram, California based educator, and student of Ouspensky's (16) *Fourth Way,* Susan Zanos (17), in her book on *Human Types: Essence and the Enneagram* talks of Lunar, Mercurial, Venusian, Martial, Jovial, Saturnine and Solar types, as well as combinations thereof. Drawing thereby on astrology as well as the work of the Christian Gnostics, what is glaringly missing, therefore, is the dynamic element built into the original Heliopolitan mythology, and storyline, specifically, and of course the backdrop of Egypt generally.

2.12.3. Inhibited Indigenous-Exogenous Social Innovation

In fact, and in reality, just like Egypt as a whole, today, Sekem as an integral enterprise has been somewhat inhibited in engaging in what we would term thoroughgoing social innovation. Thereby it would be recognising and releasing its indigenous GENE-IUS, by combining indigenous and exogenous knowledge, and value. For notwithstanding its Heliopolitan grounding, duly reinforced by Heliopolis University for Sustainable Development which it has established, the home grown Ennead has been hitherto neglected. Instead Sekem has drawn generally on so-called "Spiral Dynamics" (18), with its hierarchy of so-called cultural "memes" from "survival" to "wisdom" oriented, born and bred by Don Beck and Chris Cowan in America, a far cry from ancient or indeed modern Egypt today.

More specifically, moreover, Sekem has drawn from their Belgian compatriot, organisational developer Frederick Laloux (19), in his seminal work of *Reinventing Organizations: A Guide to Creating Organizations Inspired by the Next State of Human Consciousness,* which builds in turn on Spiral Dynamics. For Laloux from the outset:

> My interest is in organizations and collaboration, not medicine or astronomy. But the conceptual question is the same: could it be that our current worldview limits the way we think about organizations? Could we invent a more powerful, soulful, more meaningful way to work together, if only we change our belief system?

Ironically, such a "soulful" approach to work, and to enterprise, could be uncovered, indigenously from within ancient Egypt, as revealed in our conclusion, thereafter merged with the exogenous. What Sawaf has suggested, above, is that it is possible to trace an unbroken line of senior Merchant Priests at least from Queen Hatshepsut down through Moses and Oedipus and the founding of the cradles of the democratic city-states of Greece. The Merchant Priesthood as such, moreover, was instrumental, he maintains, in the founding of the European world, and arguably, also, the United States of America.

Sadly though, what Sawaf is alluding to, as a source of individual and communal learning, as well as economic and enterprise development, is long lost to the modern-day Egyptian, and indeed African, if not worldly-wise consciousness, as we fail to connect with our prior natural and communal grounding, and indeed centering, in "north" and "west" Africa, integrally as it were.

At their best, value-based *communal* societies are *infused with vision*, embodying a unique contribution to the world; at their worst rigid dogma prevails.

We now turn to our second source of communal grounding, this version duly enriched by the formidable French anthropologists, Griaule and Dieterlen, lifetime researchers into the life and work of the Dogon peoples of West Africa.

2.13. References

1 **Lessem** R and **Schieffer** A (2015) *Integral Renewal: A Relational and Renewal Perspective.* Abingdon. Routledge
2 **Rice** M (1997) *Egypt's Legacy: The Archetypes of Western Civilization 3000–30 BC.* London. Routledge
3 **Naydler** J (2009) *The Future of the Ancient World.* Rochester, Vermont. Inner Traditions
4 **Jung** C.G. (1991) *The Archetypes and the Collective Unconscious.* London. Routledge

5   **Gadalla** M (2007) *Ancient Egyptian Culture Revealed.* Greensboro. USA. Tehuti Research Foundation

6   **Amadiume** I (1997) *Reinventing Africa: Matriarchy, Culture and Religion.* London. Zed Books

7   **Bauval** R (2007) *The Egypt Code.* New York. Arrow Books

8   **Bauval** R and **Osman** A (2015) *The Soul of Ancient Egypt: Restoring the Spiritual Engine of the World.* Vermont. Bear and Company.

9   **Lachman** G (2011) *The Quest for Hermes Trismegistus: From Ancient Egypt to the Modern World.* Edinburgh. Floris Books

10 **Abouleish** I (2005) *Sekem: A Sustainable Community in the Egyptian Desert.* Edinburgh. Floris Publications

11 **Gadalla** M (2007) *op cit*

12 **Weber** A (2019) *Enlivenment: Towards a Poetics for the Anthropocene.* Cambridge. Mass. MIT Press

13 **Sawaf** A and **Gabrielle** R (2007) *Sacred Commerce: The Rise of the Global Citizen.* Ojai, CA. Sacred Commerce

14 **Bauval** R and **Osman** A (2015) *op cit*

15 **Naranjo** C (2004) *Enneagram of Society: Healing the Soul to Heal the World.* Nevada City. CA. Gateway Consciousness Classics

16 **Ouspensky** P D (2000) *The Fourth Way: Teachings of Gurdjieff.* New York. Random House

17 **Zannos** S (1997) *Human Types: Essence and the Enneagram.* Maine. Samuel Weiner

18 **Beck** D and **Cowan** C (2005) *Spiral Dynamics: Mastering Values, Leadership and Change.* Chichester. Wiley-Blackwell

19 **Laloux** F (2014) *Reinventing Organizations: A Guide to Creating Organizations Inspired by the Next State of Human Consciousness.* Brussels. Nelson Parker

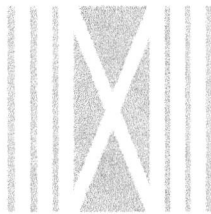

CHAPTER 3

Seeking the Primordial

The five elements, which make up five clans, together allow an entire village to form a cosmological wheel. The village can then balance itself by keeping the various elements in balance, that being its principal task. Such an elemental wheel exists in each person, moreover, just as it is present in each clan and community. Each person needs to keep the water of reconciliation flowing within the self, in order to calm the inner fires and live in harmony with others. Each person needs to nourish the ancestral fire within, so that one stays in touch with one's dreams and visions. Each person needs to be grounded in the earth, to be able to become a source of nourishment to the community. Each person needs to remember the knowledge stores in one's bones—to live out one's own unique genius. And each person needs to be real, as nature is real, keeping in touch with a sense of mystery and wonder, and helping to preserve the integrity of the natural world. To be out of balance in any of these areas is to invite sickness to come to dwell within.

Patrice Some, *The Healing Wisdom of Africa*

3.1. Introduction

3.1.1. Ancient Cosmology: Our Afrikological DNA

As we indicated in our opening chapter, the very divisiveness of "north" (rich) and "south" (poor), if not also "east" (communist) and "west" (capitalist), not to mention also specifically university and community, as well as generally globalisation and localisation, is transcended once we (1) move from such two opposing worlds to four integrating ones. Indeed for American software engineer, and cosmologist extraordinaire, Laird Scranton (2), whose writings span ancient China and Egypt, Neolithic Scotland and the land of the Dogon, although the term *ancient cosmology* is often closely linked with religion, it properly *refers to systematized cultural beliefs about how processes of creation occur, and to the ways in which these processes were understood by ancient cultures.*

Any distinct cultural perspective, moreover, from which these processes are explained, is called, for him a *creative tradition,* for us re-GENE-ration, specifically recognising and releasing gene-IUS, thereby altogether Synergising in this case Dogon moral Inspiration (local) with a Universal truth (global). Such an archaic tradition, that dates back to 10,000 BCE, serves to fuse together, in retrospect and prospect, the pre-modern, the modern, and the trans-modern. Indeed for Iranian-American contemporary public intellectual Reza Aslan (3) in his recent book on *God: A Human History of Religion*:

> This is essentially what our prehistoric ancestors believed. Their primitive animism was predicated on the belief that all things—living or not—share a single essence: a single soul, if you will. The same belief spurred the ancient Mesopotamians to deify the elements of nature, long before they began to transform those elements into individual, personalized gods. It lay at the heart of the early Egyptian belief in the existence of a divine force that manifested itself in both gods and humans. It is what the Greek philosophers meant when they spoke of "one god" as the singular, unified principle steering all creation. All of these belief systems can be viewed as different expressions of the pantheistic conception of God as the sum of things. But one can find the same belief in nearly every religious tradition. It is deeply embedded, for example, in Chinese Taoism, where the divine principle is presented as the ground of all being.

In this chapter then, we shall be drawing on such a primordial, though evergreen, cosmology, for our complementary grounding, following in ancient Egypt's formidable footsteps, now basing our origination on the renowned Dogon peoples of West Africa.

3.1.2. The Dogon as an Ideal Point of Entry

The well explicated cosmology then, that Scranton draws on, constitutes for us an ideal Afrikological point of entry. For Dogon culture (see also the opening quote from Some), offers many advantages for use as a touchstone for a study of this primordial type: *the Dogon are remotely located, effectively distanced from corrupting outside influences, their cosmology encompasses a rich set of archetypal symbols, myths, themes and practices,* their tribal ethic emphasizes purity of language and preservation of original traditions and themes. Meanwhile those traditions embrace a set of practices that have significance for at least three religious traditions: those of ancient Egypt, of Buddhism and of Judaism.

Perhaps more importantly, Dogon cosmological beliefs were carefully documented by a team of French researchers over three decades. This team was so dedicated to its subject that its lead anthropologist, Marcel Griaule (4), succeeded in gaining both initiated status within the Dogon esoteric tradition and honorary citizenship in the tribe itself. This emerged out of his longstanding *Conversations with Ogotomelli: An Introduction to Dogon Religious Ideas,* Ogotomelli thereby being a Dogon African sage.

3.2. The Science of the Dogon: Decoding the African Mystery Tradition

Dogon Words and Symbols Shared with the First Egyptian Dynasty

Scranton (5) then became interested in Dogon mythology and symbolism in the early 1990s. The Dogon are a modern-day African tribal people who live along the cliffs of the Bandiagara escarpment, south of the Sahara desert, near Timbuktu and not far from the Niger river in Mali, West Africa. The tribe consists of approximately 100,000 people in 700 villages. Highly suggestive of an ancient lineage for the Dogon people are their religious rituals and practices which in key ways mirror those of Ancient Egypt, on the one hand, and Judaism on the other. Furthermore, *the Dogon myths are expressed in words and symbols that are shared with the Amazigh, the tribes of hunters who lived in Egypt prior to the beginning of the First Egyptian dynasty.* Perhaps most significantly, Dogon mythology is documented in tribal drawings that often take the same shape as the ancient pictograms used in Egyptian hieroglyphic writing.

Prior Structures of Civilized Knowledge

Some of course will think it absurd to suggest that the people of 3400 BC were learning theories of advanced science at a time when they hardly had mastered the skills of stonemasonry. *What is believable,* for Scranton though, *is that the structures of civilized knowledge were presented to mankind in a form that would orient us towards a larger understanding of the sciences.* Indeed hints about the origins of the universe, the composition of matter, and the reproductive processes of life were incorporated into this framework.

It is distinctly possible, then, that there is new science to be found in the Egyptian hieroglyphs, those remarkable 5000-year-old drawings whose mysteries could well provide important clues to modern scientists.

3.2.1. Themes of the Ancient Creation Stories

Surface and Deep Story

The oldest creation stories centre then on a surprisingly constant set of themes. Firstly, *if we look at the themes that appear in the Dogon religion, we find that they can be grouped into two distinct storylines*, which Scranton calls *the surface story and the deep story.* In other words, the universe actually consists of two creations, one we can see and one that we cannot. The same pattern can be seen in the dominant Egyptian creation traditions of Heliopolis and Hermeopolis. The surface storyline included some or all of the following: first, a self-created god emerges from the waters of chaos. The Dogon called such Amma, and the Egyptians Amen (Atum). This self-formed god/goddess creates four sets of masculine-feminine pairs. In Heliopolis these eight, overall, con- stituted the so-called Ogdoad: Shu and Tefnet, Geb and Nut, Isis and Osiris, Seth and Nephythis. For us (6) such a "surface story" is constituted of the "topsoil" (inclinations) and "subsoil" (institutions) of a society.

The deep story includes more intimate details, for us drawn "topographically" from a societal "bedrock" (ideologies) and core (images). Typically the un- formed universe, for the Dogon, is described as an egg that contains all of the seeds, or signs of the world. In some cultures these signs are represented as the letters of the alphabet, but in others they are simply identified as the seeds of the world to come. *Implied throughout are a basic set of principles.* Both describe an initial set of emergent godlike entities created in pairs.

Pairing of Male and Female

A second guiding principle is the pairing of male and female. The self-created god, in many societies is both male and female. We can see this pairing also reflected in the traditional organisation of Egypt into two lands, one called Upper Egypt and the other Lower Egypt. In modern Dogon culture, a plot of land is divided between those who farm (Pax Communis) and others who forge the tools and implements (Pax Scientia) of farming. In contemporary guise this is more conventionally associated with the ancient Chinese cosmol- ogy of *yin* (feminine) and *yang* (masculine), the acknowledgement of which we (7) have acknowledged as a keynote of transformation.

Cardinal Points of the Earth – North, South, East and West

*A third concept of great importance to the earliest religions is the idea of the cardinal points of the Earth—north, south, east and west—*which is central to our integral approach generally, and to our Communiversity specifically. Such can be seen, for example, in the Great Pyramid of Egypt, deliberately aligned with the four cardinal points, for us Community (south), Sanctuary (east), Academy (west) and Laboratory (west).

3.2.2. Dogon Symbols and Meanings

The Eighth Ancestor

Amma or Amen (Atum) then represents, as it were, the first living cell, which emerged from the waters of the ancient ocean, described by modern scientists as a kind of primal soup. A pairing is then formed by mitosis, a form of cell division. This process of splitting results in a matching pair of new cells, each with the same chromosomal makeup as the original cell.

The eight ancestors of the Dogon, much like the first eight emergent Egyptian gods and goddesses, could be seen as an example of the more complicated reproductive process called meiosis. *The Dogon describe the journey of the eighth ancestor as entering the womb of the earth, and it is a journey each of the eight ancestors must make during the process of transformation.* Once inside the womb, the eighth ancestor gains knowledge of the Word of the female Nummo, which with the male Nummo takes the shape of a spiralling coil. This coil is the textbook image of the DNA molecule—the double helix which is depicted in our own TCA (Trans4m Communiversity Associates) logo (www. tc-a.org) that we know is the medium of transmission for the genetic "word", DNA being constituted of four nucleotides.

The Four Quantum Forces

Further examining the Dogon symbols, now as they relate to quantum physics, Scranton notes that the four creative stages—*bummo, yala, tonu* and *toy* (see below)—might have a bearing on quantum physics, in relation to the four types of force-carrying particles the physicist Stephen Hawking (8), described in his *Brief History of Time,* as also cited by one of us, Anselm Adodo, in his *Nature Power* (9) in the opening chapter, which can be aligned with our GENE generally, and our Communiversity specifically:

> ... The first category is the *gravitational force.* The force is universal, that is every particle feels the force of gravity, according to its mass or energy ... our Communal Grounding

> the next category is *electromagnetic force,* which interacts with electrically charged particles like electrons ... The electromagnetic attraction between negatively charged particles and positively charged protons in the nucleus causes the electrons to orbit the nucleus of the atom ... our Emergent Transformation Journey

the third category is called the *weak nuclear force*… exhibiting a property known as spontaneous symmetry breaking. This means that what appear to be a number of completely different particles at owe energies are in fact found to be all the same particle, only in different states … our Navigatory Academy

the fourth category is *the strong nuclear force,* which holds the quarks together in the proton and neutron, within the nucleus of the atom… our Effecting Laboratory.

The gravitation is so weak and undetectable as to be a seed (bummo–grounding–learning Community). The electromagnetic force defines the outline of the object (yala–emerging–re-GENE-rative). The weak nuclear force at states of high energy refines the component particles (tonu–navigating–research Academy) and the strong nuclear force binds or draws the atoms together (toy–effecting–integral Laboratory).

Dogon Quantum Forces Parallel to Contemporary String Theory in Physics

String theory came to the forefront of scientific thought in the early 1980s, whereby particles were conceived as vibrating, oscillating, dancing filaments. Just as the strings of string theory, as such, are thought to give rise to the four quantum forces, so the Dogon tell us that the spider gives birth to four seeds, or *sene na,* which for us indeed constitute the seeds of our Communiversity.

We now turn more specifically to Dogon parallels to Egyptian mythology.

3.3. Dogon Parallels to Foundational Cosmology

3.3.1. The Heliopolitan Cosmology

The many persistent similarities between Dogon and Egyptian religious symbols (see next chapter) and lifestyles lead to a natural suggestion that modern Dogon society could actually represent a contemporary remnant of ancient Egyptian culture. For French 20th century Egyptologist Serge Sauneron (10) in his book *The Priests of Ancient Egypt:* "The Egyptians never considered their language—that corresponding to the hieroglyphs—as a social tool; for them, it always remained a resonant echo of the vital energy that had brought the universe to life, a cosmic force. Thus study of this language enabled them to "explain" the cosmos. "

Moreover, in *A History of Ancient Egypt,* another contemporary French Egyptologist Nicholas Grimal (11) provided a description that reflects the surface storyline of the Dogon:

In the beginning was Nun, often translated as "chaos", containing the potential for the seeds of life. It was from this chaos that the sun emerged. It appeared on a mound of earth covered in pure sand emerging from water, taking the form of a standing stone, the "benben", the focus of a cult at Heliopolis, considered to be the original site of creation.

We know, moreover (see chapter 3), that the first emergent gods of the Heliopolitan tradition were Geb, Nut, Shu and Tefnut—respectively associated with earth (Geb), water (Nut), wind (Shu) and fire (Tefnut), followed by Isis and Osiris, Seth and Nephythis, altogether constituting the eightfold Ogdoad. With Neith as the mother goddess, moreover, we therefore have at the very foundation of Egyptian religion the unmistakable symbol, according to Scranton, of a primordial thread symbolising the four categories of quantum particles, expressed in virtually the same terms as that of the Dogon.

3.3.2. Releasing Gene-ius

For English Egyptologist Wallis Budge (12) moreover, early last century, in his *Legends of the Egyptian Gods,* we find the ancient Egyptian equivalent of the creation of matter, known as "laying the foundations". As such, again duly aligned with our re-GENE-ration:

- firstly the hieroglyphic counterpart of the Dogon word *bummo,* the act of conception, is *bu maa,* a synonym for *maat,* based on the roots word *maa,* which means to "perceive"—our grounding: *learning community*
- secondly, the Egyptian counterpart of the Dogon *yala* is *ahau,* which means "delineation of posts or boundaries"—our emergence: *regenerative sanctuary*
- thirdly, the Dogon *tonu,* an "approximation of what is to be created" is the Egyptian *teni,* which means "to estimate"—our navigation: *research academy*
- finally, the Dogon creational stage, *toy,* is *tematu,* which means in ancient Egyptian "complete", the same notion as the God Atum (to be complete), which for us is transformative effect: *integral laboratory.*

These four phases, in turn, can be related to the above four quantum forces: the gravitational force (grounding), the electromagnetic force (emergence), the weak nuclear force (navigation), and the strong nuclear force (effect). These then in turn can be aligned, as we have seen, with the four constituents of our Communiversity: Community, Sanctuary, Academy, Laboratory.

The Cult of the Feminine Principle

Scranton's comparative studies, moreover, strongly suggest that many of the classical ancient symbolic traditions from Africa, Egypt, India and Asia derived from a common source, ultimately pointing back to the archaic Gobeki Tepi site in Turkey (dated around 10,000 BC) and thereafter to the deities of the archaic Sakti Cult of India. This Cult, sometimes referred to as the "Cult of the Feminine Principle", is said to have originated in mountain regions to the north and west of India, in the Fertile Crescent.

The cult, which like the Dogon survives today, is considered to have been ancestral to the Vedic, Buddhist and Hindu religions of India, and reflects cosmological concepts that lie at the heart of the Egyptian and Dogon creation traditions. Traditions of the Sakti Cult are preserved in India by an ethnic group called the Tamil, and concepts of the tradition, expressed in the words of their Dravidian languages, also comprise one of the many sub-groups of the Dogon language.

Interaction Between Non-Material and Material Energy

Cosmological beliefs of the Sakti Cult, then, rest on one of the earliest philosophies to emerge, an ancient precept called *Samkhya,* which provides the philosophical foundation for the Vedic, Buddhist and Hindu religions, and is seen as a companion philosophy to the yoga tradition. Consistent with what we know about the Dogon outlook on processes of creation, Samkhya is described as both dualistic and non-theistic. In the broadest of strokes this primordial philosophy defines two eternal realities: a "witnessing consciousness" called *purusha* and a "womb of creation" called *prakriti.* In the mindset of philosophy, the processes of material creation are catalysed when the consciousness of "purusha" is infused into "prakriti".

The notion then that *the processes of material creation depend on an interaction between non-material and material energy, conceptualised as a male/female duality* is one that also plays a foundational role in Dogon cosmology. In the Buddhist tradition, moreover, similar concepts of the implied duality of the universe are expressed through the notion of co-existence of two distinct worlds of creation, one that is *spiritual* (a world of *formlessness* or "non-manifestation") and one that is material (a world of *form* or "manifestation").

As Scranton's cosmological studies have progressed, he has come to understand that a great number of symbolic aspects of the ancient creation tradition are metaphors for a single theme: reconciling the non-material with the material universe. At the most essential level of interpretation, we interpret the terms *above and below,* or *heaven and earth* as metaphors for the two universes, *combining the geometric figures of the circle (symbolic of the Heavens) with the square (symbolic of the Earth).*

Granary, Stupa and Communiversity Aligned with the Cardinal Points

The Buddhist "stupa" in fact is a ritual shrine which can be cosmologically likened to the Dogon granary. Architecturally, the granary is four-sided, and the steps of the four stairways correspond to zoological classes of animals, and so reflect an intellectual organisation for society that also seems scientifically rooted. As an integral aspect of their symbolism, *the base plans of the Dogon granary and the Buddhist stupa, like our communiversity, are each aligned to the cardinal points of north and south, east and west.*

3.4. Dogon Cosmology as Centre-piece

3.4.1. The Four Elements and the Centring Aether

Scranton's entry point into *primordial structural differences* then begins with the Dogon concept of four "clavicles" (collar bones). These are described as being ovoid (curved like an egg) and attached to one another "as of welded together". The Dogon (9) say that what separates them is four "angles" or direction of space. *These are seen as precursors to the four classic primordial elements of water, fire, wind and earth.*

Ancient Greek philosophers such as Plato and Aristotle promoted the concept of an aether and debated the significant aspects of its existence, including the question of whether it should be treated as the first of the primordial elements alongside water, fire, wind and earth. In the Tamil language the concept of aether was expressed by the world *akacam*, while in Buddhism it was referred to as *akasa* which can also mean "space". According to architect and philosopher Adrian Snodgrass (13) within Buddhism it is *considered "the quintessential and central element", and one that conceptually precedes the four elements, and is synonymous with the notion of Enlightenment.*

It is reasonable then to think, according to Scranton, that the Dogon word *atay* has a bearing on the same concept. For French anthropologist Genevieve Calame-Griaule (14), then, the meaning of the word applies to oscillating motion, which the Dogon compare with a creeping plant. Aligned with such, for the Dogon furthermore, is the *yu* seed, considered by them the smallest grain.

From the viewpoint of the Dogon Amma's (tribal God) then clavicles precede the four primordial elements in very much the same way that the aether is said to precede them in Buddhism. In fact the Dogon term for "clavicle" is *anu*, a word that also implies the notion of bonding in loving friendship. From this perspective the "yu" seed, which is compared to two clavicles bound together, implies the notion of two people locked in a loving embrace, which Scranton sees as one of the central metaphors of the archaic creation tradition. In fact, the Kabbalistic (Jewish mysticism) outlook aligns with both the Dogon and also Egyptian definitions in interesting ways. First, it relates to the name of the Dogon white millet seed, or *yu*, as providing a phonetic root for the Hebrew letter *Yod*, standing for God. We also see such reflected in the Egyptian mouth glyph.

These are further linked with Dogon and Kabbalistic characterizations of matter as a Word that issues from the mouth. In each of these cases we see the ancient concept of an aether that is placed conceptually as prior metaphoric acts of creation, each with symbolic associations to seeds and plants. A seed, of course, represents a potential for life. The concept of aether, moreover, is also recognised in Islam, where it is again counted alongside the four elements, to which we now more fully turn.

3.4.2. Bummo, Yala, Tonu, Toymu: Our GENE-and-Communiversity

Taking On From Where Ancient Egypt Left Off

In Dogon cosmology, symbolic references made to water pertain to matter in its initial wavelike stage—our Community; those to fire relate to an act of perception—our Sanctuary; wind refers symbolically to the concept of vibration—our Academy; and statements about earth pertain to mass or matter that is fully formed—our Laboratory. The series of symbolic categories that defines that pattern for other four-stage metaphors is expressed, as we have seen, by the terms *bummo, yala, tonu,* and *toymu* which can be aligned with our GENE. By literal definition the term *bummo* means "trace", *yala* means "mark" or "image", *tonu* means "reflection" and *toymu* means "complete".

Architecturally speaking the term *bummo* (similar to the Egyptian *bu maa*) refers to the initial concept of the building to be constructed (grounding Community). It is represented by the most tentative outline of the building marked by dots. The term *yala* (in the Egyptian *ahau*) refers to the next (emergent Sanctuary) conceptual stage of the same plan, this time defined more precisely with additional points, plotted to mark the major features of the structure. The third term *tonu* (in the Egyptian *tennu*) indicates a plan (navigation/Academy) in which the dots have been connected, and whose outline features have thereby been fleshed out. The final terms, *toymu* (or in the Egyptian *temau*) refers to the final structure in its completed (Laboratory effect) form.

One, Two, Three and Four Dimensional

Moreover, for Scranton, the Dogon term *bummo* combines the Egyptian phoneme *bu* (meaning "place") with the Egyptian word *maa* (meaning "to perceive") and so takes it to imply "place perceived". Dimensionally speaking, the concept of "place perceived" could reasonably refer to a *geometric point*, a figure that is understood to be one-dimensional. The term *yala* then refers to the perspective of a geometric line, thereby a two-dimensional construct. Similarly the Egyptian word *ahau* can refer to "a period of time", whereby the concept of measurable time coincides with that of measurable space.

Following the same line of reasoning, we find that the Dogon term *tonu* refers to three-dimensional space. We see this because the Dogon term *to* means both "arc" (implying the concept of "surrounding") and "to be the interior of", while *nu* refers to "waves or water", that can fill a three-dimensional space. The last of the four Dogon terms *toymu* means complete. The Dogon term *temu* in fact refers to "fording a stream on pebbles" and so suggests the concept of the formation of particles from waves. We now turn specifically to the mysterious notion of "The Pale Fox".

3.5. The Pale Fox

Dogon Social Organisation is Based Primarily on a Four-Part System

The *Pale Fox* was the follow up work of the French anthropologists Marcel Griaule and Germaine Dieterlen (15), after their prolonged *Conversations with Ogotomelli*, referred to hitherto. As such they took the "four-fold" nature and scope of Dogon cosmology further on. For them as such, *social, political and economic organisations are interdependent with the system of Dogon beliefs, this being a function of the general apprehension in the social life of the supernatural world, the world of the living, and that of the ancestors.* Social organisation, our Communiversity being one embodiment of such, is based primarily on a four-part system, not unique to the Dogon in Africa, who consist of four tribes.

The four great Dogon tribes are called Dyon, Arou, Ono and Domno. Theoretically they are considered to be the replica of the four mythical lineages of humanity's four male "ancestors", respectively Amma Serou, Lebe Serou, Binou Serou and Dyongue Serou. Within this lineage an individual is always situated in relation to four ascendant and four descendant generations.

Dogon Personhood: The Body as a Microcosm of the World

The Dogon notion of a "person" then, *dime*, is very elaborate. A man is constituted of a body, that is specifically of four "body souls", indeed four alternating male and female "sex souls", and of a composite vital force: *nyama*. Eight symbolic seeds (four souls of alternating sexes) stand then for the organisation of the world within the body of (wo)man conceived of as microcosm: they represent, as gender alternates, the four elements in turn (air, earth, water and fire) and the four cardinal points.

The Dogon, moreover, have four given names, associated with these four body souls. Besides these given names, a Dogon has the right to bear several mottos: those of his people, his tribe, his region, his village and his quarter. Finally, he inherits the personal motto of his *nani* (ancestor). All of these mottos are related to his life force, *nyama*.

Dogon Thought: An Indigenous Explanation of Physical and Human Nature

Like other African societies moreover, *the Dogon have analysed the world around them, and made a synthesis of the facts, beings and things.* Having observed and studied everything within their range of perception, they have constructed an indigenous explanation of the manifestations of nature (anthropology, botany, zoology, geology, astronomy, anatomy and physiology), as well as social facts (social structures, religious and political structures, arts, crafts and the economy).

The world is conceived as a whole then, this whole having been thought, realized and organised by one creator God—*Amma*—in a complete system which includes disorder. *The originality of such thought lies in the fact that it postulates a series of correspondences between elements, grouped in categories, that can be broken up and linked together.* As such the symbol plays the role of conveyor of knowledge—anticipating the biosemiotics we will be alluding to extensively in chapter 5—a succession of symbols leading from that of the female soul to that of the lizard to that of the shawl. Thus the Dogon will have learnt, with the help of a connecting line, a long series of ideas and actions that he or she evokes, semiotically (16) so to speak.

Leaving no room for what we might call chance, every element or event is charged with meaning in relation to and in interaction with others, simultaneously in space and in the present and future time. Actually it is not a matter of the analysis of static facts but rather a general understanding of something live, viewed from a biological, indeed biosemiotic, standpoint. The entire universe is moving: man on earth is in motion, and life, even inside the smallest seed of grain, is in motion. God moreover holds a primordial place in this mythology and cosmology; he alone is considered to be unique and perfect: he created the world; he can destroy it and make another. The Dogon do not incessantly repeat "Amma-God is great", but their beliefs and all their institutions demonstrate it.

3.5.1. The Elements of Dogon Fourfold Social Structure

In their social structure, then, the Dogon have deliberately constructed a system of kinship and marriage, to begin with, based on four lineages and five generations. The make up of these mythical lineages, firstly moreover, correspond with the cosmogenic division of the four elements, and cardinal points, and to the four tribes. In the development of these four lineages over five generations the individual is always situated in relation to four generations before and after his own.

Secondly, the present world is conceived as having come out of a first seed formed by God. This seed contains the essence of creation, including the four basic elements (air, earth, water and fire), as we saw above, and the "word" of the creator, that is to say, life manifesting itself within eight segments (the four-fold "body" constituted of alternating "sexes") animated by a motion which is both vibratory and spiralling. All farm labour then, from seeding to garnering, and the accompanying rituals, are in keeping with such.

Thirdly, for the Dogon, as for other societies of West Africa, the least ordinary object reveals in its forms and designs the conscious experience of a complex cosmogony. *A basket intended for carrying things, for example, represents, when turned upside-down, the ark on which humans descend from heaven to earth, the square bottom of the object representing space and the cardinal points.* In religious life, moreover, both individually and collectively, the rituals serve as re-actualisations of mythical events. For us then, our GENE, our "integral worlds", our Communiversity all represent such four-folds.

3.5.2. Dogon Initiation: Four Degrees of Development – Forward to Clearward

The Dogon therefore, who have classified everything, have established a hierarchy by degree of instruction of initiates, which could be likened to our GENE. Their *knowledge spans four degrees which are from least to most important,* the *giri so, benne so, bolo so, so dayi.* The *giro-so,* "fore-word", is a first source of knowledge, analogous to our communal learning, with simple explanations. The *benne-so* "side-word", secondly, includes the words *win giro-so* and the deeper explanations of these, which is where our Sanctuary comes in. The *bolo-so* "back-word", thirdly, completes the preceding knowledge on the one hand, and furnishes syntheses, resonant with our research Academy, applicable to greater parts of the whole on the other. The *so dayi,* finally, the "clear-word", concerns itself with the edifice of knowledge in its ordered complexity, exemplified by our Laboratory.

But initiation is not only an accumulation of knowledge, nor even philosophy, in a manner of thinking. It is of an educational nature, for it forms or models the individual at the same time he is assimilating the knowledge. But it is still more than this in its character; by making the structures of the universe understood progressively it leads the initiate to a way of life as conscious and complete as possible in nature and within his society, in the world as it is conceived and organised by God.

Myth moreover presents a construction of the universe—from that of the stellar system down to that of the smallest grain, with man in between, himself a microcosmic image of the world. It is from this perspective also that the psychological element comes into play. The emphasis is placed, by the Dogon overall then, on *the personage of the Fox: independent but dissatisfied to be so; active, inventive, and destructive at the same time; bold yet timid; restless, sly, indifferent, he is the incarnation of the contradictions inherent in the human condition.* He or she then is the entrepreneur, or leader, for us the *intenhaka*, in duly African guise. In this scheme of things it is of course important to know and understand the structure of the universe; but it is also a matter of living it, in the fullest sense of the world, in body and spirit.

3.6. Creation and Morphology of the Signs

3.6.1. The Primordial "Egg": Kize Nay, "Things Four" and Sibe Nay, or "Angles Four"

In the beginning then, before all things, was Amma, God, and he rested upon nothing. "Amma's egg in the ball" was closed, but made up of four parts called "clavicles". In their original sense the four clavicles are also the prefiguration of the four elements, *kize nay,* "things four": water (*di*), air (*ono*), fire (*yau*) and earth (*minne*). Likewise the ideal bisectors which separate them will mark the collateral directions, *sibe nay,* or "angles four", that is to say space. Thus all the fundamental elements and future space were presented in the morphology of the primordial "egg".

Amma's egg is represented in the form of an oblong picture covered with signs, called "womb of all world signs", the centre of which is the umbilicus. From the meeting point of the two axes extended two intersecting signs, forming bisectors making the four cardinal directions. An element is attributed to each sector. Counter-clockwise they are earth, fire, water and air. In the Dogon word (idea) all things are manifested by thought; they are not known by themselves.

All Things are Manifested by Thought

In the form of point *a*, according to Griaule and Dieterlen, a sign passes through the "master-signs" corresponding to it in the earth sector, where it receives the life force, *nyama,* which gives it form *b*. Via the fire sector it takes on *c*. Then it comes into contact with the signs of the air sector whereby it takes on *f*. In the water sector it takes on *g*. Continuing to turn it describes a spiral plane, in the course of which the four parts separate to each take on a separate appearance. Again semiotics comes into play.

Amma then, in beginning things, through the work of thought was divided into four, permitting the rise of the four elements. And having sprung into existence these become conscious of themselves.

From Signs to Drawings: Bummo, Yala, Tonu, Toymu

After the first series, as we saw above, the abstract signs or "trace" *bummo* (our grounding) will become the second series, that of the *yala* "mark" *or* "image" executed in dotted lines. Therefore, for example, when one builds a house one delineates the foundation with stones placed at the corners: these stones are the *yala*, the "marks" (our emergence) of the future dwelling. The term *yala* also means "reflection", which expresses the future form of the thing represented. The third series of signs is that of the *tonu* (our navigation), "figure" or "diagram". The *tonu* is a schematic outline; it is a sketch, the rough draft of the thing being represented. The fourth series (our effect) consists of the "drawings" or *toymu,* as realistically representative of the thing as possible. When one has finished building the house this is the *toymu* of that house, in our case the Communiversity, constituted semiotically of *Bummo* (Community), *Yala* (Journey), *Tonu* (Academy) and *Toymu* (Laboratory).

The difference that exists between these are the stages of creation. *The bummo are shown by zigzagging lines, the yala by dashed lines, the tonu is shown in a circle of four segments, and the toy evinces both the final stage and their animation.*

We are now ready to conclude, duly connecting grounding with our centering.

3.7. Conclusion

The Four Open Clavicles Show the Four Cardinal Directions

Amma's open clavicles, surrounded by figures recalling the essential elements of his work, are represented by a figure in black, called "drawing in the centre of the formation of Amma's world". *The four open clavicles show the four cardinal directions or the collateral directions we find: to the northwest the resurrected Nommo in human form; to the southwest the Fox; to the northeast the ark; to the southeast, man.*

Everything having been accomplished, Amma decided to keep to himself the twenty-two principle signs (like the number of letters in the English alphabet) representing the elements and essential stages of the second creation and also the "life" of the universe; he placed these signs in his open clavicles at the four cardinal points. For the most part, then, he does not intervene directly; when a sacrifice is offered on the altars bearing his name, his deputies will be called upon, for they have—by his will—the power to act. This brings us form philosophy/cosmology to praxis/communiversity.

Afrikology and Communiversity in Nigeria

As we shall see in chapter 6, as noted by African poet and philosopher Sanya Osha (17), the presence of four or more elements can also be found in the Yoruba of Nigeria, co-author Anselm Adodo being one such. The pantheon of Yoruba gods, as such, has strong reminiscences of both Dogon and Egyptian cosmology, and its attendant transformation cycle of elements. For the Yoruba, the so-called four estates, four winds, four days of the week, four walls of the Yoruba kingdom and a divine foursome of Shango/Oya/Oba and Oshun prevailed. We now turn from local grounding to local-global emergence, and specifically to African Creation Energy, and thereafter to African philosophy, drawing, again in both cases, on West African traditions in a contemporary light. Indeed then, in our penultimate chapter through Adodo's Paxherbals, we put such theory into practice.

3.8. References

1   **Lessem** and **Palsule** S (1997) *Managing in Four Worlds: Competition to Cocreation.* Chichester. Wiley-Blackwell

2   **Scranton** L (2017) *Seeking the Primordia: Exploring Root Concepts of Cosmic Creation.* New York. Self Published

3   **Aslan** R (2017) *God: A Human History of Religion.* London. Transworld Publishers

4   **Griaule** M and **Dieterlen** G (1975) *Conversations with Ogotomelli: An Introduction to Dogon Religious Ideas.* New York. Galaxy Books

5   **Scranton** L (2002) *The Science of the Dogon: Decoding the African Mystery Tradition.* Vermont. Inner Traditions

6   **Lessem** R et al (2013) *Integral Dynamics: Cultural Dynamics, Political Economy and the Future of the University.* Abingdon. Routledge

7   **Lessem** R (1998) *Integral Dynamics: Management Development through Cultural Diversity.* Abingdon. Routledge

8   **Hawking** S (2011) *A Brief History of Time: From Big Bang to Black Holes.* New York. Bantam

9   **Adodo** A (2020) *Nature Power: Natural Medicine in Tropical Africa.* Abingdon. Routledge

10 **Sauneron** S et al (2000) *The Priests of Ancient Egypt.* Ithaca. Cornell University Press

11 **Grimal** N (2007) *A History of Ancient Egypt.* Chichester. Wiley-Blackwell

12 **Budge** W (1985) *The Egyptian Book of the Dead.* Mineola. New York. Dover Publications

13 **Griaule M** and **Dieterlen** G (1986) *The Pale Fox.* Baltimore. African World Books

14 **Snodgrass** A (2005) *Interpretation in Architecture: Design as a Way of Thinking.* Abingdon. Routledge

15 **Calame-Griaule** G (1999) *Le Renouveau de Comte.* Paris. CNRS

16 **Lotman** Y (2009) *Universe of the Mind: A Semiotic Theory of Culture.* Indianapolis. Indiana University Press

17 **Griaule M** and **Dieterlen** G (1986) *op cit*

18 Sanya **Osha** (2018) *Dani Nabudere's Afrikology.* Dakar. CODESIRA

PART THREE

*Local-Global Emergent
Foundation*

CHAPTER 4

African Creation Energy

God who made us African and gave us unique cultures and a system of thought obviously intended such to be our working tools. How else can the African contribute to a world civilization if he did not do so from his native ways like Europeans and Asians from theirs.

Jonathan Chimakonam (1), *Introducing African Science*

EMERGENT FOUNDATION: TRANSFORMATION JOURNEY

- Altogether *building on prior communal grounds*, you are enabled, through an extended, individual, technological and societal transformational journey, to co-*evolve your Calling, in a particular Context, via Co-creation, making a Contribution.*
- What emerges is what is regenerated within you and between yourself and others; whereby you become porous and permeable, *continually open to new possibilities, through your inner, and your organisation's/ society's outer, Calling.*
- Emergence stimulates transformation, whereby you develop and evolve cross-catalytically, involving *deconstruction and reconstruction*, and an intermittent and discontinuous, but *flowing wholeness, lodged within a Contextual field.*
- The emergent, *far-from-equilibrium* developments give rise to a new *dynamic balance, weaving together Cocreatively*, past and future,

indigenous and exogenous; destroying static concepts of structures and systems, leading to a new self.

- *When fully functional*, process-driven, emergent individuals, communities, organisations, and whole societies, *make a transformative innovative Contribution*; when dysfunctional they unpredictably lurch from one state to another.

4.1. The African Creation Opener

4.1.1. The Meaning of African Creation Energy

Having centred ourselves in our integral worlds, and thereafter locally grounded what will become newly global Afrikology in the legacy of ancient Egypt, on the one hand and in Dogon primordial wisdom, on the other, we move locally-globally on, firstly the primordially laden African *science of sciences* (chapter 4), as we shall now see, and then, secondly, philosophically and transformatively onto *Atuolu Omalu*. Our first port of emergent call as such is now the remarkable body of work of so-called *African Creation Energy*. Therein we will focus on the longstanding African past, present and future, scientifically and technologically, on our overall transformation journey.

The chosen term African Creation Energy (2), for Ghanean African American Osiadan Borebore Oboadee, who embodies such, has hidden "Etheric" meaning. The word "Africa" comes from the Afro-Asiatic word "Afar" meaning "dust", which represents the "Earth". The etymology of the Word "Creation" comes from the word "Crescent", which represents the "Moon" and the word "Energy" represent the "Sun", which is the primary source of energy in the planet.

The letters used to abbreviate "African Creation Energy", A.C.E, not only spell the English ACE, meaning "First" or "Primary" or "Original", but also represent the three fundamental geometric shapes of the Triangle (A), the Circle (C), and the Square (E), combining to form the ancient Alchemic symbol of the "squared circle". Utilising African Creation Energy, Osiadan Borebore Oboadee has used the "Squared Circle" as a metaphor and symbol to represent the unification of dualities necessary to bring about the birth and creation of a new paradigm.

4.1.2. Nature, Physics and Energy

The Conservation of Energy

The word "Physics", in fact, is an ancient Greek word meaning "Nature". One of the laws of physics (nature) is called *Conservation of Energy*, stating that *energy cannot be created in the sense that it comes from Nowhere and Nothing into existence*, and *energy cannot be destroyed* in the sense that it ceases to exist, *but energy can transform from one state into another.* Gradual of anything, therefore, involved a gradual process of growth and change over time in which a metaphorical seed, kernel or node grows and transforms into another form, figure or structure.

Yoruba Ashe to Ancient Egyptian Sekhem

African Creation Energy therefore, for Osiadan, is the energy, power and force that created African people and that African people use, in turn, to create. Amongst the Yoruba people of Nigeria, this energy is called *Ashe*, which means "the power to make it happen", personified by the Yoruba "Orisha". Amongst the Akan people in Ghana this energy is called *Tumi*, the web of energy and power that exists through space and all of creation, woven by the Akan deity of wisdom, "Ananse". In the Congo, such energy is called *Dikenga* (see below), referring to the thermodynamic process of transformation of energy depicted in their cosmogram "Yowa". Among the Mande people of West Africa, *Ama* is used by the blacksmiths to forge technology for the wellbeing of the whole village. In Ancient Egypt and Nubia, African Creation Energy was called *Sekhem,* as we saw in chapter 2.

We now turn to the origins of technology.

4.2. The Origins of Science and Technology

4.2.1. Technology is to Build or Construct by Uttering Reasonable Speech

The etymology of the word "Technology", in fact, comes from the Greek word "tekhne", meaning "system, process, method or craft", and also has origins in the Proto-Indian-European word "Tek", meaning to "shape, contrast, build or weave". The suffix –logy in the word "technology" comes from the Greek word "logos", meaning "word, speech, utterance or reason". Thus *the etymological sense of the word "technology" is "to build or construct by uttering reasonable speech". In Africa, the Ancient deity that created or "constructed the universe by utterance" was the Egyptian deity PTAH, the Opener.*

Technology as such, for Oboadee, does not just refer to material objects such as tools, instruments, utensils, apparatuses, and machines, but also to immaterial mental objects such as concepts, systems. The manifestation of knowledge into the physical world by way of Creativity in the form of "Technology" is the objective indicator of human knowledge and capability. Thus the most advanced form of technology at any given point of time is called "State of the Art" which indicates the "State of Mind". There is an old saying: "You know the tree by the *fruit* it produces", likewise, you know a knowledge or science by the Technology created from it.

4.2.2. Technology is the Study of How Nature's Resources are Used By All

The study of the history of *technology is the study of how, for all creatures, nature's resources are used*. Birds, for example, use nature's resources to create nests, spiders to create webs, bees to create hives, and beavers use nature's resources to create dams; all of these are examples of technology for their respective species. The creative process then, for Oboadee, that began with the creation of the universe, planets, stars, mountains, valleys and oceans of Nature, continues with the creative endeavours of Nature's creatures in the form of ant mounds, human skyscrapers, and many other creations by many other creatures.

The history of human technology, then, began in the location of the origin of humanity, in Africa. Exoterically, or operatively, harnessing the power of fire provided early humans in Africa with the means to increase food supply, have warmth and light at night, and develop and create other tools needed for survival. Esoterically or speculatively, considering that "Fire" is a metaphor for "Light", *"Energy"* or "knowledge", then the statement "harnessing the power of fire" is symbolic of using energy and applying knowledge, which is "Technology" by definition.

4.2.3. "Nature Technology" Impacts Community, Environment, Planet, Universe

Using "Right Wisdom", moreover, in the Creation and formation of "Nature Technology" means not only considering the desired result of technology but also considering how such impacts the community, environment, planet and universe. Just as the waste from an organism can serve as fertilizer which can be used to grow and create something new, the waste, by-product, or undesired effect of "Nature Technology" mechanism or organism is harnessed by the "Nature Engineer" to serve as fertilizer from which some new desired thing can germinate and grow, to continue the desired cycle of creation.

We now turn to the so-called "Science of Sciences and Science in Science", and to the origins of African Creation Energy, that is to its Ghanean-American founder Oboadee.

4.3. Science of Sciences and Science in Science

4.3.1. Towards a Science Based Way of African Life

Exposed to Nuwaupu as the Science of Sciences

Osiadan Borebore Oboadee (2) was raised in the Islamic religion, though it was always evident to him, even at an early age, that there were inherent, powerful, and more reasonable truths and explanations about life and existence within *science* that were not provided by his religious beliefs. It was only after 17 years of having been raised an orthodox Sunni Muslim that his father brought home books on *Nuwaupu*, written by *Amunnub Reakh Ptah.* These books dealt with questions and contradictions found within the three Monotheistic religions: Judaism, Christianity and Islam. Osiadan still practiced as a Muslim for the next 9 years until 2007. During that time he obtained a BSc in Electrical Engineering and a Masters in Mathematics.

Nuwaupu then is the science of sciences and the science in sciences, drawing on the original creative forces from Africa. By studying Nuwaupu, Osiadan was able to trace his roots to Egypt, the Sudan and Ethiopia and then onto West Africa.

Speculation Precedes Operation

Studying the "Science of Sciences" and the "Science in Sciences" dictates that the process of "speculation" precedes the process of "operation". This the speculative nature of one's "way of life", cultural practices, religion, theology cosmology and philosophy, shapes and forms the mind and mentality as the base of all assumptions, hypotheses and beliefs about reality and living. Hence a "scientific-based" culture, philosophy or "spiritual science" should lead to a great success when moving into the operative mode of using and applying one's beliefs. Therefore it is no surprise, for Oboadee, that Asian and Indian cultures that have a "scientific-based" philosophy and "way of life" also excel in achievement in the operative fields of Science, mathematics and Technology.

As such, having the "Science of Sciences" (speculative) and the "Science in Sciences" (operative) as a base for African culture should definitely lead to creation, development, and the production of African technologies, he says, that will greatly improve the quality and standard of life for African people worldwide. In fact his works are intended to motivate the African reader to embrace their traditional "science based" culture and philosophy, so they may become *creators* of advanced technologies, enhance their wellbeing, and quality of life.

Society Reaping the Benefits of a "Spiritual Science"

Since science is the one thing that people can agree upon regardless of their religious, philosophical and theological beliefs, then, for Oboadee, a *science-based philosophy, religion or way of life* will ultimately unite the peoples of this world. The methodologies and practices of S.O.S.A.S.I.S can be found in the interpretations of African culture and philosophy, as well as in all other cultures around the world. Unfortunately "scientific method" and the "mathematical method" have become trivialized and mundane. However, for him, these methods are the operative expression of the oldest philosophy on the planet which started with the African people.

For the Christian Catholic religion, as above, an "eight-pointed" star or "squared circle", with a centre obelisk, sits in the middle of St Peter's Square in Vatican City. For Oboadee, Peter means "rock", phonetically similar to "Pater", and thereby to Ptah. Muslims they perform an act called *Tawaf* circling round the "squared circle" of the Kaaba. For the Jewish people they regard the *Temple of the Mount,* as the eight-sided *Dome of the Rock* as the resting place of the Divine Presence of God. These, for him, are all speculative interpretations of the original African "spiritual science". In religion, prayer can be likened to the "external calling" or *empirical method,* and meditation to "internal speculation" or *rational method.*

A "Spiritual Science", as such, is nothing more than a methodology developed as a way and guide to life. The application of S.O.S.A.S.I.S, as such, in the social sciences for Oboadee can lead to peaceful households, functional families, thriving economies, proper political science and government. The application of science, in that guise moreover, involves the development of culture. The basic purpose of a "spiritual science" or cosmology or "cultural philosophy" is to set up a foundation for a society as to how to live life right, speculative philosophy thereby setting the precedence for a culture's operative science.

Thus the return to ancient and traditional African culture and philosophy with S.O.S.A.S.I.S as a basis should place Africa, according to Oboadee, at the forefront of emerging technologies such as solar power, wireless energy transfer, electric cars, artificial intelligence, quantum computing and holography, eventually, when also as a foundation for African culture, philosophy, economy and government, leading to an African scientific and industrial revolution. The Science of Sciences and Science in Science, as such, is the method, the means, and the programme of life, creation, education and learning. In Ancient Egypt, both science and spirituality were intricately woven into the fabric of society. For example, Ptah was seen as a master craftsman and a divine representation of the unseen God of Amun. When one adopts a balance of science and spirituality, therefore, a dynamic Balance can be obtained as society will reap the benefits of a "Spiritual Science".

4.3.2. African Philosophy and Science

Ptah to Buddha

Etymologically, in fact, the word "Africa"" either comes from the Afro-Asiatic word "Afar", meaning "dust" or "Earth", or from the Arabic word "Faraqa", meaning to divide or separate, aligned with the very Latin meaning of "science", as such. Also on mythology the name Ptah, as the Ancient Egyptian God of Technology, means "to open, separate or create", synonymous also with "to grow", which is said to be the meaning of the Hindu deity "Brahma". The tone, utterance, breath, vibration or pulsation that Ptah uses to create is called HU, whereas Braham creates through AUM. The breath of "vibration from the mouth" is called Atman, the "world soul", in Hinduism, which is phonetically similar to ATUM, the son of Ptah. In addition the name Buddha could have come from a tonal morphology of Ptah to "Phutah". Moreover, the Hindu triad of Brahma, Shiva and Vishnu who represent Creation, Destruction and Preservation share many characteristics with the African Memphite triad of deities Ptah, Sekhmet and NeferTum who represent the same principles respectively.

Memphis was an Ancient African Industrial City

In fact the city of Memphis was an Ancient African Industrial city that existed for the purpose of developing, growing and creating Science and Technology. This city, which was the centre for Ptah, gave rise to scientists, engineers, architects, physicians, "social engineers" and philosophers.

The scientific "method", for Ptah, or "science of sciences", involved forming a hypothesis or belief (imagination) in the heart (Sia), carried out through experimentation, by speaking the hypothesis into existence with his tongue (Hu). After the hypothesis of the heart Sia has been tested with the tongue Hu, the creation exists and can be observed and experienced, and the cycle of scientific creation continues. Philosophically, the concepts of the Heart of Ptah called Sia, and the tongue called Hu, are comparable to the Greek concepts of Nous, representing the World Soul, and the Logos, representing the Word.

Duality of "the Two Ladies": Empiricism and Rationalism

In Egyptian mythology, moreover, *The Two Ladies* are *Wadjet* and *Nekhbet*. Wadjet represented one land, "Lower Egypt" (Northern Egypt) and Nekhbet represented "Upper Egypt" (Southern Egypt). Unifying the "two ladies", symbolically, represented "unification" or the coming together of opposite dualities, "aggressive and passive, mental and physical, the Observer and the Observed, in Science, the external world of nature and the internal world of the mind."

This duality of "the two ladies" in modern science represented the philosophical debates between *empiricism,* supported by Aristotle, Locke, Hume, Bacon and *Rationalism* supported by Socrates, Descartes, Kant and Spinoza. While these concepts of *Experience* and *Reason* were polarised in the philosophies of Heliopolis and Hermeopolis, they were unified in the philosophy of Memphis, with *Ptah* at the centre. Whereas *Re* represented the Sun, life and Empiricism (external experiences), *Tefuti* represented the Moon, the underworld, and Rationalism (mental experiences).

The Cycle of Transformation and Scientific Method

At the same time, in the cycle of transformation, the "Movement of the Sun" in the Science of Sciences of Ancient African Culture and Philosophy had four major points: the *Rising Sun*, the Sun at *High Noon*, The *Setting Sun,* and the Sun in the *Underworld.* One of the most obvious "tools" from what Oboadee calls S.O.S.A.S.I.S (Science of Science and Science in Science) is the navigational compass with the four cardinal directions North, East, West and South (NEWS) and the intermediate directions NE, NW, SE, SW, ultimately sub-divided into eight (there were eight deities in the Egyptian Ogdoad).

Starting, overall then, from the point of *Experience* (our south-east), information is received by way of senses in the mind. The mind then uses *Comprehension* (our north-east) and analogous reasoning to understand, comprehend, and "make sense" of the information it has experienced. Analogies, similes, mathematical objects, mythologies, parables, words, abstractions, number and shapes then become *Theories* (our north) which the mind can process. The mind then begins to *Analyse* (our north-west) the abstractions using inductive Reasoning to see how the information can be used for the benefit of society, moving onto *Experimentation* (our west), tests, trials, attempts. The *Result* (our centre) is then experienced and the cycle repeats itself.

FIGURE 4.1. THE UNIFICATION OF SCIENCE

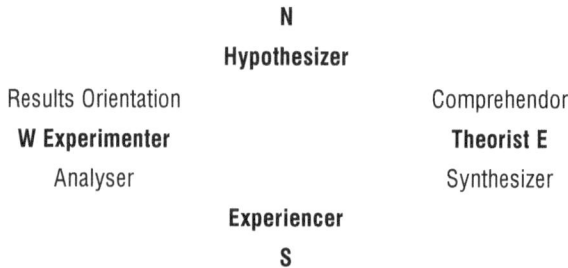

N

Hypothesizer

Results Orientation   Comprehendor

W Experimenter   **Theorist E**

Analyser   Synthesizer

Experiencer

S

Personifying all of such, more fully, as in the Figure above, spanning all eight sub-divisions of the compass, in a transformational cycle, Oboadee starts with:

- The *Experiencer,* responsible for speaking and acting out everything she sees, hears, smells, tastes and touches, also being an excellent communicator.
- The *Comprehendor* is very observant, and an excellent listener. He creates metaphors, similes, and analogies to aid in comprehension.
- The *Theorist,* thirdly, is responsible for interpreting and translating all information into writing, coming up with signs, symbols and diagrams and shapes, to represent the information received.
- The *Analyst,* being inquisitive and probing, is responsible for analysing and questioning the information given to her, having strong inductive reasoning.
- The *Hypothesizer* generates hypotheses which should serve to explain the information given to her, using logic and reason to determine such.
- The *Synthesizer* is responsible for coming up with ways test the hypotheses, combining Rational and Empirical approaches.
- The *Experimenter* performs the experiments, in the field, to test the hypotheses, using the models and methods developed by the Theorist.
- The *Results Oriented* person, finally, reviews the consequences of the experiments performed; her reports are decisive definitive and conclusive.

4.4. Science, Technology and Engineering

4.4.1. Heka, Hu and Sia: The Three Principles of African Creation

In Ancient Africa, Oboadee goes on to say, the process of Engineering used Science and Mathematics to create Technology symbolised by the deity Ptah, using *Hu* and *Sia* (see below) to perform *Heka* respectively. "*Heka*" translated as "Magic" in Ancient Africa was associated with authority and influence over nature's resources, also then *representing the concept of working with, manipulating, weaving, forging, forming, transforming,* and thereby creating with chemicals, minerals, elements, components, various forms of matter. "Heka" then, originally considered "Magic", is more closely *associated with the modern concept of Engineering.*

In fact the word "mechanism", "machine", and the word "magic" have the same etymological origin from the Proto-Indo-European word "magh" meaning "to have power", or "to be able" which is Heka, which can also be aligned with *energy* which shares an etymological root with the Greek word "egon" meaning "to do work". In Ancient Africa then *Heka*, along with the concept of *Hu* (the *creative force*, energy, vibration, drive, reason or purpose symbolized by utterance and speech) and *Sia* (insight, comprehension, awareness, knowing, *wisdom and understanding*), were *the three principles that the African Creation God Ptah used to create.*

4.4.2. The Word Engineer is Linked to "Gene" and to "Generator"

Moreover, it is interesting to note that *the word Engineer is linked to "gene"*. This also implies that Engineering ability is linked to "genes". Traditionally Africans viewed the ability to practise Heka (engineering) with certain genetics and generations—hence *generators*—whereby certain *elect* individuals are responsible for tribal wellbeing. Just as single-cell organisms combine to form organisms and multi-cell organisms, multi-component mechanisms like clocks require simpler mechanisms like gears to be developed, individual principles and ideas make up overall "mental technologies".

Meanwhile just as harnessing the power of Fire proved to be the greatest technological achievement for early humans. The greatest technological advancement in modern human technological development has been the ability to harness the power of electricity. In fact the use of electricity on Earth is visible from space which means the earth is emitting light (electromagnetic radiation) like a sun due to electrical technology. This book, for Oboadee, seeks to liberate and empower the African reader by providing instruction on how to obtain power in the form of electricity using concepts associated originally with PTAH.

The word "electricity" comes form the Ancient Greek word "Electron", which is actually a compound word consisting of the words "Elect", which has its etymological origins in *Lexis* and *Logos* (which was *Hui,* the creative utterance of Ptah in Africa) and "tron", which is similar to "tek", as "something that performs action".

4.4.3. African Creation "Gods" of Technology

PTAH Was the God of Craftsmen, Artists, Builders and Engineers

PTAH then was considered the God of craftsmen, blacksmiths, artists, architects, builders and engineers. In the city of Memphis in Egyot, PTAH was part of a triad including his wife Sekhmet and his son NeferTum. By definition of function, the role the African deity PTAH in African philosophy is equivalent to "Logos" (creative utterance or logic) and "Nous" (intention of the mind or Reason, which the Egyptians believed existed in the Heart). The name PTAH has been translated as "Creator". Although this deity was known by all the people in Ancient Egypt, the study of the art and science of the "school of PTAH", was restricted to an elite priesthood.

Scientifically *lightening*, or electrical discharge, is the visual representation of the sound of thunder. The etymology of *thunder* comes from the Swedish words "Thor Din". Thor was the European version of PTAH. Other European versions of the Egyptian God include the Irish Tuireann and the Celtic Taranis. PTAH is also associated with the Arabic word *Fataha,* meaning "Opening", and which is the title of the first or opening chapter of the Holy Qu'ran. It has also been suggested that the name PTAH and Buddha, as "the awakened one" are interlinked. *The description of PTAH creating by imagining or visualizing creation "in his heart" and then causing the creation to come into being by "Speaking it with his tongue" means that PTAH served as the Architect* who designed the Blueprints and the Builder who formed the Structure; the Engineer who drew the schematic and the Technician who put it together.

The various craftsmen and engineers in Ancient Nubua considered PTAH to be the patron of their respective crafts, and the most skilled and talented considered themselves to be "high priests". One of the most notable craftsmen to be given the honour and distinction of the "sun of PTAH" was the polymath Im-hotep, an engineer, architect and physician form Egypt's 3rd dynasty, who invented the papyrus scroll, was architect of the first pyramid, and wrote journals on Medicine, Anatomy, Biology.

The Union of Human and Natural Creation

There are in fact many similarities between the Nubian triad of PTAH (Creator), Sekhmet (Destroyer) and Nefertum (Completer) to the Hindu triad of Brahmin (Creator), Shiva (Destroyer) and Vishnu (Preserver). Traditional Akan beliefs in Ghana establish significant relationships between the Creator, his creations and the Akan people. The Akan believe the creator puts his creativity into the Soul (Kra) of the people, so Human Creations are just as much part of Nature as "Natural" creations. This *union of Human and Natural creation is shown in the symbol called Abode Santaan, the "all seeing eye of the Divine Creator":* the symbol incorporates the eye, the rays of the sun, the double crescent moon and the stool. The sun, moon and eyes depict natural creation and the stool human creation.

The oral tradition of most West African tribes says that they migrated there from Egypt, the Sudan and Ethiopia. Ancient Egypt indeed was a melting pot of mainly African, Mesopotamian and much later European, to name a few. In West Africa, because the science, art and technology of Metallurgy were essential to survival, wellbeing and the quality of life, blacksmiths were respected for their "magical" engineering skills. It was also believed that they had the ability to manifest the spirit of *Gu* (PTAH). The Yoruba refer to Gu as *Ogun,* the God of vitality, of both survival and medicine.

Studying and observing nature, then using and applying the information, led to mastering the Earth, elements, ground, chemicals and substances of nature, applying such to Create things necessary for survival, wellbeing and quality of life, this being the role of inventors, engineers and technologists. In the religious sense "Gods" of technology served as Healers, Providers, Sustainers, Protectors.

4.4.4. Applied African Alchemy and Electro-Chemistry

Philosopher's Stone and Dikenga Cosmogram

Traditionally in Africa blacksmiths, or "Suns of PTAH", were the individuals in the community that had knowledge of the minerals and elements of the Earth and nature. Whether the elements were combined to make medicines for Healing, or Metallurgy to make tools and buildings, the application of this knowledge was paramount to survival and wellbeing. This is why Im-hotep was a Builder, Architect, Physician and Healer. In ancient times in Africa, two of the sciences used were called Alchemy and Geomancy. While Alchemy dealt with transmuting different elements, geomancy dealt with interpreting the "divine" features of the Earth, rocks, soil, sand. Operative Geomancy led to geology, the same way operative Alchemy led to chemistry. Speculative Alchemy, as the "philosopher's stone", or the "Great Work", had four stages:

- Red – unity of the finite and infinite (G)
- White – burnout of impurity, the moon, female (E)
- Yellow – enlightenment, the sun, male (N)
- Black – change, dissolution, individuation (E)

The fourfold Dikenga cosmogram of the Congo depicted Atomic cycles in Nature, depicting the flow of Energy as in Thermodynamics.

Alchemy and Geomancy/Chemistry and Geology

The words Alchemy and Chemistry are originally derived from Khemet meaning the "Black Land" of Ancient Egypt. The investigation of the matter and material of nature begins with Geology as Mineralogy and Herbology, and the classification of elements, nutrients, minerals, and chemical substances and compounds. Further analysis leads to the Atomic level and the smallest particles of matter. The application of African Alchemy in modern

Chemistry and Chemical Engineering has had the greatest impact, for African Creation Energy, on modern technological development in the field of Electro-Chemistry, which makes electricity, electrical power and energy possible.

The Djed Pillar and Voltage

The *Djed* Pillar, as an Ancient Egyptian symbol, is said to represent "Stability". The Pillar is shown as a column with four parallel, horizontal bars across the top. The three empty spaces between these symbolically represent *Hu, Heka,* and *Sia,* which, as we have seen, are Ancient Egyptian concepts of Creativity (Hu), Engineering (Heka) and Insight (Sia). The Djed Pillar, moreover, was originally associated with PTAH. The Djed Pillar, specifically then, can be constructed as a source of "Stable" DC Voltage. The Djed symbol, furthermore, is the origin of the Phonecian letter Samekh and the Greek letter Xi, currently used as a symbol for DC Voltage Sources in electrical circuit diagrams.

In the book *The Ankh, African Origin of Electromagnetism,* the writer Nur Ankh Amen (3) describes how Alessandro Volta, the European credited with the development of the first electric cell, discovered a Djed Pillar while pillaging ancient Egyptian relics, thereby discovering the principles whereby the Djed produced a stable electric current. The Electrochemical Cell would correspond to a single horizontal bar on the Djed Pillar, and the stacking of the four bars would construct a pile battery.

4.4.5. The Ankh and the Current

The *Ankh* is an Ancient African symbol called "The Key of Life". The Ankh symbol is shown as a loop or coil, or circle "O" at the top, united with a "T" or cross at the bottom, which symbolised the unification of the dual principles of Male–Female, Life–Death, Circle–Square, Positive–Negative. For us, of course, the cross symbolises the four worlds and the circle integration. The unification of the dual elements in the field of Electro-Magnetism, the negative and positive charges, is a "key to electricity".

The Waas and Power

The *Waas* is an Ancient African symbol that was used as a hieroglyphic in writing and as a sceptre carried by deities, pharaohs and priests that represented *Power.* The top and bottom of the Waas is shaped to resemble the head and tail of an animal. In modern terms such "Power" is defined in Physics (which means *Nature*) as the rate at which work is performed and energy converted.

Ptah's Law of Electronics

The Djed, Ankh and Waas symbols, then, that make up the staff of PTAH serve as both theoretic (metaphoric and symbolic), as well as functional (applicable and useful) symbols and tools that, for African Creation Engineering, can be relevant to Electronics.

FIGURE 4.2. PTAH'S LAW OF ELECTRONICS/OHM'S LAW

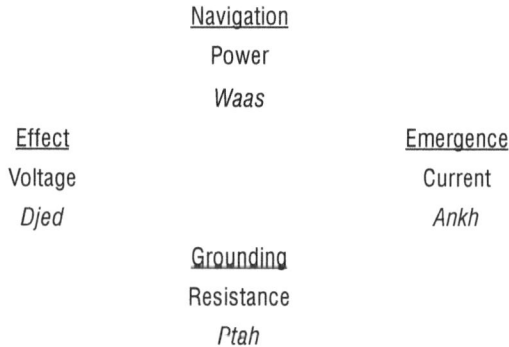

Navigation
Power
Waas

Effect		Emergence
Voltage		Current
Djed		*Ankh*

Grounding
Resistance
Ptah

The modern mathematical equation that states the relationship between Voltage, Current, Power and Resistance, known as Ohm's Law, can be aligned respectively with Ptah, Ankh, Waas and Djed, as shown below, together with our GENE.

The Four Elements

In Ancient African Alchemy, the four classical elements, four directions of four vibrations, were considered the fundamental building blocks in Nature. They represented the energy of everything in Nature: Earth, Water, Air and Fire. In modern science these conform to Solid (Earth), Liquid (Water), Gas (Air) and Plasma (Fire). Within each of these are sub-atomic particles which move and vibrate constantly. When the vibration is large enough to be detected by the human ear we call it sound.

In the Ancient Egyptian Djed or Ennead cosmology these four elements are constituted as Geb (earth or solid), Tefnut (moisture or liquid), Shu (air or gas), and Set (fire or plasma), with HU as the vibration of Creation.

FIGURE 4.3. THE FOUR ELEMENTS

N
Navigate
Air

W	*IUS*	**E**
Effect	Integrate	Emergence
Fire	*Sound*	*Water*
Plasma	Vibrations	Liquid
Set	*Hu*	*Tefnut*

S
Grounding
Earth
Solid
Geb

Underlying the four elements, then, was a fifth *quintessential* one, *ether.*

4.5. Ether Engineering

4.5.1. The Quintessential Element

Hidden Genius

For Osiadan Borebore Oboadee (4), furthermore, humanity has acknowledged the existence of a fundamental and *quintessential* element of energy that permeates the totality of Nature. In Ancient Alchemy, Ether was conceptualised as the *Fifth Element*—thereby *Quint-essential* of Earth, Water, Air and Fire—"essential" meaning element. For the Yoruba, *Ashe* refers to such hidden, ethereal power. In Arabic the word for unseen, invisible or hidden is *Ginn*, which is related to Genius, and to Engineer. Technology, as such, is the operative manifestation of spirituality. Knowing that Ether is "spirit", then Ether Engineering empowers the practitioner.

Matter and Antimatter

One of the attributes of Ether is that it is primordial, essential and fundamental. In modern science such elementary particles of nature are the smallest building blocks that make up all matter in existence. However, there are also antiparticles of non-existence. In Ancient African culture in Egypt there were the Principles of the Primordial state at the beginning of creation, represented by eight deities called the Ogdoad: four males and four females, collectively called Nun or Nu. The "Underworld" in Ancient Egypt, *Duat*, was also connected with Nun, and possibly with anti-matter.

4.5.2. Electrons and Electricity

The PTAH of Technology

After anti-matter, the smallest fundamental particle that most people are able to have experience of is the Electron. Electrons are the workmen of Nature. The flow or movement of Electrons is called Electricity. In his book on the PTAH of Technology, which we have aligned with our GENE, Oboadee aligned Ptah (G), Ankh (E), Waas (N), Djed (E), and with the modern mathe-matical symbols V, I, P and R respectively representing Resistance (G), Voltage (E), Power (N, Current (E), measured in Ohms (G), Amperes (E), Watts N), and Volts (E).

The Ether of the Mind: Quantum-sphere, Noopshere, Cyberspehere

Just as the electron is the smallest fundamental particle to rise from the primordial abyss of anti-matter, it is said in Ancient African cosmology that PTAH rose from the primordial abyss of Nun. Also, just as the movement of the vibration of electron causes light, it is said in Ancient African cosmology that "speech" or vibration from Ptah gave birth to Atum or Atum-RE symbolic of light. In the Memphite Theology, PTAH is also representative of the mental faculties of the mind, consciousness, and Reason. The relationship between thoughts, reason, electrons and electricity is that thoughts and reason are actually electrons flowing in the brain. A thought is an electrical signal sent between neurons and your brain, via electrons.

Thus both conscience and consciousness are composed of Ether in the form of flowing electrons. Comprehending the fact that thoughts and reason are composed of the fundamental electrons called the electron, then we must also comprehend such relative to the ether of the mind, through three creations:

- The *Quantum/sphere*, the realm of electrons
- The *Noosphere,* the realm of human and biological thoughts
- The *Cybersphere,* the realm of computers and mechanical thoughts

Therefore it is no surprise that the ability of computers to speak or network with one another through the flow of electrons and electromagnetic radiation has been termed *Ethernet*.

4.5.3. The Thermodynamic Cycle

Sekhmet "the Powerful One" Daughter of the Sun God RE, Moderator of Ma'at

In modern science, *Thermodynamics* is the study of heat, energy, temperature, pressure and work. Mastering the science of thermodynamics enables the practitioner, for Obaodee, to comprehend life and death, energy and transformation, and the processes of Creation in general. In Ancient African cosmologies, the power of heat (meaning of thermodynamics) was personified by the goddess *Sekhmet whose name literally meant "the powerful one". She was the daughter of the sun God RE, the wife of PTAH, and the moderator of Ma'at or Equilibrium.* The priests and priestesses of Sekhmet were doctors, physicians and healers. Called also *Nyanbinghi* by Central Africans, she symbolised, also, various female freedom fighters, as the feline goddess.

The Fourfold Thermodynamic Cycle

There are four laws underlying contemporary thermodynamic cycles. African cosmologies are replete with theologies and theories related to such, inspired by studying the daily cycles of the sun, as a major source of heat and energy.

The Ancient Egyptians acknowledged Thermodynamic Cycles by personifying the "four states of the sun" as Kheper-Re, Aton-Re, Atum-Re and Amun-Re. Other examples include the "Gye Nyame" of the Akan in Ghana, the Dikenga Congolese cosmogram, and the Lusona cosmogram in South Africa (at the top is God, left is the Sun, right is the Moon, and bottom is the Human), and the diasporan Nuwaupu (Revolution in the south-east; Origination in the north-east; Dorigination in the north-west; Evolution in the south-east). In fact, for the Dikenga cosmogram the transformation through each of the four points, starting from the centre, called "coming and going", is similar to Entropy, which literally means "turn to the centre".

The "Father of Thermodynamics", Nicolas Carnot, who was part of Napoleon's fleet in the conquest of modern Egypt (Carnot died aged 36) developed the so-called "Carnot cycle', which can be likened to the Dikenga *cosmogram*:

- Expansion: *Tukula/falling*
- Heat Removal: *Luvemba/falling*
- Compression: *Masoni/rising*
- Heat Addition: *Kala/rising*

Each thermodynamic position not only refers to a state of energy but also Mentality, Personality and Spirit, thoughts or consciousness being the transfer of electrons.

4.5.4. Thermodynamics to Hydrodynamics

In Ancient Egypt, the personification of the wind, air and atmosphere and gases in general was the deity named *Shu*. Shu was the husband of the goddess *Tefnut* who represented Moisture or Liquids in nature. The Ancient Egyptian story of *Shu* (Gases) and *Tefnut* (Liquids) being husband and wife and both being children of RE (Sun, Fire or Heat), establishes a parable that shows relationships between modern scientific concepts like *steam, condensation and evaporation* which are transitions between gases and liquids caused by heat. The application of the science of Thermodynamics as it applies to transitions between liquids and gases led to the development of the development of one of the earliest forms of Steam Engine, accredited to *Hero* of Alexandria, phonetically similar to *Heru* of Ancient Egypt.

4.5.5. Electromagnetic Radiation

In modern science, the term "Resonance" is used to refer to things that vibrate or oscillate at a certain frequency. Thus the etymological sense of the word "Resonance" is to "Resound", to sound again, or the "sound of Re". In the Heliopolis cosmology of Ancient Egypt, the "sound" or "utterance" emitted from the Sun deity RE was called HU. The deity *Hu* was the personification of Creative Utterance, tone, pulsation, sound or Vibration. *Hu* is comparable to the concept of *Aum* in Hinduism. In the Memphite cosmology, it is said that the African Creation deity PTAH uttered the creative tone *Hu* to initiate creation.

4.6. Conclusion

4.6.1. From Teaching to Construction

The etymology of the word "teach" is to speak, tell or say, and that of "technology" is to build or construct by uttering reasonable speech, showing the close relationship between Teaching, Technology and "speech", that is HU, the creative "tone" of PTAH. Whereas teaching is speaking to "instruct", technology is speaking to "construct". *African Creative Energy is about constructing.* The purpose of its "African Liberation project" then is to free minds, energies and bodies of African people from mental captivity and physical reliance on inventions and technologies that were not developed by African people.

Creative expressions, then, such as music, art and fashion, solely for the purpose of aesthetics and entertainment should come only after Creative Energy is used for the purpose of creating, developing and inventing everything needed for survival and wellbeing. Therefore, the solution to Liberate African people from dependence on Western technology is to engineer and invent African technology. In fact religion, money and technology are the three most captivating forces that Africans need to be liberated from in order to advance, and all of these, inherently for Osiadan, fall under the umbrella of "Technology", leading to invention and creation.

4.6.2. Invention or Creation Like an Offspring has its Creator's Nature

The importance of liberating African people from such dependence is because an *invention or creation is like an offspring; it comes from a creator and therefore has its creator's Nature and likeness.* A "brainchild" in the form of a concept, idea or invention is just like an actual child in that certain traits and characteristics of the creator are passed onto the creation. Therefore, a person, place, or thing has the nature and likeness of whoever created it. For this reason *African Creation Energy must reinvent the metaphorical wheel whenever necessary,* albeit also aligned with other worlds.

We now turn from local-global emergent foundation, in science and technology to the historical and transformative foundation of contemporary African philosophy, before we turn to newly global emancipatory navigation, that is to Afrikology itself, evolved out of African Studies, with which one of us, Anselm Adodo, is intimately involved in Nigeria, that is at Ibadan University.

4.7. References

1   **Chimakonam** J (2012) *Introducing African Science: Systematic and Philosophical Approach.* Bloomington. Author House
2   **African Creation Energy** (2010) *Ptah Technology: Engineering Applications of African Sciences.* www.AfricanCreationEnergy.com
3   **African Creation Energy** (2010) *The Science of Sciences and The Science in Sciences.* www.AfricanCreationEnergy.com
4   **Amen** N A (2001) *The Ankh, African Origin of Electromagnetism.* Brooklyn. A and B Books
5   **African Creation Energy** (2012) *E.T.H.E.R. Engineering.* www.AfricanCreationEnergy.com

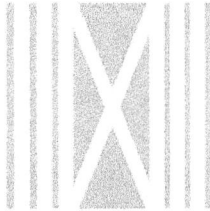

CHAPTER 5

Creativity and Conversationalism

5.1 Introduction: The African Philosopher as Society's Gadfly

> In Western philosophy the starting point for an account of person-hood, then, is usually epistemological and psychological. Knowledge is the possession of a particular individual and the question then becomes how such knowledge can be accounted for, or even "captured". In African thinking the starting point is social relations—selfhood is seen and accounted for from this relational perspective. The West has used an individualist and objectivist framework that has given it a civilization where the individual is powerful, where liberty is a good that is absolute, where there is room for the play of free enterprise, where scientific and technological progress covers the world with its achievements. In Africa things are quite otherwise, since African civilization has been traditionally characterised above all by solidarity, communitarianism, traditionalism and participation, though of course today in Africa things are changing.
>
> Coetzee and Roux, *Philosophy from Africa*

5.1.1. African Philosopher as Society's Gadfly

Now, we turn from local grounding in ancient Egyptian and Dogon, primordial cosmology, and thereafter locally-globally to African Creation Energy building on such, to historically emerging African philosophy, in the modern era. Atuolu Omalu (Omalu translated as "knowers" in Igbo) becomes a call then, coordinated by leading University of Calibar based African philosopher Jonathan Chimakonam (2), a fellow countryman of Anselm Adodo in Nigeria, now though based at the University of Pretoria in South Africa, together with leading philosophical colleagues, to properly define Africa's place, to find it and take it in the international community. It is a compass, he says, to retrace steps where they are derailed and chart a new course.

As a society's gadfly, the African philosopher is once again reminded of his sacred social, political, cultural, economic, leadership and, above all, intellectual duty to mould the renaissance of Africa. He or she cannot perform these duties if (s)he did not get their bearings right. *Such philosophy, and as we shall see on its historical transformation journey, just like our integral rhythm of research and innovation,* evolves from origination (ethno-philosophy) towards transformation (integrativist), albeit that it does not reach a point of ultimate, economic and enterprise, effect. Indeed, in Adodo's Transformation Studies, in Nigeria, while we start out on such an African philosophical and natural-cultural journey, we end with technological and enterprise laden praxis.

5.2. African Ethno-Philosophy and Nationalist Idealism

5.2.1. Ethno-philosophy as a Local Source of African Uniqueness

For the first such fellow philosopher included in Chimakonam's overall work, Ada Agada (3), based at the University of Nigeria, Nsukka, and author of *Existence and Consolation: Reinventing Ontology, Gnosis, and Values in African Philosophy,* so-called "ethno-philosophy" (our grounding and origination) has come to be the dominant current in African philosophy, from which no African philosopher, he says, has broken completely. This is the case because it has established itself as the foundation of African philosophy, in much the same way that Greek monism and the world of Plato and Aristotle constitute the foundation of Western philosophy. Such *ethno-philosophy has its sources in traditional cosmologies, proverbs, communal wisdom, cultural practices and religious beliefs, thereby emphasizing Africa's uniqueness,* asserting a unique mode of African "emotive" knowing.

5.2.2. Only On A Foundation of Tradition a Truly African "Modernity" Can Be Constructed

The publication of Placid Tempels' (4) *Bantu Philosophy* in the 1940s, in fact, marked the birth of the ethno-philosophical enterprise. John Mbiti's (5) *African Religion and Philosophy* confirmed the viability of the enterprise. Such ethno-philosophy, for Agada, is firmly traditionalist, and he profoundly respects it as systematic, original thinking, thereby aligned for us with grounding and origination, although from the singular, local perspective of every particular tribe or ethnic group. Every other current in African philosophy, for him, takes its bearing from such. Even the nationalist thinkers like Nkrumah (6) and Senghor (7) who used philosophy largely as a tool of political engineering and social action found their bearing in ethno-philosophy (for us linking grounding with effect, though missing the GENEtic steps in between). Ethno-philosophy, for Agada then, will remain a source of inspiration for innovative individual thinkers who African philosophy patiently awaits as its future. *It is, moreover, on such a basis of original tradition that a truly African "modernity" can be constructed.*

5.2.3. Ethnophilosophy, Philosophical Sagacity and the Joy of Being

So-called "philosophical sagacity", he goes on to say, is basically a philosophy of culture whose content is ethno-philosophical. For Agada as such it fails as a constructive alternative to ethno-philosophy. Innocent Asouzu (8), again based at Calabar University's prolific Department of Philosophy in Nigeria, is the thinker, as we shall see moreover, has noted that it is not a thing of shame that African philosophy is compelled to borrow elements from Western thought (for us assuming local-global proportions). For disparate philosophical traditions are complementary, missing links of reality. His so-called Ibuanyidanda philosophy leads Asouzu to such radical ideas in African philosophy, as notions of the joy of being as well as the principles of integration and progressive transformation. The question that remains for the 21st century, overall then for him, is how we can think innovatively, and, for us also, how we can act accordingly.

Nationalist Idealism: Negritude, Conscienscism, Ujaama

Straddling our grounding and effect then, with the cultural concept of *negritude*, Leopold Senghor (9) achieved fame as one of the most original and important thinkers to come out of Black Africa. Likewise, with the idea of *consciencism*, as we have seen, Nkrumah called for the recovery of a new Africa that would be able to stand on its own feet. Thirdly, with the notion of *ujaama* (familyhood) Nyerere (10) enunciated a socio-political and economic philosophy for a resurgent Africa. These three African political philosophers (thereby for us the global-local politically, if not also economically, racing ahead of the local-global) believed that socialism was the ideal socio-political model for an Africa that was emerging from the backwater of colonial rule.

Nkrumah regarded the African liberation struggle as a historical movement towards Africa's self discovery, renaissance, and eventual self-sufficiency. The doctrine of *consciencism* is his chief contribution to African philosophy, encapsulating the new spirit of Africa, *the new personality that has emerged from the dilemma of a continent that has been forced into confrontation with imposed external value systems like Christianity, Islam and Western civilization.* The authentic African value-system, having encountered these foreign ones, can no longer be the same. It is necessary for a new African personality to emerge that has resolved its conflict with foreign imposed value-systems. *Consciencism* realises such.

Rejecting the doctrinaire leanings of Nkrumah, Nyerere proposed his model. For him ujaama represented African socialism—an egalitarian and humanistic ideal rooted in the traditional family system operative in traditional African societies. Since the extended family system embodies brotherhood and mutual dependence the Marxist perspective of a vicious class struggle does not apply. The economic failure of ujaama, however, suggests that Nyerere over-romanticized the African past, and failed to fuse the past and present, to establish a viable East African future, notwithstanding, also, the top-down approach he took to ujaama, which was thereby bound to ultimately fail.

African Logos is a Living Intelligence while European Ratio is Cold, Rigid, Static

Senghor (11) is in fact, for Agada, the most original of the African political philosophers. As such, the African perceives the universe as an interconnected and dynamic whole. Indeed Senghor's reason is a sympathetic one, not the discursive *and analytic reason of the European.* The African reason, as we have seen, is closer to the *logos* of the Greek rather than the Latin *ratio*. The *logos* is a living intelligence, emotive, flexible, and inter-penetrative, while the *ratio* is cold, rigid and static.

All three philosophers—Nkrumah, Nyerere, Senghor—assert the humanistic essence of their philosophical concepts—consciencism, ujaama, negritude —and all are rooted in ethno/philosophy. For Agada, Senghor comes closest to giving Africa a constructive alternative (for us further evolution of the local towards the local/global) to ethno-philosophy, in his concept of a uniquely black intellect, but he left the question of the future (for us newly global emancipation and thereafter global-local transformation) unanswered.

So where, according to Agada, do we go from here?

There is No Shortcut to Greatness for African Philosophy

Agada, as we have seen, has taken a bird's eye view of some of the more notable developments in African philosophy, while maintaining that ethno-philosophy will always ground African philosophy. Such philosophy will only grow, however, when individual thinkers come to challenge the unhealthy dominance of ethno-philosophy with their constructive alternative programmes, and for us move, ultimately transformatively, on. The project of individual thinking with a constructive bent will constitute, he says, the major preoccupation of African philosophers in the first half of the 21st century, through such Nigerian scholars as Asouzu, Ozumba, Chimakonam, and Agada's own *Consolation Philosophy* building on that of Asouzu. For us, moreover, such philosophy needs to be linked with political, economic and indeed technological (see chapter 5 that follows) praxis.

Set against that, in Europe and America, he says, philosophy journals and books, overall then, have become mere talking shops. This fruitless argumentation has been going on for decades without making much progress. That said, the Western and Oriental philosophies are much older and far more sophisticated than African philosophy. Western philosophy in its current written form in fact has existed for over two thousand years and has produced many iconic system builders. Analyses from Western philosophy continue to feed on the great systems developed by these iconic thinkers of originality. It is then sheer foolishness, Agada maintains, for Africans to exaggerate the role of philosophical analysis in their own tradition when its tradition has existed in reliable written form just half a century. *Philosophising is a serious business; it is a heavy burden indeed. There is no shortcut to greatness for African philosophy.*

To make the tradition great African philosophers must not then overlook what is happening in Western philosophy and start their own work from scratch. That said, the foundation, our origination, has already been laid by ethno-philosophers. The present though demands great innovation, diversity and originality. The time has come for the individual thinkers to lead the charge of African philosophical thought, and to provide a constructive alternative, or for us a further evolution, to and from ethno-philosophy, coupled of course with philosophy-in-action. Innocent Asouzu is one such innovative philosopher, as is Chimakonam is himself, both oriented to complementarity, morality and overall integrality, as we shall now see.

5.3. Complementary Reflection in African Philosophy

5.3.1. Ibuaniyidanda as Local-Global Complementary Reflection

Reflection In and Beyond African Philosophy

Asouzu (12) then, based at the University of Calibar philosophy department, explores *The Methods and Principles of Complementary Reflection In and*

Beyond African Philosophy. It is not, as such, an exclusivist, hegemonic type of dialectic that seeks to render contents absolutist. It is neither a type of liberal dialectic that seeks solace in unfettered relativism. On the contrary, it is a complementary, comprehensive type whose method, system and principles consider all existent realities as missing links. Thereby it has the capacity to neutralise extremist forces of divisiveness that infringe on the unity of being and consciousness.

All missing links thereby assume mutual authenticating character in a way that makes each indispensable in the affirmation of the being of the other, as this relates to the relationship of human beings and communities to each other. This is why, moreover, in the absence of some sort of institutions established to regulate conflicting views and expectations that we encounter in the world, the chances of upholding the unity of being and consciousness remains slim.

Bringing Missing Links of Reality in a Mutually Related Mode

The *ibuanyidanda* approach then does not pretend to be identical to the philosophies of any ethic groups, races or geographical regions of the world. Instead, in doing such complementary reflection Asouza draws inspiration from a wide network of relations, constituted of diverse actors and factors. His philosophy (for us integral economics as such) seeks to sensitise stakeholders, not only concerning the vastness of opportunities accruing then from mutual complementarity, but also demonstrating why a collective response to most problems of the world is something indispensable.

Research method, for Isouzu as such, is the disposition needed to relate to missing links of reality in a mutually related mode. It is the capacity to focus on the *ibuanyidanda*ness of any phenomenon, be it "missing links of reality" related to persons, communities, institutions, the ecosystem, and all things both spiritual and material. Existence therefore is all it takes to have all missing links harmonised.

Ibuanyidanda and Some Challenges of Ontology

For Aristotle, on the other hand, the essence of the human person is reason or rationality in itself, whereby the world is constituted of, for Asouzu, the profoundly misleading notion of the irreconcilability of categories and opposites, which lies at the foundation of "Western education". Thereby human beings and communities, and indeed for us enterprises and economies, must contest with each other for scarce resources, tending to denigrate all things that stand in their way of such. In contrast with such an Aristotelean perspective, *Ibuanyidanda sees existence as the capacity to be in mutual complementary relationship with all things. It is another way, in Igbo, of saying "I cannot be alone"* (ka so mu adina).

Since human beings often seek to carve out niches for themselves to uphold privately motivated interests, they are easily drawn, quite instinctively, to such an exclusivist, bifurcating "competitive" ontology. In our bid to focus on all, in a particular group that people have in common, Asouzu maintains, we easily forget their specific differences, so that we are bound to polarize the world into arbitrary emotional, cognitive and ideological blocks, the division between static and dynamic being one such polarisation.

Ontology beyond a Static-Dynamic Dichotomy

Placid Tempels in fact hints at the tendency for human consciousness to oscillate between transcendence and world-immanence. On account then of his unintended ethnocentric interest, Tempels focuses on only one side of his ambivalent interest which aims at portraying the Bantu as animists whose dynamic ontological experience is different from a static Western ontological one.

Quite surprisingly as such, for Asouzu, the very things that enter into Tempels' debased Bantu notion of being, in his "vital force theory" is what many researchers have elevated to a "dynamic notion of African being", carried away by the notion that there is a realm of reality that is exclusively African. Caught by such ethnocentrically induced zeal may seek to reclaim for Africa a dynamic notion of being, but it is unfortunately all too often associated with a debased, superstitious, magical ontology. Reducing African science to a study of the nature and character of dynamic supernatural forces, it is thereby targeted against a "static" Western motion of reality: that of the naturally exact, applied sciences. In this derogatory way, for Asouzu, the distinction between static and dynamic is artificial.

There is, for him then, another way the attribute dynamic can remain credible. It is in a dynamic complementary harmonised mode. In this mode, *being can be grasped in the dynamism of its essentiality as missing links that link to each other in a relationship of mutual complementarity, as reinforced by ibuany- idanda philosophy and method.*

A Synthetic-Analytic Transformation

In the case of practitioners of African philosophy, Asouzu goes on to say, many such theories are built on observational statements like: *ibu anyi danda* (no load is unsurmountable for the *danda*, ant in igbo), or *njiko ka* (togetherness is the best strategy), thereby "I am because we are; and since we are, therefore I am". Many believe that statements of this type express the ideas of intimate belongingness for which Africans are known. As such, they assume that viable theories can be constructed based only on these ideals observable in African living which such statements seek to express. Such theories then are exact replicas of empirical indicators. When such theoreticians are caught in these questionable assumptions they are unlikely to invest much effort to rid theories of such pre-scientific predilections, for us moving from the local, and local-global, to the newly global, thereby remaining beclouded by sense experience.

The method of *ibuanyadanda* (complementary reflection) strives to overcome biases of this type, for Asouzu, and those imposed by uncritical reliance on data of sense experience. Cognisant then of the descriptive synthetic root of the expression *ibu anyi danda*, and all such expressions, there is a need to transform them by exploring more fully their universal connotations, making room for the co-existence of, for us "local-global", opposites. Whereas the synthetic expresses the "basic rule of *danda*", the synthetic-analytic variant offer the groundwork for the principle of *ibuanyidanda* philosophy, whereby *anything that exists serves a missing link of reality*. In the same way, it formulates the principle of progressive transformation.

We now turn specifically from Calibar University based Nigerian philosopher, Asouzu to another, Chimakonam himself (more recently the latter has moved to Pretoria University Department of Philosophy).

5.3.2. Cogno-Normative Complementary Epistemology

A Simple Look Behind Only So We Can Effectively Surge Forward

For Chimakonam, our pursuits in African philosophy should be to open up the mind of the African fortuitously closed by historical events. This opening should usher in a transformation in the way the African thinks—not necessarily by extinguishing the flame from African traditions and igniting another from her present but by *delicately and pragmatically adapting elements from the past that are relevant in building a transformed framework sufficiently formidable for the futuristic journey which Africa must now make* (for us releasing African GENE-IUS).

Thus in constructing an authentic and modern African philosophy, a momentary backward glance (to our Grounding) is inevitable. But it is *a simple look behind only so we can effectively surge forward* (thereby for us, locally-globally Emerge). Scholarly agitations which tend to over-price African pre-colonial traditions to the *inimical point of perpetual excavations are perpetually off the mark*. At the point where Africa stands today there is no vision behind, only memories, there is no road in front, only signposts.

If we are to find our way to the open country of dreams and visions, he says, we must move forward not backwards, and the African philosopher must free himself from too many loads from his nostalgic past, taking up only a handful of necessities from his past tradition so he can travel light and fast (for us Navigate "newly globally") so he can wiggle through the small doorway at the end of the globalized tunnel.

The Moralized African Knowledge Needed to Transform Society

If the pursuit of research then is to serve the narrow purpose of proving to others that Africans knew how to think consistently in pre-colonial times, it is difficult to see how such could be of value in the sort of transformation required today. *We need some sort of Cartesian "cogito" upon which the future should be built, not merely an African theory of knowledge but a critical theory of transformation* (for us origination to transformation arguably along a "southern" relational path, philosophically, economically and enterprise-wise). Knowledge as such is a form of power—for growth, innovation, transformation. *Others might ask such questions as what is knowledge, as a philosophical pastime, but the African epistemologist must ask them in order to transform his society.*

Thereby it is up to the world to emulate what Africa has offered itself, that is when Africa has made the most of its ideas. Ironically globalization becomes the undoing of one who appropriates but has nothing to be appropriated – such is the African situation, for Chimakonam, today. *Yet in our world today, civilization hinges on scientific knowledge. The religious man, for example, needs the microphone, transportation and the mass media. However, scientific knowledge in the African episteme must be moralized.* That said, the African philosopher must avoid building his new society without moral fibre, whereby he cannot ignore traditional beliefs. That said, the African philosopher must invent himself in the mode of the ancient Greeks, who were philosophers, theoreticians and scientists alike (for us adding polity and economy to the mix). The roles which the philosopher has to play in Africa are diverse, from social, economic, political, and scientific to historical but undergirding them is the interest of humanity.

Incorporating Morality and Complementarity

Chimakonam's theory of so-called *"cogno-normative" or complementary epistemology,* then, following in Asouzu's footsteps, might be regarded as African in two respects: first because it *seeks to solve nagging African problems and* second *because it contains the logical structure of African thought it excludes the spiritual perspective.* While not disagreeing that before colonialism Africa had its own episteme, the question he raises is what exactly did Africa have in pre-colonial times that is worth "local" philosophical acknowledgment in these "global" modern times? For whatever has previously been perceived as knowledge from the gods implies that the human being is incapable of generating his own. So what do we want to sift, locally-globally, from the African past?

In constructing then his theory of cogno-normative epistemology Chimakonam sifts from the past the idea that whatever is useful needs to have positive moral worth, as such positive moral content is necessary for action. The other element he sifts from purified African thought is complementarity. Altogether then, to avoid increasing knowledge in the direction that will increase Africa's misery, *he constructs an episteme that, on the one hand, is both cognitive and normative, and on the other, implies the complementarity of philosophy and science.* The gauntlet that needs to be picked up, as such, is how do modern African philosophers come to possess knowledge which Wiredu (13), for example, considers to be in the heads of non-Africans?

Connected with the Current Existential Situation and the "Useable" Past

How then might we construct a new episteme for Africa? Some of the deconstructionists like Hountondji (14), de-constructing especially ethnophilosophy, have advocated a system building that would be in keeping with the philosophical standards of the West. However as they, in Chimakonam's view, put nothing in its "Westernised" place there was a need for another deconstruction. So what followed, for him, were the so-called "conversationalists": Asouzu, Ozumba, Agada and himself. *Such a thereby integral form of "knowing" cannot be unconnected with the African's current existential situation and the demands of the cultural biases of his "useable" past.*

In the first existential respect, the African, for him, lives in a world that is poor, wretched and needing urgent political, economic and social reinvention. Secondly the African needs a particular set of knowledge to begin his journey of recovery. The knowledge to overcome poverty, racism, and the effects of colonialism needs positive moral content. Having seen what knowledge divorced from morality has done for the West, the African needs to not make the same mistake. In fact *to achieve well-rounded development Africa needs strong institutions, not strong individuals. Competence, creativity, synergy are the types of abilities needed* for such.

As the philosopher is the gadfly of the society, ever studying it and noting its worries and needs, he or she is called upon to construct the modern episteme, including prototypical traditionally laden narratives from, and for, the modern Africa. It is, moreover, through critical conversations that such should arise, both particular and generalised, emerging altogether, as African. To re-open the African mind to this intellectual reality is the duty of the modern African philosopher, nay epistemologist.

Africa Must Seek Knowledge that will not only Improve but also Preserve Life

The cogno-normative or complementary epistemology then has it as its goal to lay great emphasis on humanity, or as such "humanistic epistemology".

This entails knowledge for humanity: its methods and procedures need to carry a human face. The point is here that knowledge is for humanity and not the other way round. Backward in almost every aspect of life then, *Africa, for Chimakonam, must seek knowledge that will not only improve but also preserve life.* Thereby the empirical and the rational need to be integrated in a mutually interdependent complementary relationship. What is knowledge then is necessarily moralizable, and thereby normative.

Chimakonam now turns from philosophy to logic, from being and becoming to knowing, for us from grounding and emergence to navigation.

5.4. The Question of Knowing in African Philosophy

5.4.1. The Three-Valued Structure of Logic Tradition in African Thought

That the corpus of works in African philosophy are today ridiculed as containing nothing original is because African philosophers are yet to develop their own logic tradition, Chimakonam maintains, to give proper shape to philosophical thoughts. A discourse, therefore, qualifies as African philosophy not because it is authored by an African. It is partly, he says, because it has an African logic tradition as its foundation notwithstanding also the issues it treats.

The logic tradition in Africa for Chimakonam (15), as he has extensively documented hitherto in terms of what he calls Ezumezu logic, is a variant of three-valued—for us neither local/indigenous nor global/exogenous (either-or) but "newly" global—logic. Indeed African Cameroonian philosopher Meinrad Hebga (16) bemoans the prevalent system of two-valued logic inherited from Aristotle. Such a classic, two-valued logic is in fact considered universal. Udo Etuk (17) calls the African "three-valued" orientation Affective logic. Chris Ijimoh (18) calls it *Harmonious Monism.* For Chimakonam as such, every logic is primarily relative, but with varying degrees of universal applicability.

5.4.2. The Ezumezu Theory of African Logic

Particular and Universal

Chimakonam then puts forward three clarifying positions:

> By African logic I do not mean a culture-bound exclusive system that holds only in African thought and is not universally applicable.

> I do not mean classical two-valued logic as the only universal logic.

As an African logic, it is not unconnected with such a universal logic, thereby containing, but also transcending, such, as Ezumezu. The two sub-contrary values, *ezu* and *izu* (true and false) are fragmented halves of the Ezumezu whole.

The Four Stages of the Ontological Quadrant

Interestingly enough then, like us, Chimakonam then traces four stages of development of metaphysics—in terms of John Heron's (19) *modes of knowing*, for us, this extends from experiential to conceptual, but *not* including the economic/practical—in what he calls the overall theory of an ontological quadrant (our integral rhythm bereft of the *transformative* effect). This holds that the being of metaphysics developed across four stages leading to the emergence of logic (not in our integral terms *enterprise*, or in Communiversity terms, our *Laboratory*).

The first *local* stage (our Grounding or origination or would-be *communal learning*) is a worldview or metaphysics that is dormant and inactive comprising of superstitions and religious concerns. The second *local-global* stage is the cosmology/ontology where metaphysics becomes active (our Emergent foundation or *transformation journey*) offering critical explanations of phenomena, questioning what is being, physical or non-physical or both, setting the stage for the emergence of two-prong or three-prong evaluations (for us from local or global—one or the other—to local/global combined). The third *newly global* stage (for us "newly global" emancipatory navigation or our *research academy* as such) is for Chimakonam the purest development of metaphysics. It is here that the diversity of cultures (our trans-cultural realities) manifest. Fourthly then for him logic (for us the transformative effect of the *Laboratory)* becomes the fourth stage at which metaphysics gives way to art, logic, etc. In our terms what is glaringly missing is the economic, the practical, the pragmatic—*global-local* transformative effect.

Sub-Contrary Valuations and the Modes

As Hegba delicately demonstrated in African thought the principle of contradiction "does not keep two diametrically opposed systems from being true at the same time, their fundamental predispositions being different". Granted that the two standard values (two-valued logic) are sub-contraries thus capable of complementing each other (for us local-global), Chimakonam breaks the modes into two, namely, first, the contextual and, second, the complementary modes of thought. Standing on their own, the two sub-contrary values, called *ezu* and *izu* or true and false are treated as fragmented halves of a whole, each being contextual. Joined together in the intermediary third value the product called Ezumezu is complementary (local-global).

Joseph Agbo takes the argument knowingly on from here, specifically now in relation to "the West and the Rest".

5.4.3. The West and the Rest of Us in African Philosophy

Injected a Western Orientation into the African DNA

For Nigerian philosopher Joseph Agbo (20), based at Ebonyi State University, on the one hand, when a people's psyche is arrested it has multiple and permeating repercussions on all physical, environmental and spiritual aspects of life and the people. No wonder Franz Fanon (21) considers the psychological effects of colonialism to be even more devastating than the economic and political ones. The colonizers, he says, took real advantage of the meaning of "education" and "domestication" and proceeded to engrave "Western" values into the flesh of the African, and effectively *injected a Western orientation into his DNA,* duly inhibiting Chimakonam's "three-valued logic".

Build Managerial Ocean-Liners with which we Africans Can Navigate the Oceans

On the other hand, he says, instead of dissipating energy, trying to pull the rug that we are all, at the same time, standing on, by trying to build a bulwark against the urging tide of globalization, we should rather put such energy into *building solid managerial ocean-liners with which we Africans can navigate the oceans.* Philosophy as such, for him, is the foundation and roof, the base and apex, the pillar and structure of the disciplines (but for us, additionally, we need a fully equipped political, economic and managerial home). Indeed Africans can in principle decide that future generations would not be caught in the same web where we whirl like spiders, detached from our roots, acting like butterflies while feeling we are birds. But it would not happen because we wish it so, it would happen when we make conscious efforts to achieve it, when we do not feel or think "jinxed".

Africa then should engage other cultures in interactive philosophy (and for us diverse forms of economy), *and then project what she has for constructive appreciation, and not evaluation.* Africa instead is experiencing the historical march of a world that has already been mentally dominated by Western metaphysics. *We must re-present realities from that tradition, distil them, and bring them into crystallisation as classic representations of our identity and contribution to global scholarship.* But scholarly reflection is not enough; there is a need for action and policy adjustments on the part of African leadership.

Chimakonam and fellow Calabar University based philosopher Godfrey Ozumba (22) now conclude by periodizing, thereby stratifying African philosophy in contemporary guise, in the latter case furthering the ontological quadrant, in ways that can be closely aligned with our own integral rhythm, whether applied in an African context to integral research, or to integral economics or enterprise.

5.5. Conclusion: Periodizing African Philosophy

5.5.1. Philosophy as a Universal Human Heritage with Cultural Colorations

Movements African Philosophy: Externalist to Integrative

For Ozumba, overall then, *philosophy is a common universal human heritage but with cultural colorations.* It is akin to water which takes the shape of the containing vessel. When we see water we know it is water but not water that collected in a vessel as opposed to a flowing stream. This is why there is a need for cultural vessels which give philosophy its different colorations. *Diverse cultural philosophies enrich our philosophical ray as do the multicolours in a rainbow.*

As we allow different cultural philosophies to unfold, we encourage a hundred different flowers to bloom, thereby enlarging our common philosophical heritage. African philosophy, therefore, is that philosophical tradition that applies the essence of philosophy for issues of African concern (for us local) but with global extension. The four movements that Ozumba has identified (he starts out with an *Externalist* carbon-copy of the effective "west", missing out "navigation", in our terms, after his *Internalist* "grounding" and *Hybrid* "emergent" prior to his ultimately *Integrative* effect) are:

1. The Externalist movement
2. The Internalist movement
3. The Hybrid movement
4. The Integrativist movement

The Externalist movement consists of those early ethnographers, sociologists, historians and philosophers who ventured into accounting for the African cultural philosophy from a Western world-view. For them whatever goes as African philosophy is a transliteration of Western philosophy. The second Internalist group emphasized the need to build a complete edifice of African philosophy rising from the roots, which includes the likes of Abraham (23) and his *Minds of Africa* and Nkrumah's *Consciencism.* The third *Hybrid* group include those trained in the West (Europe and America) struggling to keep their African identity against cascading torrents of Western intellectual heritage. Here we have philosophers like Wiredu and Hountondji.

The last movement (our transformational) is Integrativist whereby for the likes of Asouzu and Ozumba all cultural philosophies are to integrate so as to achieve a broader and deeper philosophical perspective. Insisting that African philosophies should form the platform for such. It opposes superstitions and anachronistic systems. It is only through critical and rigorous examination that the wheat can be sifted from the chaff of every possible philosophical material.

It Would Be A Misnomer to Pose the Same Philosophy for Africa and Europe

Ozumba believes then that Western philosophy can serve as a model for African philosophy but not to the point of assimilation or complete integration. *The structure of environmental, political, social and cultural needs of Africa today is not the same as those in Europe, so it should be an utter misnomer to pose the same philosophy for both continents.* We need to root out those elements from the West which don't fit into our African architecture and replace them with African philosophical insights. *The fact that we have not done that is why, for Ozumba, Western democracy, economics, logic and religions are not working in Africa.* To craft the African alternative is the job of a conscienticised, decolonised and re-Africanized African philosopher.

All societies face societal and environmental befuddlement, and the extent of their successful confrontation of these challenges is not due to the extent of their philosophical endowment, per se, but the extent to which this endowment has been explored and put at the service of enhanced human wellbeing. We now turn back to Chimakonam, with his fourfold philosophical stratification, following from his earlier "ontological quadrant", as articulated above.

5.5.2. The Philosophers Seek to Solve the Problem of their Time

The History of African Philosophy Began with "Frustration" and Not With Wonder

Chimakonam, like his Calibar based philosophical colleague, Ozumba, periodizes African philosophy in four phases of development, and indeed transformation—albeit somewhat different from the latter—which we have aligned with our own integral rhythm, from origination to transformation. As such *the history of African philosophy began with "frustration" (and not with wonder as it was in Western philosophy). The frustration was born out of a caricature of Africa as culturally naïve, intellectually docile, and rationally inept.* This has a wider implication that touches on sensitive issues like the identity of the Africa, his place in history as well as his contribution to civilization.

Original Grounding: Discover African Identity: First Epoch of African Philosophy

Thus began the history of systemic African philosophy with the likes of Leopold Senghor, Kwame Nkrumah, William Abraham, John Mbiti, already cited, and some expatriates like Placid Tempels and Marcel Griaule (see chapter 3). The history, it is important to remark, is a very short one. Soon after colonialism, actors realized that Africa had been sucked into the global matrix unprepared. *During colonial times, the identity of the Africa was presupposed to be European, his thought system, standard and even his perception was structured by the colonial shadow which stood towering behind him. The question then that trailed every African was: who are you?*

Of course the answers from a European perspective were savage, primitive, less than human. It was the urgent need to contradict these European inventions of Africa and of the Africans that led the returnee Africans in search of African identity. So, *to discover or retrieve African identity in order to initiate a non-colonial or original history for Africa* in the global matrix and start a course of viable economic, political and social progress that is entirely African *became the focal point of the first epoch of African philosophy*, as a systematic exercise.

Placid Tempels, the European missionary, wounded by the pitiable African condition elected to help and in his controversial book, *Bantu Philosophy*, sought to create Africa's own philosophy as *a proof that Africa has her own peculiar identity and thought system, that the African is not savage or primitive*. However, it was George James, another concerned European, who attempted a much more ambitious project in his *Stolen Legacy*. In his work there were strong suggestions not only that Africa has philosophy but that so-called Western philosophy, the bastion of European identity, was stolen from Africa. However there has been no proof that the Egyptians were black! After these two Europeans, Africans began to attain maturation. John Mbiti, Julius Nyerere, Leopold Senghor, Kwame Nkrumah, as ethno-philosophers and nationalist idealists, as we saw above, to name a few opened the doors of ideas. This, for Chimakonam, was the first era.

Emergent Foundation: Traditionalist Versus Modernist: Middle Philosophical Era

The middle era of African philosophy is characterised by the great debate between the Traditionalists and the Modernists. The latter include Kwasi Wiredu and Paulin Hountondji. This middle period then gave way to a later one which had as its focus the construction of an authentic African episteme.

Emancipatory Navigation: Critical Reconstruction and Eclecticism: Later Period

Two camps rivalled each other: the *Critical Reconstructionists as evolved Modernists, and the Eclectics as evolved Traditionalists.* The former sought to build an African episteme untainted by ethnophilosophy whereas the latter sought to do the same by a delicate fusion of relevant ideals of the two camps. Eventually the Eclectics won the day.

Transformative Effect: Conversationalism and Creativity: Contemporary Period

This heralded a new era or Contemporary period in African philosophy. The focus becomes *conversationalism, concentrating on individual creativity.* Altogether, and also in our GENEtic terms, then, we have, as per our integral research-and-innovation trajectory from origination to transformation, an:

1. G: Early period: 1920s to 1960s: *Ethnophilosophy and African Nationalism*
2. E: Middle period: 1960s to 1980s: *Traditionalists-and-Modernists*
3. N: Later period: 1980s to 1990s: *Critical Reconstruction and Afro-Eclectics*
4. E: Contemporary Era: 1990s to Date: *Conversationalism and Creativity*

Overall, *the philosophers seek to solve the problem of their time* (and we would argue the same should apply to economic and managerial thinkers and practitioners), in the four phases outlined above and elaborated upon below, duly aligned with our GENE, and again with our integral rhythm underlying, if you like re-GENE-ration, albeit in philosophical terms without yet the socio-economic overlay to go with it.

In fact, and if you like for us, the problem with the original African nationalism, of say an Nkrumah or a Nyerere, is that it never underwent the full GENE cycle, and has never been recognized and renewed, as such, since. Arguably, moreover, African nationalism did not start (Senghor being an exception) with *local* grounding (though ethno-philosophy did), before emerging as local-global, and thereafter, "newly-global", being for us the key to emancipation.

Chimakonam then goes into more specifics, for each phase of the African philosophical, four-fold cycle, from the early to the contemporary eras, revisiting what has been said at the outset of this chapter, also now for us on our GENE-tic terms.

5.5.3. Grounding/Origination: Local Ethnophilosophy and Nationalist Ideology

Ethnophilosophy

This is the initial era (for us locally grounded) Chimakonam calls cultural/ideological excavation aimed at retrieving and reconstructing African identity from the raw material of African culture. The schools that emerged and thrived were ethnophilosophy and nationalist/ideological. The British colonial system has sought to erode native thought while the French has pursued assimilation. The British then educated their colonies in English language and culture, strictly undermining the native languages and cultures. The products of this new social system were then given the impression that they were British even through second class. Suddenly, however, *colonialism ended and they found to their chagrin that they were treated as slave countries in the new post-colonial order.*

Some of the actors in this period were not native Africans like George James and Placide Tempels but were touched by the insincerity and cold-heartedness of the departing colonialists. For Tempels, in his *Bantu Philosophy*, "being is force, and force is being". John Mbiti, in his *African Religions and Philosophy*, African philosophy could be likened to Tempels' vital force of which African religion is the outer cloak. For William Abraham, in his *Mind of Africa*, as for Tempels, and Mbiti, *the lost African identity could be found in the seabed of indigenous African culture in which religion featured prominently.*

Nationalist Ideology

On the other hand, there were those who sought to retrieve and establish once again Africa's lost identity through economic and political ways, including Nkrumah, Nyerere and Senghor. These actors felt that *the African could not be decolonized if he did not find his own system of living and social organisation. The question that guided their study therefore became what system of economic and social engineering will suit us and project our real identity?* Nkrumah advocated African socialism, forged from the traditional structure of African society which is communal. Systematising such will yield an African brand of socialism. Senghor charted a similar course, drawing on African culture and language Nyerere argued that cultural imperialism had to be overcome, by developing a socio-political and economic ideology from the petals of African culture, and traditional *ujaama*—family/hood—values.

5.5.4. Emergent Foundation: Local-Global Philosophical Sagacity/ Professional Universalist/Afro-Hermeneutic/Literary-Artistic

While the Traditionalists sought to construct an African identity based on excavated African cultural elements, the Universalists sought to demolish such structures by associating it with ethnophilosophy. The (for us emergent "local-global") schools then that thrived in this era included Philosophical Sagacity, Professional Universalist, Afro-Hermeneutic, and Literary/Artistic. On the one hand there were the promoters and on the other hand the demoters of the African philosophers of the early period. The former denigrated "ethnophilosophy" and the latter defended an African identity that was tooted in it as true and original.

In 1978, Odera Oruka (24) a Kenyan philosopher presented a paper in Ghana on "Four Trends in Current African philosophy" namely: Ethnophilosophy, Philosophical sagacity, the Nationalist Ideological school and Professional Philosophy. Later he added two further schools: Hermeneutic and Literary/Artistic. The ethnophilosophers were prominently represented by Kwame Gyekye (25) in Ghana; Philosophical sagacity by Marcel Griaule on the Dogon; the Nationalist-ideological by Nkrumah, Nyerere and Senghor; the Professional school of Hountondji and Wiredu; the Hermeneutic school by Serequeberhan (26); the Artistic-Literary by Achebe (27), Soyinka (28) and Ngugi wa' Thiong'o (29).

5.5.5. Emancipatory Navigation: Newly Global Authentic African Philosophy: Critical Reconstructionist/Afro-Eclectic

The later period (or "newly global" emancipatory navigation), for Chimakonam, heralded the emergence of the Critical Reconstructionist and Afro-Eclecticist movements. The former desired a new episteme untainted by ethnophilosophy and the latter sought to reconcile different approaches. However, dying in its embryo, thereby failing to distinguish itself sufficiently from Western philosophy, critical reconstructionism became eclecticism. For Nigeria's Uduigwomen (30), founder of the Eclectic school in 1995, there was a need to unify the goals of Particularists and Universalists, thereby giving rise to an authentic African philosophy. While the particularists supply the raw material of culture, the universalists provide the analytical structures and conceptual frameworks.

5.5.6. Global-Local Transformative Effect: Conversationalism and Creativity: Fusing Tradition and Modernity

The Creation of Critical Narratives by the Fusion of Tradition and Modernity

The New Era or Contemporary Period (for us now effectively "global-local") of African philosophy began in the 1990s and took shape in the new millennium. The orientation of this period is conversational philosophy. By conversational philosophy Chimakonam means the *rigorous engagement of individual African philosophers in the creation of critical narratives by the fusion of tradition and modernity*. It was the Nigerian philosopher Innocent Asouzu who, going beyond previously botched attempts erected a new model of African philosophy.

In fact the mansion of Western philosophy was not built in a day and was once like the African thatched house. When we now read the speculations of Homer, Hesiod and even the Ionian philosophers, we wink in amusement. Plato's eugenics for example, Aristotle's disparaging attitude to slaves and women, represent the thatch houses of European philosophy. For Hountondji to advise Africans to abandon their hatch house instead to seek ways of turning it into a befitting mansion is the height of philosophical indolence. Iroegbu (31) then, in his *Metaphysics: The Kpim of Philosophy* inaugurated a reconstructive and conversational approach in African philosophy.

He engaged previous writers in a critical conversation out of which he produced his own thought (Uwa ontology) bearing the strain of African tradition and thought, but remarkably different from ethnophilosophy. Iroegbu then inaugurated this drive but it was Asouzu who made the most of it. His theory of *ibuanyidanda* ontology or complementary reflection maintains that "to be" simply means to be in complementary relationship. Every being, therefore, is a variable with capacity to join in mutual interaction. In this capacity every being is seen as a missing link serving a missing link of reality in the network of realities.

Other emerging theories of conversational and reconstructive African philosophy came after. These include njikoka philosophy or integrative humanism credited to Godfrey Ozumba. Njikoka philosophy sees the question of being as central to African philosophy. "To be" therefore is to be in mutual, integrative relationship. Being is only being in a network of other beings. Within the network of reality, every being is necessary. Also, with the critical deconstruction that occurred in the latter part of the middle period and the attendant eclecticism that emerged in the later period, the stage was set for the formidable reconstructions and conversational encounters that marked the arrival of the New Era of African philosophy.

It is Time For Our Research Academies to Turn a New African, Integral Leaf

All of such, in the final analysis for us, while philosophically rich, and transformatively enriching, in such overall philosophical guise, has not been matched politically, economically and enterprise-wise, thereby duly and integrally stratified as such, in any shape or form, so instead we are preoccupied by one-dimensional "flatlands"—in America's leading integral philosopher Ken Wilber (32) terms)—that is leadership and entrepreneurship, ad infinitum. While philosophy then, most especially of late in Nigeria, as we have seen, flourishes, and indeed has evolved integrally, polity, economy and enterprise lag dramatically behind, and the very universities that should be serving to evolve such, remain equally left behind, stuck, more often that not, in an impoverished Western enclave. *It is time for our Research Academies, especially, to turn a new African, integral leaf.*

To further enhance such our overall, African integral process, we now turn "newly globally", by way now of emancipatory navigation, to Afrikology, aligned retrospectively, via one of us, Anselm, with the Institute for African Studies at Ibadan University in Nigeria, and prospectively, via the other of us, Samanyanga, with Manicaland State University for Applied Sciences in Zimbabwe.

5.6. References

1 **Coetzee** P & **Roux** A (2000) *Philosophy from Africa.* Oxford. Oxford University Press

2 **Chimakonam** J (2014) *Atuolu Omalu.* Unanswered Questions in Contemporary African Philosophy. Lanham. University Press of America

3 **Agada** A (2015) *Existence and Consolation: Reinventing Ontology, Gnosis, and Values in African Philosophy.* St Paul. Minnesota. Paragon House

4 **Tempels** P (2014) *Bantu Philosophy.* Orlando. HBC Publishing

5 **Mbiti** J (1975) *African Religion and Philosophy.* New York. Holt, Rinehart, Winston

6 **Nkrumah** K (1996) *Consciencism: Philosophy and Ideology for De-colonisation.* New York. Monthly Review Press.

7 **Senghor** L (1964) *On African Socialism.* London. Pall Mall Press

8 **Asouzu** I (2007) *Ibuanyidanda: New Complementary Ontology.* Zurich. Lit Verlag

9 **Thiam** C (2017) *Return to the Kingdom of Childhood: Re-visioning the Legacy and Philosophical Relevance of Negritude.* Columbus. Ohio. Ohio State University Press

10 **Nyerere** J (1969) *Nyerere of Socialism.* Dar es Salaam. Oxford University Press

11 **Souleymane** B (2011) *African Art as Philosophy: Senghor, Bergson and the Idea of Negritude.* Calcutta. Seagull Books

12 **Asouzu** I (2004) *The Methods an Principles of Complementary Reflection In and Beyond African Philosophy.* Calabar. University of Calabar Press

13 **Wiredu** K (2009) *Philosophy and African Culture.* Cambridge. Cambridge University Press

14 **Hountondji** P (2002) *The Struggle for Meaning.* Buckingham. Open University Press

15 **Chimakonam** J (2019) *Ezumezu: A System of Logic for African Philosophy and Studies.* Zurich. Springer

16 **Hegba** M (1998) *Rationalité d'un Discours Africain sur les Phénomènes Paranormaux.* Paris. L'Harmattan

17 **Etuk** U (1989) *Destiny is Not a Matter of Chance.* Bern. Peter Lang

18 **Imijoh** C (2016) *Harmonious Monism.* Bloomington. Indiana. XLIBRIS Publishing

19 **Heron** J (1994) *Feeling and Personhood.* Abingdon. Routledge

20 **Agbo** J (2017) *Love: It's the Blood of the Church.* United States. www.xulon Press

21 **Gibson** N (2003) *Fanon – The Post Colonial Imagination.* Cambridge. Polity

22 **Ozumba** G and **Chimakonam** J (2014) *Nijoka Amaka: Further Discussions on the Philosophy of Integrative Humanism.* Ughelli. Nigeria. Third Logic Option Publishing

23 **Abraham** (2015) *Mind of Africa.* Accra. Ghana. Sub-Saharan Publisher

24 **Graness** A and **Kresse** K (Eds) (1997) *Sagacious Reasoning: Henry Odera Oruka in Memoriam.* Bern. Peter Lang

25 **Gyekye** K (1997) *Tradition and Modernity: Philosophical Reflections on the African Experience.* Oxford. Oxford University Press

26 **Sereqeberhan** T (1994) *The Hermeneutics of African Philosophy.* Abingdon. Routledge

27 **Achebe** C (2006) *Things Fall Apart.* London. Penguin Classics

28 **Soyinka** W (2012) *Of Africa.* New Haven. Yale University Press

29 **Ngugi wa Thiong'o** (2009) *Something Torn and New: An African Renaissance.* New York. Basic Books

30 **Uduigwomen** A F (Ed.) (2011) *Philosophy & the Rise of Modern Science.* Vancouver. El-Johns Publishers

31 **Iroegbu** P (1995) *Metaphysics, the Kpim of Philosophy.* Madison, CN. International Universities Press

32 **Wilber** K (2006) *Integral Spirituality.* Boston. Shambhala Publications

PART FOUR

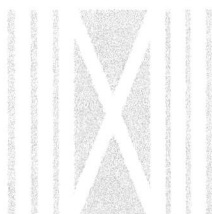

Newly Global Navigation

CHAPTER 6

African Studies to Afrikology

Knowledge has been fundamentally reinvented a number of times in the history of the West. In each case one new institution has replaced the knowledge based institution that preceded it … Today the laboratory and the research university still stand as the most evolved and overlapping intermeshed institutions of knowledge. But since the central dynamic in the history of knowledge has been for a single institution to supersede its predecessor, the time is ripe for reinvention.

McNeely and Wolverton (1), *Reinventing Knowledge*

EMANCIPATION: RESEARCH ACADEMY: SOCIAL INNOVATION

- Profound theories are produced by a research academy, as a *complex system or network* rather than a simple structure, with interconnected knowledge substance and processes, leading to *social innovation*.
- Alternative epistemologies enhance the notion of complex order by connecting individual disciplines into linear and *cross-linear relationships;* such systematic linkages *interconnected substance and process.*
- Without such differentiating and integrating systems, emergent philosophies and concepts, institutions and practices, remain disconnected lacking in coherence; *interlinked substance and process gives direction to innovation.*

- While substance draws on *biosemiotics, anthropology, oikonomics, and management;* process draws on *descriptive method, phenomenological methodology, feminist critique and participatory action research.*
- At best, systematically undertaken *social research is ethical,* 'doing right', with collective benefit to all; at their worst it is alienating and bureaucratic.

6.1. Introduction

6.1.1. Afrikology: Deconstructing and Reconstructing Knowledge

We now turn from our localised grounding, and communal learning, to our local-global emergence, through a transformation journey—practically exemplified by Adodo's Transformation Studies in Africa (TSA), currently a masters and potentially also a PhD program, at Ibadan University in Nigeria— onto now emancipatory navigation. Such is reflected in a prospective research academy, underpinned by humanities based African Studies evolving towards integral, all round Afrikology, specifically in Nigeria (Ibadan University) and Zimbabwe (MSUAS).

In the 1990s we (2), that is Ronnie Samanyanga Lessem, as an Afro-European, and Sudhanshu Palsule, as an Anglo-Indian began our transforma-tion journey (see opening chapter) *from local identity to global integrity,* recog-nising that the "north-west" then dominated over the "south-east". We thereby sought to co-evolve, out of a spirit of co-creation, *four worlds,* newly globally so to speak (south, east, north and west), rather than just one, that is globalisation, or two, so-called "developed" and "underdeveloped" ones. Such "four worlds", plus an integrating centre, underlie (as illustrated in each of the boxed inserts heading up this book's chapters), for us two authors Lessem and Adodo, in integral theory and in transformative practice, via now Transformative Studies in Africa (see above), our *Deconstruction and Reconstruction of Knowledge and Value Out of Africa.*

Such "Afrikology" then, as identified by its originator Dani Nabudere (3), while emerging *out of Africa,* is not exclusive to such, but speaks to and for the south and east, north and west, altogether, albeit from a new "southern" centre. As such, for us, it is invariably Grounded locally (Egyptian-Dogon), Emerges locally-globally (South-East-North-West), Navigates newly globally (Afrikology), and Effects transform-ation, specifically social innovation, glob-ally-locally (Africa–Worlds/wide).

6.1.2. Local Identity (Communal Learning)/Global Integrity (Communiversity)

How does this fit into our current, auspicious context? As we look at the state of the world today, taking due heed of Boris Johnson's Brexit in Britain (the withdrawal bill from the EU was finally ratified at the time of writing in December, 2019), Trump's America (the Democrats have just voted to impeach him), accompanied by civil wars in Yemen and Syria, rampant unemployment in Southern Europe and Southern Africa, the story goes on and on, we see, not a "clash of civilizations" but rather a "clash between the local and the global".

To that extent, and Afrikology-wise, we pursue a transformational course from local identity (communal learning) to global integrity (communiversity), rather than flip-flopping between the local and the global, which results in the likes of "Brexit". In our own TCA (Trans4m Communiversity Associates) language we journey from ID (local Identity) to CD (Communiversity). To that extent we overturn the conventional notion of a "uni-versity", with its standardised, universal—some would argue, as we shall see "colonial"—connotations, and start from communal home, the commons.

As such, and overall, the ever increasing advance of "climate change", alongside the hazardous loss of biodiversity, is leading to something of a world-wide wake-up call, that we are indeed part of a "world-wide web", not only technologically, but especially, oikologically. We need then, in our terms, to start from the *natural/communal* "South", as constituting the very grounds for, and of, the *technological/ economic* "west" (which is where we ultimately need to end), as a Communiversity, emerging *Out of Africa*, rather than out of Europe, the USA or China, inclusively rather than exclusively, thereby originating in, and through, a local community, rather than a globalised individual.

In a conversation some years ago with our friend and colleague Mfuniselwa Bhengu (4), ex-Chairman of the Afrikology Institute in South Africa, he communicated in an e-mail exchange (April 5, 2016):

> When you Africanise, you are localizing, but when you are Afrikologizing you are globalizing ...Therefore, Afrikologising is an inclusive process of transformation and societal innovation.

In other words, we are revisiting humankind's origins, emerging out of Africa, but thereafter encompassing the whole world, or our worlds as a whole. Indeed in our (5) own *integral worlds* approach, as such, we have distinguished between different "southern" and "eastern", "northern" and "western" worlds, or Realities, each in their own right. More specifically, we have identified the following worldly *realities,* each then serving to constitute, in our Communiversity *Pax Africana* terms:

- "southern" *nature and community,* embodied in a *learning Community*
- "eastern" *culture and spirituality,* infusing a *transformation Journey*
- "northern" *science and technology,* informing a *research Academy*
- "western" *enterprise and economy,* associated with an *integral Laboratory*

And more generally the:

- "centre" with an all round *polity* underlying our overarching *Communiversity.*

Of course each "world", as a whole, has its latent, if not actualised, "south" and "east", "north" and "west"—what we term overall *integrality*—but it is a question of relative emphasis in each particular societal case.

> A major shift occurred in the four-element system between the time it was conceived and the ontologies of Graeco-Roman late antiquity, medieval Byzantine, Arabic and the Early Modern Derivative. The system became fixed, rigid and standardised, as though the issue of transformation no longer mattered. As such, the elements no longer mutated from one substance to another, even when interacting with other elements. The latter signalled the emergence of the state, science and organized religion as major organizing factors in culture and society. It also implied the entrenchment of transcendence over immanence.
>
> Sanya Osha (6) *Dani Nabudere's Afrikology,*
> *A Quest for African Holism*

6.1.3. Re-GENE-ration: Realities, Realms, Rhythm, Rounds, Rhizome

Needless to say, the way the world is currently constituted, whereby the "west" (even China and India today, at least economically if not in the Chinese case politically, mimic the "west") rules over the rest, means that such *integrality* is inhibited, in economy, polity and academe. To that extent, we (7) have evolved what we term our integral, and indeed transformational *rhythm* of social innovation, or more specifically social re-GENE-ration, thereby GENE-IUS-wise, whereby we are:

- <u>G</u>rounded locally in the natural and communal "south": *Origination*
- <u>E</u>merge locally-globally in the cultural and spiritual "east": *Foundation*
- <u>N</u>avigate newly globally in a scientific/technical "north": *Emancipation*

- Effect *Transformation* globally-locally enterprise-wise in the "west"; pursues
- Synergise *Integrally* by combining moral Inspiration with Universal truth

Altogether constituting societal re-GENE-ration, from origination to transformation, starting out in the "south": hence the relevance of Afrikology, as for us a philosophy, and also praxis, of wholeness.

Through a "centre" that holds, in Achebe's (8) terms, as opposed to his *Things Falling Apart,* we underlie, moreover, the recognition and release of GENE-*IUS*. In depicting such gene-IUS as above, we have referred to moral Inspiration (local) and Universal truth (global, duly Synergized (local-global-local). We regard Afrikology, thereby, as a means of centering the "south", within and across our four particular *integral worlds*, that is altogether (our 4 R's) involving integral:

- *Realities:* South, East, North and West
- *Realms:* Nature, Culture, Technology, Enterprise
- *Rhythm:* Grounding, Emergence, Navigation, Effect
- *Rounds:* Self and Community, Organisation and Society

Building up now towards our relational Centre, we add a fifth such R, the:

- *Rhizome:* Ancestry, Generation, Substance, Land and Memory

Such builds, more generally, on the work of renowned ecological anthropologist Tim Ingold, from his (9) book on *The Perception of the Environment: Essays on Livelihood, Dwelling and Skill.* Ingold, in turn, draws from the "progenerative" approach of the contemporary French philosophers Deleuze and Guattari (10), whereby, for Ingold, drawing on their work:

> I believe that a relational model, with the rhizome rather than the tree as its core image, better conveys the sense that so-called indigenous people have of themselves and their place in the world ... from a relational perspective persons should be understood not as procreated entities, but rather as centres of progenerative activity variously positioned within an all-encompassing field of relationships ... Ancestors as such can be ordinary humans who lived in the past, spirit inhabitants of the landscape, or original creator beings.

We note also Ingold's emphasis on *Livelihood, Dwelling and Skill,* as opposed to, for example, the conventional approach to generating jobs, employment, enterprise and so forth, a subject to which we shall return. How then is such, institutionally if not inter-institutionally, to be achieved?

Polity and Communiversity

We (11) have argued hitherto, in our *Idea of the Communiversity*, that there is no effective agency in a particular society, to promote re-GENE-ra-tion, from the Ground up, or more realistically, for us, middle-up-down-across (12), as originally cited by the renowned Japanese organisational psychologists, Nonaka and Takeuchi (13) in their work on *The Knowledge Creating Company*. For Nonaka then, alluding to the great Japanese manufacturing enterprises in their heyday, like Sony or Honda, in times of crisis, instead of hiring and firing new personnel, or indeed the incumbent CEO, as is characteristic of the corporate "west":

> Rather than reactively fighting for survival with their backs to the wall, physically and economically through typically downsizing, they proactively set out to create a new future. Such a proactive approach, moreover, involves both re-cognizing and re-newing the capability of the enterprise as a whole, to create new knowledge, disseminate it throughout, and embody it in products, services and systems.

In our terms, societally as well as organisationally speaking, it is newly inclusive knowledge and *value* that we seek, rather than, exclusively, individual entrepreneurship or leadership, in pursuit of such. Thereby we (14) draw on *Nhakanomics,* societally, and, in an African context, *intenhaka's* (15), specifically, the term *nhaka*, in the indigenous Shona language meaning "legacy". Such an "integrator" then, not only bridges the proverbial gap between research (natural and social sciences) and development (economy and enterprise), in our case here serving to bring about social innovation, but also between nature (ecology and community) and culture (arts and humanities).

To that extent we need to draw on an inter-institutional combination of community, journey, academy and laboratory, locally and globally, middle-up-down-across, serving as the antithesis to the proverbial, duly "westernised" university as an "ivory tower". Ironically though, as we shall see, it is in the economic "west", though in this case building on the natural, cultural and scientific "rest" that the Communiversity is ultimately actualised.

6.2. Newly Global Afrikology as Emancipatory Navigation

6.2.1. Reclaiming the Future

For Nabudere (16), then, a Ugandan African contemporary philosopher, and the originator of Afrikology, Western knowledge systems cannot be understood outside of the African communality of knowledge. In fact one of us

(Samanyanga) had the privilege of meeting Dani in South Africa a decade go, just before he died, when he gave a speech at the African Heritage Centre in Pretoria. Immediately Samanyanga was struck by the breadth and depth of his philosophical orientation. In fact they had agreed to meet again in Uganda, to carry on the conversation they had begun on Africa-in-the-world. Then sadly Nabudere passed away.

Professor Nabudere had been in fact Minister of Justice in 1979 and of Culture, Community Development and Rehabilitation in 1979–1980 in the Interim Government of Uganda. He was President of the African Association of Political Science from 1983 to 1985 and Vice-President of the International Political Science Association from 1985 to 1988. He was engaged in a collaborative arrangement with the University of South Africa in joint research projects under the umbrella theme of "Reclaiming the Future". He was the founder and principal of the Marcus Garvey Pan-Afrikan Institute (MPAI). Over the last ten years of his life, Nabudere was working on setting up grassroots organisations to assist rural communities and raise their voices over issues that concern their lives. Indeed Samanyanga was first introduced to him by his friend and colleague Mfuniselwa Bhengu, cited above, an ex-Parliamentarian as well as African cultural and economic historian, with a special interest in Ancient Egypt.

6.2.2. All Phenomena Originate From Primordial Substance

For Bhengu (17), the so-called *Ubuntu* mind, born and bred in southern Africa where he is based, is also, for him, originally connected with the Ancient Egyptians, with whom, for him, his Zulu people are closely linked, as are, as we have seen (chapter 2), the primordial Dogon people of Mali. As such:

- all phenomena originate from primordial substance or, in Zulu, *Qqobo,* that is infinite reality or ultimate value, for us lodged in a local *community*
- perpetual evolution, that is growing forever into the future (*ukama njalo* in Zulu) is the destiny of the person, of all phenomena and the cosmic order, as is the case for our so-called local/global transformation *journey*
- *Imvelo* (the cosmic order) has three pillars of being: the Law, the Environment and the Person. Law moreover metamorphoses into art, religion and philosophy, altogether for us lodged in a newly global research *academy*

Added to such, for us, is also the integral *laboratory.*

These laws of Ubuntu emanate from ancient principles of *Maat*—balance or justice—duly adapted by the Ancient AbeNguni, Zulu peoples (see also chapter 1), to which we add, Communiversity-wise, a now global-local laboratory, building on what has come before. Where then, for Bhengu, does Afrikology come in?

6.2.3. On the Meaning and Scope of Afri-cology

The word, "Afrikology" is not ethnic nor racial but a validation of a human knowledge of communal—including natural—living. It is "*Afri-*" because it is inspired by what Nabudere calls, "*ideas originally produced from the cradle of human kind located in Africa*" and so, it is not Afrikology because it is African (although to some extent it is). It is also "*ko* (logy)" because it is based on *logos*, the word from which the world was originated, but at the same time, an episteme, a worldly-wise eco-logical knowledge and consciousness. Consequently, it does not strive for superiority but a reclamation and validation of its rightful position, as a whole. It seeks to avoid any claim to an overarching epistemic superiority, but stands for plurality of epistemic directions, for us "southern" and "eastern", "northern" and "western" communi-*versity* (harbouring di-versity). Knowledge therefore is an interpretation that is always situated within a living communal tradition and our inescapable historicity.

How then does such "Afrikology" compare with the better known *African Studies*, that proliferate in universities around the world, and how does our Communiversity add knowledge-and-value to such?

6.2.4. Afrikology, Communiversity and Collective Knowledge

For Nabudere then, university based African Studies, like the *Area Studies* of which it formed a part, and other such studies including Oriental, Middle Eastern, Latin American, Chinese and Japanese as well as Slavonic Studies, have represented an exogenous, Euro-American, attempt to understand "the other", arguably, he says, so as to be able to better exploit their resources, if not also colonize their minds. To that extent, Nabudere advocated that such exogenous areas studies be replaced by indigenous-exogenous *Afrikology*. We then add our Communi-versity as a vehicle for such. This is not only for the African people by the African people, but also, and more especially, for the world as a whole, serving thereby to recognise and release the GENE-IUS, of each and every particular individual and community, organisation and society, albeit in an overarching worldly-wise (diverse worlds) context.

More specifically, the utterance of the Word from the heart by the tongue is an act of *divine speech* and communication, giving meaning to things.

Moreover, and as such for Nabudere, the work attributed to ancient Egyptian-Greek mystical figure Thoth Hermes was a collective knowledge, an ancient "mystery stream", produced communally by the African people from ancient times up to the point it was received by the Ancient Greeks. They then tried to individualize his authorship, via Hermes, the "messenger God", from which *hermeneutics,* the foundation of what we (18), in our *Integral Research and Innovation,* have termed the *path of renewal,* is derived.

6.2.5. On Eurocentrism

According to Egyptian development economist Samir Amin (19), moreover, latterly a Director of the World Social Forum based in Dakar, in the Senegal, in his book on *Eurocentrism: Modernity, Religion and Democracy,* Plato, who spent a great deal of time in Egypt, did not—during his stay—develop a full understanding of the Egyptian mystery stream. The Greek departure from the Egyptian source begins in a sustained way, more concertedly though, with the writings of Aristotle and his classifications of the components of the universe.

From this moment, the Western narrative, for Nabudere as for Amin and for Chimakonam (see previous chapter), generally, and the European academic curriculum, specifically, began to be superimposed on the African one, and began to marginalize such African communal knowledge, and also as such *African Creation Energy* (see chapter 4) and value as a metaphysical creation.

This fragmentation of language and thought, with the "north-west" eclipsing the "south-east", as it were, lies at the root of the current human malaise, for Nabudere, and educational malaise, for us, and disorientation. This can be overcome, for him, by a return to the original epistemology, and for us also, such original communal to communiversity praxis, born and bred in Africa, as per *Afrikology.* This is realised, on the one hand philosophically and conceptually, through the power of the word and the hermeneutic tradition, for Eritrean American Tsenay Serequeberhan's (20) via *Hermeneutics of African Philosophy.* As such:

> Post-colonial Africa poses the challenge of self-transformation and the concrete actualization of its chimerical "independence". It does so, furthermore, in view of the suffering millions that have been victimized by the *lived actuality as opposed to the hoped for ideality* of an "independent" Africa.

On the other hand for Nigerian poet and philosopher, Sanya Osha (20), research fellow at the Institute for Economic Research in Innovation, at Tshwane University of Technology in Pretoria, South Africa:

"Nabudere's philosophy of Afrikology traces the historical, cultural, scientific and social links between the "Cradle of Humankind" and the contemporary world, with a view to healing the seismic severances occasioned by violence, false thinking, war, loss, and dispossession in order to accomplish an epistemological and psychic sense of wholeness for an African collective self."

6.2.6. Towards Transdisciplinarity and Trans-sectorality

Indeed Plato created eternal essences which were outside the control of the senses of human beings, and by so doing he created a vacuum between the eternal essence (the philosophical or conceptual "forms") and everyday matter (the material or practical "reality"), something we seek here to overcome.

According to Senegalese anthropologist, physicist and philosopher Cheikh Anta Diop (22), *The African Origin of Civilization*, the principle feature of the mechanistic order was that the world was regarded as constituted of separate entities, for us separating nature and culture, technology and enterprise, on the one hand, and community and sanctuary, academy and laboratory/enterprise on the other. These existed *outside of each other*, independent in their *integral* existence in time and space. For Diop, as for Nabudere:

> By contrast, in a living organism, each part grows in the context of the whole, so that it does not exists independently, nor can it be said that it merely interacts with others, without itself being essentially affected in the relationship.

To that extent, the differentiation between education (academe–university), and economy (enterprise–business), without their subsequent unification (communiversity) has done us no favours. The advent of *Afrikology-and-Communiversity* then, as an integral worldly-wise whole, as opposed to "African Studies"*-in-University*, as an African "area study" part, constitutes such complexity-plurality, serving to integrate—deconstruct and reconstruct—our duly centred "four worlds" of knowledge and value, out of Africa.

6.2.7. The Heart is the Locus of Reason

Nabudere then looks at some of the theories and practices that are still to be found in African and other societies, but which help one understand the integrated nature of reality and knowledge. For the Congolese African philosopher Theophile Obenga (23), as for *African Creation Engineering* (see chapter 4), it is ancient Egypt's Ptah who conceived of all things in the heart, and *it is the heart which was the locus of reason,* for him. *The heart for the Ancient Egyptians was the seat of intelligence, reason and intellectual perception.* Thus, for

Obenga, it was the heart that conceived the name to be attached to things, and it is the tongue and the mouth that uttered or proclaimed what the heart had conceived through reason.

Interestingly enough, moreover, such a "heart-felt" approach to research and education coincides with that of the renowned, contemporary English research philosopher, and originator of *Cooperative Inquiry*, John Heron (24), based today at the South Pacific Centre for Human Inquiry in Auckland, New Zealand. For him, while there are altogether "four modes of knowing", equivalent to our GENE—experiential (Grounding), imaginal (Emergence), conceptual (Navigation) and practical (Effect)—what then grounds our knowledge and learning is:

> ... emotional confidence, fulfilment and positive arousal as the most important constituents for individual learning ... Individual people and whole societies learn and develop more effectively when they are enjoying themselves and what they are doing; when they are satisfying some felt need or interest, and are emotionally involved in what has personal and societal relevance to them; when they feel good about the whole idea of learning and development as well as the exercise of their learning competence; when they feel confident, secure and in a low threat, co-operative, non-competitive position.

We align, or ground, such heart-felt emotion with nature-and-community, or communal learning, through which our Communiversity grounds itself, whereafter spirit emerges (Sanctuary), mind navigates (Academy) and body effects (Laboratory).

6.2.8. CIRD-A – Beyond University-Based African Studies

What is then required, for Nabudere, is a new holistic and at the same time ethical conception of reality that has roots in primal, for us communal, grounds. Afrikology as such, for him, is a transdisciplinary, and for us inter-institutional, epistemology that can take us out of the limits of African Studies-and-academe in isolation, rooted in the humanities, most especially in the arts and history, but excluding the communally based natural and social sciences, as well as, for us, business and management studies.

Our prospective Centre for Integral Research and Development out of Africa (CIRDA)—to be hopefully established between Trans4m Communiversity Associates and Da Vinci Institute in South Africa—includes all of such.

It is in that guise, moreover, that we take heed—for all his general acknowledgment—of Osha's (25) also critical comments on Afrikology:

> Nabudere fails to take into account the mechanisms, practices and institutions that, in the course of knowledge generation, have all been transformed during the process of human development. He provides no indication as to how to re-incorporate our ancient African heritage.

In other words, our *integral* approach to recognising and releasing GENE-IUS, as we shall see, necessitates an individual and collective approach to not only local origination, and local-global foundation, but also newly global emancipation and ultimately global-local transformation: a Communiversity. In that guise, and for example, for African American Clyde Ford (26) in his *Hero with an African Face: Mythic Wisdom of Traditional Africa,* the African Bambara society are carriers of a tradition known as *doma* or *soma* meaning "those who know", and who are thereby in touch with the very "grounds" of knowledge:

> As a rule, the master of knowledge is a "general practitioner" versed in the sciences of plants, of the earth, with its agricultural and medicinal properties, of water, and of astronomy, cosmogony, psychology, and other subjects. What is involved, in fact, is the eminently practical science of living, which consists in mobilizing the energies available so that they serve life.

We now turn to that very knowledge substance which is conventionally absent from African Studies lodged in the Humanities, that is Afrikologically for us Biosemiotics (see chapter 1), Economics and Management, if not also Anthropology. As such, African Studies, normally lodged in such subject matters as African art and sculpture, music and literature, if not also ethno-medicine, as well as African philosophy and history, is now amplified—in our overall scientific and technological Afrikological context—by such science (natural and social) and technology. We start with the new discipline of what we term Oikonomics, as a "southern" re-visioning of economics.

6.3. The Substance of Afrikology

6.3.1. The Nature of Oikonomics

Oikonomia – The Art of Household Management: Alias Kumusha

For the American economic historian Ingrid Rima (27), in *The Development of Economic Analysis,* the modern word "economics", interestingly enough, has its origin in the ancient Greek word "oikonomia", which means "the art of household management". We then take on, oikonomically, in southern

European (ancient Greece) guise, from where she leaves off, adding a further dose of anthropology (nature, culture), of biosemiotics (nature, culture and science) and also management studies (enterprise) to such oikonomics.

In reviewing such Rima describes how Aristotle undertook to examine what is probably the first economic issue to have been subjected to formal inquiry: what sort of wealth getting activity satisfies material needs as a desirable goal of human activity? *For Aristotle in that respect, retail trade—as opposed to household trade—which is exchange for the purpose of making money, is unnatural.* What is natural is the pursuit of "autarky" or self-sufficiency. This has echoes today (see Nhakanomics) of our integral *kumusha*.

Onto The Economics of the City State: Towards Ubuntu

Greek thinkers moreover, like Aristotle, from their particular socio-political perspective, believed that a "good life" is the purpose of existence, and that it is best achieved within the city-state or "polis". The state (polis in ancient Greek), rather than the individual, just like for us now the learning community takes precedence over the individual, is omnipotent. The theory underlying that, in contrast with today's conventional pre-emphasis on mathematical economics, embraced ethics, sociology, economics and political science. *The search for the good life was at the same time the search for the ideal state, and also a co-evolution of culture, polity and economy, in the specific context of such a "city-state".* In today's southern African terms, the equivalent of such, is *ubuntu*.

Co-evolution of Economics and Ethics

More than a millennium later, the European Churchmen considered avarice or lust for earthly things as one of the seven deadly sins; only those economic activities that maintain individuals in the rank order in which God has placed them were regarded as proper. Within this framework, society was seen as an integrated whole in which God, nature and man each had a preordained place. It was therefore essential that human affairs be conducted in accordance with the principles of "distributive" (rank) and "commutative" (fairness) justice. Thomas Aquinas' *Summa Theologica* (28) survives as a masterwork of economics because it confronts the coexistence of ethical and economic questions, in of course a Christian, indeed Catholic, European context. Then everything fundamentally changed, as we entered the 17th century.

The Wealth of Nations: Liberalism, Atomism, Self-Regulation

In moving from such a socio-political and then cultural-religious to a scientific core, for Rima, once it thereby became recognised in 17th century Europe that the physical universe obeys certain laws that can be discovered by observation and experimentation, it was only a matter of time before it was asked whether the same laws might not be applied to modern society, governing social and economic phenomena. The English political philosopher John Locke and the Scottish moral philosophers, among them David Hume, Francis Hutchison and his most famous pupil Adam Smith (29) in the 18th century, sought to identify the natural laws ruling the behaviour of society. Developments in the natural sciences, physics and astronomy, were thus influential in establishing the point of view and methodology for studying the behaviour of the social sciences, and for co-evolving an economic system accordingly.

Economic thought had then entered a transitional phase in the second half of the 18th century. The newly emerging attitude was one of increasing liberality: *the gradually evolving idea that the economic system is a self-generating, autonomous mechanism that does not require management from above, but functions best when allowed to regulate itself.* In fact Smith, being enamored of Newton and the picture he created of a mechanical and perfectly harmonious planetary universe, along with many other economic thinkers of the time, tried to apply the same kind of conception to the universe of people. People as such become things. Apart from its general principle of self-interest, this is economics' most dehumanizing idea. *Instead of the economy being for people, it implies that people are for the economy.* His devotion to the classical physical sciences unwittingly obscured his at least partial intent, to advance the rights and dignity of the workers. In time this would give birth to the antithesis to such, that is Marxism.

Marxism: Combining Socialism with Historicism

Overall, Marx's (30) objective was to lay bare the economic law of motion of modern society. He maintained that the prime mover of social change is to be found in changes in the mode of production. For him, the mode of production includes not only the technology surrounding the physical means of production, but also the social relationships deriving from the whole complex of the socio-economic, political and cultural institutions that accompany a given stage of development. Hence, Marx's economic position was very different from that of the equilibrium-seeking demand-and-supply oriented.

Unlike Hegel, Marx saw the arena of conflict to be the material world, within its existing social system, rather than locating it in the realm of ideas, for us, in culture and spirituality. Thus, Marx began the *Communist Manifesto* (31) with the observation that "the history of all hitherto existing society is the history of class struggles". In the meantime, for over a century and a half, there has been a prolonged interregnum, reaching across to this very day, when mainstream economic theory steered off into murky, indeed marginal waters, which would ultimately lead to the so-called "neoclassical" era, vividly resurrected in the past few decades.

Reverting to Neoclassical Neoliberal Economics

The premise, therefore, that individuals are capable of maximizing behavior in the "free" markets in which they operate, whether as producers or consumers, has become the "Leitmotif" of the tradition associated with the Chicago School of Economics, in which Friedman has been the most prominent member. Chicago economists are first and foremost advocates of an individualistic market economy. The Chicago school's view of human nature, in such a context, is that of being universally responsive to market incentives.

The necessity of encouraging the emergence of individual "entrepreneurial personalities" in so-called "underdeveloped" countries is therefore a matter of special concern to the Chicago School (32). The counterweight to such, as we have seen, is anthropology, although, ironically, one of the world's leading cultural anthropologists, Margaret Mead, was also based in the University of Chicago, but in the anthropology department, and never the twain—anthropology and economics—did meet!

Capitalism in the Web of Life: Life Making as Oikeios

That said, coordinator of the World-Ecology Research Network, at Binghamton State University of New York, Jason Moore (33) identifying his fields of teaching and research as political ecology, agro-food studies, historical geography, social and spatial theory, environmental history, environmental humanities, political economy, world history, neoliberalism, recently published his seminal work on *Capitalism and the Web of Life*. Therein and thereby he alludes to what he terms *Oikeios*. In this spirit Moore understands "capital" and "capitalism" as producers and products of such. From this *Oikeoitic* perspective we are led to such questions as how firstly is humanity *unified* with the rest of nature within the web of life? Second, how is human history *co-produced* history, through which humans have put nature to work—including other humans —in accumulating wealth and power? In that sense he is revisiting Aristotle's *oikos* in 21st century guise, for us taking then a newly "southern" *oikonomic* turn. We now turn from such nature based oikonomics to nature and culture, via anthropology.

6.3.2. Nature and Culture: Anthropology

Anthropology: Why It Matters

As such an anthropological nature-and-culture takes precedence over, but does not preclude, technology and enterprise. In fact anthropology, in its respectively ecological, cultural, social and economic guise, includes all of the above. How then has anthropology evolved, especially over the course of the last century and a half, since this social scientific discipline was born, and why is it so important today, as an integral part of the overall *oikonomic* knowledge substance upon which we need to ultimately Afrikologically draw (incidentally not a single business school around the world draws substantively on anthropology)?

Contemporary English ecological anthropologist, Tim Ingold (34), in his latest book on *Anthropology: Why It Matters,* terms it a field of holistic study that would seek to bring to bear, on the problem of how to live and work, the wisdom and experience of all the world's inhabitants (as opposed to conventional economics with its strongly western connotations), whatever their backgrounds, livelihoods, circumstances and places of abode. He calls anthropology, following in the footsteps of African American historian Chancellor Williams (35): a discipline-in-the-making. Whereas philosophers are reclusive souls, more inclined to turn inwards in a studious interrogation of canonical texts of thinkers like themselves (though Chimakonam would disagree), anthropologists, in contrast, "philosophize in the world". For Williams then:

> One of the greatest discoveries of this age was made in the field of anthropology, not physics. It was the discovery that in the rush from primitive life man actually left behind some of the more fundamental elements needed for a truly civilized life. Chief among these was—and of course is—the sense of community, direction and purpose. This is why Africa is very important now. It can profit if it sees the precipice towards which we are drifting, and takes the opposite course in an effort to build a different kind of society on a spiritual foundation.

Never in history, Williams goes on to say, has this kind of anthropology been more needed. For the world remains in the grip of a system of production, distribution and consumption that, while grotesquely enriching a few, has left countless millions of people surplus to requirements, condemned to chronic insecurity, poverty and disease, and also wreaked environmental destruction on an unprecedented scale. Not without reason have some declared the onset of a new era in earth's history the Anthropocene.

Identity in Community

An anthropology worthy of the name must, moreover in Ingold's view, be founded on the principle that we inhabit one (we call "integral") world. But this world is not the globe of corporate finance, of international telecommunications, of "the West". It is a world not of similarity but of manifold difference (our transcultural Realities). For anthropology, the challenge is to spell out, with clarity and conviction, alongside such differences, the one-ness, for us the substantive *integrality*, of such a world.

In that context, interestingly enough, the very term "community", from the Latin *com* ("together"), plus *munus* ("gift"), means not just "living together" but "giving together". *We belong to communities because each of us, being different, has something to give. Identity in community is thus fundamentally "relational"*: who we are is an index of where we find ourselves, at any moment, in the give and take of collective life.

Anthropology's Purpose

Anthropology's purpose, for Ingold then, is to draw on what we learn from our education with other people to speculate on what the conditions and possibilities of life (and for us economy and enterprise) might be. Thanks to the wealth of human experience they bring to the table, anthropologists have hugely important things to say. Anthropology as such, which is speculative and experimental (for us going all the way from origination to transformation), could have the potential to transform lives.

For Zimbabwean social anthropologists Mawere and Nhemechana (36), anthropology then, for them, can very well be used in postcolonial Africa to help Africa decolonise and develop. What is needed therefore is to adjust the discipline and thereby turn it into a powerful apparatus for African liberation and scholarly growth, for us—bearing in mind Ingold's first obstacle above—revisiting economics in the light of anthropology, as well as vice versa:

> In a context, where transformation has become the battle cry, it is necessary to mobilise the discipline of anthropology, as a prerequisite for a thereby transformed economics, in order to understand the ramifications for global transformation on Africans. Furthermore, in a world where there is not only resurgence of indigenous knowledges, but also where Euro-modernity is increasingly troubled, there is need to revive the discipline of anthropology that renders local "alternatives". Local "alternatives" to the Western neoliberal economies need to be supported through anthropological researches; local anthropological jurisprudence needs to be supported so that they provide "alternatives" to Western forms of politics and economics that is increasingly criticized

for its legal imperialism; local social security systems need to be supported through anthropological research since they provide "alternatives" to faltering Western social security systems.

African people have resorted to informal or non-formal sectors of the economy for survival, speaking less to industrialisation than to de-industrialisation, as, since the neoliberal era, it has been losing ever more industries. Thus anthropology, being the study of non-industrialised societies, is becoming ever more relevant and conditions for its growth as a discipline on the continent. The discipline is best placed to resurface "alternative" industrialisation; dwellings, systems, foodstuffs, understandings of weather and climate, mining and smelting systems. It is suited to resurface "alternative" economies for which scholars at a global level are searching ... anthropology promises, in the future, to be relevant not only in studying microscale, local sciences but it is also relevant in studying the nexus between the local and the global; its future is in liberating Africa by providing the grit for the intellectual crucible for liberation and decolonisation. If global capital thrives on denying and closing off alternatives for humanity, anthropology promises a future where alternatives are resurfaced for humanity to choose from.

We now turn from oikonomics and anthropology to so-called Biosemiotics, thereby combining nature and culture with science and technology.

6.3.3. Nature and Culture, Science and Technology: Biosemiotics

The Advent of the Semiosphere

For the recently late Danish biochemist Jesper Hoffmeyer (37), the semiosphere is a sphere, just like the atmosphere, the hydrosphere, and the biosphere. It penetrates every corner of these other spheres, incorporating all forms of communication:

> Sounds, smells, movements, colours, shapes, electrical fields, thermal radiation, waves of all kinds, chemical signals and so on. In fact our ecological awareness is still stuck at the physico-chemical level, where energy currents, biomass, and food chains constitute standard categories. Yet all plants and animals live first and foremost in a world of signification.

One of the pioneers of research into the "sensory worlds" of animals was the Estonian born, German 20th century biologist Jakob von Uexkull (38). The way he saw it, animals spend their lives locked up, so to speak, inside their own subjective worlds, each in its own *Umwelt*. Modern biology employs the term "ecological niche" under which a given species lives. One might say that *the umwelt is the ecological niche as the animal itself apprehends it.* Von Uexkull then saw, long before anyone else, that a biology that would be true to its subject matter would have to direct its searchlight explicitly on the perceptual worlds of organisms, their *Umwelts* as he called them. The Umwelt is the subjective or phenomenal world of the animal.

The idea that animals possess internally experienced or phenomenal worlds that they then project back on the outside world, however, has never been well received by mainstream 20th century biology. Organisms are treated as black boxes, operated upon by the external forces of mutation and environmental selection. What went on *inside* the black box (morphologically, physiologically, psychologically) was no longer seen as part of the *generative dynamics of nature.*

Biosemiotic Technology

Overall then, for Hoffmeyer, we may say that the Stone Age was characterised by a technology that rarely, in any systematic way, used energy forms surpassing human muscular power. The technology and social organisation of agricultural societies were designed to obtain the maximum yield from available biological energy sources (for example photosynthesis). Industrial production transcended these limitations by developing means of energy transformation of almost every conceivable kind (including nuclear) and accordingly based huge productivity on the consumption of seemingly infinite sources of artificial energy. *Finally, the kind of society we are now entering appears to be one that will derive its enabling power more than anything else from the ability to produce the technological means for ever more sophisticated command over the semiotic dimensions of nature.*

We now finally turn from Oikonomics, Anthropology and Biosemiotics to Management Studies.

6.3.4. Finance/Enterprise Bereft of Nature/Culture: Management Studies

Regression to Leadership and Entrepreneurship

In the 1980s in fact, *In Search of Excellence,* California's Tom Peters and Robert Waterman (39), ex McKinsey management consultants, burst onto the managerial stage, urging the business establishment to "go back to basics", thereby promoting individual entrepreneurship, if not also leadership, over and above management. Enough, they said, of all that institutionalised "management bureaucracy". It is high time, they argued, that we restore the individual leader, and entrepreneur, to their jointly rightful place as "king of the castle", as the dynamic duo behind any form of enterprise. Entrepreneurship, since that fateful time, also then coinciding with the Thatcher-Reagan neo-liberal era, has become the masculine order of the business—and indeed the social (social entrepreneurship)—day, with individual Leadership becoming its effective handmaiden.

Leadership Eclipses Management

At the same, and from the 1980s onwards, there has been an absolute pro-liferation of books written on *Leadership*, now dwarfing those on management, on the business bookshelves. For Harvard sociologist Rakesh Khurana (40), in his (Khurana was based at Harvard Business School before more recently mov-ing next door to Harvard University itself) seminal work *From Higher Minds to Hired Hands: The Social Transformation of the American Business Schools and the Unfulfilled Promise of Management as a Profession:*

> The substitution of market for professional and managerial logics has served to delegitimate management. In the process the business schools themselves, in the dramatic transformation of American capitalism, provided the ideological justification and the revolutionary cadres for the overthrow of the old managerialist order, and its replacement by a neo liberal utopianism that valued what were taken to be ineluctable market processes over the contingent concerns and decisions of human actors, including managers and their constituents other than shareholders.

More specifically then, and as a result:

> In the 1990s, Harvard shifted from its emphasis on general manage-ment to "educating leaders who make a difference in the world". One of the central features of a bone fide profession, is a coherent body of expert knowledge built upon a well-developed theoretical foundation. The renowned American business executive and writer Chester Barnard in fact observed in the 1930s that the "Great Man" view on leadership generated "an extraordinary amount of dogmatically stated nonsense". Leadership, as such, lacks a usable body of knowledge to go with it.

By-Passing Conservation

In fact, the extent of this historic "western" regression is born out, even more emphatically, when we follow the path laid out, developmentally, by American legal environmentalist, Jedediah Purdy (41), based at Columbia University in New York. For Purdy points out that:

> In 1909 the National Conservation Commission published a "Report on National Vitality: Its Wastes and Conservation". It opened with the assertion: "The problem of conserving our natural resources is part of

another and greater problem—that of national efficiency which depends not only on the physical environment, but on the social environment, and most of all on human vitality". Progressives warred against spoliation of human bodies and energies as much as they did against the waste of timber and coal. President Woodrow Wilson then, in his first inaugural address, elaborated on this conservationist theme, described the 19th century legacy as both "riches" and "inexcusable waste", the latter evident in the failure to "conserve the bounty of nature" and in "the human cost of lives snuffed out, of energies overtaxed and broken". The Progressive's response to such social waste—resource conservation, public-health regulation, and labour laws—figured in Wilson's language as a single remedy: "to purify and humanize every process of our common life" by replacing short-sighted self-interest with a commitment that law shall "keep sound the society it serves".

This conservation and management movement—the two were explicitly intertwined—emerged in the United States over a century ago, in fact at the very same time that the first management schools were being created in the early part of last century, as Rhukana points out, born out of the same kind of generally "conservationist" social, if not also ecological, ethos. How times have changed. For American business journalist Duff Macdonald (42), as cited above, in his book on *The Golden Passport: Harvard Business School, Limits of Capitalism and the Moral Failure of the MBA Elite*:

> The appropriate ambition for a business-minded Harvard graduate at the time, early last century, was to engage in business to serve the public sphere, more than the private one. The idea was that HBS could be a force for good, consistent with academia's joint historical aims of developing expertise and a commitment to positive social change ... In the 1980s then HBS graduates were heading for Wall Street. By then the School had abandoned its three-quarter century mission of trying to educate an enlightened managerial class, and threw its lot in with Wall Street as it went about dismantling the edifice of American industry that HBS had helped to build. HBS had nurtured the professional manger from the time of his birth, and then it helped to kill him.

Intriguingly enough, one of us, Ronnie Samanyanga, originally *out of Africa,* and a graduate of that self–same HBS, in the 1970s while based in the UK, working with a group of management consultants in corporate social affairs, in our (43) book on *Business Survival and Social Change,* reflecting inadvertently on the American conservationist tradition, made the case for *a new business ethic—the elimination of waste in all aspects of an organisation; activities ... associated with the balanced development of all assets.* Needless to say we were seemingly, paradoxically then, both before and after our time.

Revisiting Management: Return to Origins

What then of management overall, in the interim? Indeed, the field of management, and the MBA to go with it—to which Samanyanga was exposed in earnest—has been invented, almost singlehandedly, in the United States in the 20th century. Ironically the U.S., again virtually on its own, now in the 21st century, has masterminded its eclipse (albeit that the MBA Masters in Business Administration has soldiered on all over the world, regardless), at the hands of individual leadership, if not also entrepreneurship. It is as if the rest of the world has watched over all of such, duly captivated, with schools of leadership if not also entrepreneurship duly proliferating without a murmur of worldwide protest.

Meanwhile the MBA, for more than a century now, born and bred in America, increasingly today cast in Tim Peters mould, has dominated over the world's business and management stage as if, like today's neoliberal order, *There is No Alternative* (TINA), in British Prime Minister's, Margaret Thatcher oft quoted words (she was referring to capitalism not MBA-ism!). Thousands of management texts have been written, ranging from the management specialisms—finance to operations, marketing to human resources—to general management, corporate strategy and organisational behaviour (altogether defined and articulated in America). What is utterly remarkable is how stable, and unchanging, such management disciplines, and the MBA programs to go with them, have been, excepting of course for massive advances in information technology, especially from the 1980s onwards.

Indeed our own (44) work on *Transformation Management: Towards the Integral Enterprise,* spanning east and west, north and south, from a functional perspective in relation to each, as well as, more recently, our (45) *Integral Kumusha,* set within a specifically African context, both represent isolated attempts to overturn this "western" dominance in the fields of management, leadership and enterprise. As such we have turned marketing into *community building* (southern), human resources into *conscious evolution* (eastern: operations into *knowledge creation* (northern) and finance into *sustainable development* (evolved western). The Transformation Studies now that Adodo has pioneered is an extension of such, in West Africa.

Management as a Social Innovation

Interestingly enough, and again paradoxically, before the neoliberal regression to leadership and entrepreneurship since the 1980s, to which we have alluded, management itself, in the 20th century period before that, was something of a social innovation. It was the formidable Austro-American management guru Peter Drucker (46), who played a major part in such. In his masterwork, written in the 1970s on *Management Tasks, Responsibilities and Practices.*

For Drucker, with *the emergence of large scale organisation, management represented the keynote, social, innovation, in the twentieth century.* Not only has such a social innovation, for us, not been recognised, generally as such, but it has not been differentiated and thereafter newly integrated, in different parts of the world. In other words, management remains "unconsciously" *north-western* American, as such drawing on economics, sociology and behavioural psychology in particular, in the same way as leadership, if not also entrepreneurship, represents, for us, a similarly unconscious *western* regression.

The Dimensions of Management: Purpose, Productivity, Social Responsibility

There are three tasks or dimensions, for Drucker, equally important but essentially different, that face the management of every institution:

- to think through and *define* the specific *purpose* and mission of the institution, whether business enterprise, university or hospital
- to make *work productive* and the worker achieving
- to manage social impacts and *social responsibilities*

A business exists for a specific purpose and mission, indeed, for Drucker, for a specific *social* function. In the business enterprise this means economic performance. *The first definition of business management is that it is an economic organ.* Management is not just a creature of the economy, but a creator as well. Only to the extent that it masters its economic circumstances, and alters them by consciously directed action, does it manage, thereby to manage by objectives. As we can see, in that "controlling" respect, Drucker is very much an embodiment of the "north" (Europe) and "west" (America).

The second task of management is to make work productive and the worker achieving. Business enterprise, or any other institution, has only one true resource: people. It performs by making human resources productive. Making the worker achieving implies consideration of the human being as an organism having peculiar physiological and psychological properties, abilities and limitations. It implies consideration of the human resource as persons and not as things. All other resources stand under the laws of mechanics. People alone can grow and develop. Only the directed, focused, united effort of free human beings can produce a real whole. We speak of "leadership" and of the "spirit" of a company, accordingly.

But *leadership*, for Drucker, *is a sub-set of management*, and effective primarily within such. *The third task of management is managing the social impacts and the social responsibilities of the enterprise.* None of our institutions exists by itself and is an end in itself. Every institution is an organ of society and exists for the sake of society. To discharge its job, to produce economic goods and services, the business enterprise has to have impacts on people, on communities and on society.

Finally, and most significantly for us here, the predominance of management hitherto, and leadership and entrepreneurship of late, have both served to reinforce a one-sided, historically regressive, "western" overtone, at the expense of the southern, eastern and even northern ones, thereby serving to inhibit worldly integration.

6.4. Conclusion: Building on the Divine Will of Africa

6.4.1. Transcultural Management

There was, in the 1980s and 1990s, a major exception to the regressive lurch to the neoliberal "west", in practical managerial and organisational terms, in South *Africa* no less. For Albert Koopman (47), while the country was still under apartheid lock-down, established his worker democracy, Cashbuild, amongst the 1600 employees in this rurally based, building supplies retailer. This was how, for him, it all started:

> Key questions went through my mind. Why do the workers actually work? What is their social or Divine Will? What went wrong in Cashbuild with respect to capital and labour? What were we actually trying to achieve as a business organism? How do we bring together the rights of people, their spiritually based humanity and the economic process as represented in the workplace? It soon became clear to us that one purpose existed in management's head and another in the workers'. Management 'up north' was pulling one-way and the people "down south" another. There was no transcendent purpose linking one with the other.

And this is what he subsequently concluded:

> I found later that this last point was in fact the spark for all endeavours, and took precedence over any of the other technical systems, rewards, or structures we introduced. It reflected the Divine Will of Cashbuild, which in its turn manifested the parallel will of the communities, which the company represented. It further reflected the difference between competitive, north-western "having" and co-operative "south-eastern" being, as fundamentally different modes of life.

TABLE 6.1.
COMPARATIVE WESTERN AND SOUTHERN MODES OF
LIFE COMPETITIVE VERSUS COMMUNAL

INDIVIDUAL COMPETITIVE	GROUP COMMUNAL
Profit for me is derived from self-interest.	Profit to me is a vote of confidence my society gives me for service rendered to that society.
I am actually exclusive from my fellow man.	I am mutually inclusive.
I prefer to be a self-actualised person.	I prefer to be a social man.
The more I have, the more I am.	I am, therefore I share and give.
I demand productivity from people.	I prefer to create a climate in which people will be willingly more productive.
I am actually an aggressive kind of person.	I am actually a receptive kind of a person.
I look you in the eye and challenge you.	I bow my head and show my respect.
My concern is for production.	My concern is for people.

Ultimately, because South Africa at large was unable to conceive of the kind of Afrikological transformation in which Koopman was engaged (see chapter 8) he left the country, in despair, in the 1990s, and has spent the rest of his days in Canada. A sad story indeed. Yet, retrospective as we now see it, this was inevitable, as there was no Research Academy to support his worthy business and economic cause, moreover one that drew upon "southern" nature, culture, technology and enterprise, locally, locally-globally, newly globally and globally-locally.

6.4.2. African Studies to Afrikology

A key problem Koopman in fact faced, in South Africa as he would have done in other parts of the world, is that his academic constituency, that is the schools of business and economics in South Africa were living on another "western" planet from where his *Southern Mode of Life* was lodged. Indeed, for four years in the 1990s, a group of us (48) under the guise of a *Southern African Management* project soldiered on with our *African management: Philosophies, Concepts and Applications*. However, notwithstanding such books we wrote on the subject, there was no academic or business institution, not Academy or Laboratory, to support us, or indeed to support Albert Koopman, other than Cashbuild in splendid isolation.

That said, departments of anthropology or African Studies, that may have been in tune with his, and our, overall "southern" ethos, were conventionally far removed from business and economics, which is why we (Samanyanga) are giving birth to ACIRET today. So the move, for us prospectively with MSUAS in Zimbabwe, if not also actually (Anselm) in co-evolving Ibadan University's Institute for African Studies, is hopefully a timely one (see Figure 6.1. below).

FIGURE 6.1. AFRICAN STUDIES TO AFRIKOLOGY

Science and Technology
BIOSEMIOTICS
Research Academy
North/*Navigate*
EMANCIPATION

Finance and Enterprise	**African Studies/Afrikology**	**Culture and Spirituality**
MANAGEMENT	African philosophy/polity, history Arts/Sciences, Indigenous Studies	ANTHROPOLOGY
Socio-economic Laboratory	Integral Studies	Transformation Journey
West/*Effect*	Local Identity/Global Integrity	East/*Emerge*
TRANSFORMATION	INTEGRATION	FOUNDATION

Nature and Community
OIKONOMICS
Learning Community
South/*Ground*
ORIGINATION

While retaining African Humanities, artistically (Ibadan) and scientifically (MSUAS) as its Centre, its critical "Southern-Eastern-Northern-Western" surrounds are very different from the typical such African, academic case. In fact what we can see above, is that whereas, the African humanities, conventionally associated with African Studies, remain a critical part of the now Afrikological, transdisciplinary whole, without management studies, and economics, if not also biosemiotics, and a new style of forward-looking anthropology to build on what has come before, there will be no emancipation, or transformation, in Africa.

Furthermore, and institutionally, with a Laboratory such as Paxherbals (see chapter 9), a Journey such a Transformation Studies in Africa (TSA), and a Learning community, our Research Academy—whether Humanities (Ibadan University Institute for African Studies in Nigeria) or Sciences (MSUAS in Zimbabwe) based—will gain all the more inter-institutional potential (see Figure 6.1. above). However, we still have one more major step to go, if the likes of a newly established CIRD/A (Centre for Integral Research and Development out of Africa) is to engage in social innovation, and that is to align substance, as above, with a social scientific process, of research to innovation. We now turn, in the next chapter, to that *Integral* or *Imvelyan* scientific process, in altogether "southern" *relational* guise, from research to innovation, origination to transformation.

6.5. References

1 **McNeely** F and **Wolverton** L (2008) *Reinventing Knowledge: Alexandria to the Internet.* New York. W.W. Norton

2 **Lessem** and **Palsule** S (1997) *Managing in Four Worlds: Competition to Co-creation.* Chichester. Wiley-Blackwell

3 **Nabudere** D (2011) *Afrikology: Philosophy and Wholeness: An Epistemology.* Pretoria. Africa Institute

4 **Bhengu** M (2016) *Amazulu: Ancient Egyptian Origin – Spirits Beyond the Heavens.* Durban. Mepho Publishers

5 **Schieffer** A and **Lessem** R (2014) *Integral Development: Transforming the Potential of Individuals, Organizations and Societies.* Abingdon. Routledge

6 Sanya **Osha** (2018) *Dani Nabudere's Afrikology.* Dakar. CODESIRA

7 **Lessem** R, **Mawere** M and **Taranhike** D (2019) *Nhakanomics: Towards Social Innovation.* Mazvingo. Zimbabwe. Africa Talent Publishers

8 **Achebe** C (2006) *Things Fall Apart.* London. Penguin Classics

9 **Ingold T** (2011) *The Perception of the Environment: Essays on Livelihood, Dwelling and Skill.* Abingdon. Routledge

10 **Deleuze** G and **Guattari** F (1988) *A Thousand Plateaus: Capitalism and Schizophrenia.* London. Athlone Press

11 **Lessem** R, **Adodo** A and **Bradley** T (2019) *The Idea of the Communiversity.* Manchester. Beacon Academic

12 **Lessem** R and **Schieffer** A (2010) *Integral Economics: Releasing the Economic Genius of your Society.*

13 **Nonaka** I and **Takeuchi** H (1995) *The Knowledge Creating Company.* Oxford. Oxford University Press

14 **Lessem** R, **Mawere** M and **Taranhike** D (2019) *op cit*

15 **Lessem** R, **Mawere** M and **Taranhike** D (2019) *op cit*

16 **Nabudere** D (2011) *Afrikology: Philosophy and Wholeness: An Epistemology.* Pretoria. Africa Institute

17 **Bhengu** M (2016) *op cit*

18 **Lessem** R and **Schieffer** A (2015) *Integral Renewal: A Relational and Renewal Pespective.* Farham. Gower

19 **Amin** S (2010) *Eurocentrism: Modernity, Religion and Democracy: A Critique of Eurocentrism and Culturalism.* Nairobi. Pambazuka Press

20 **Serequeberhan** T (1994) *The Hermeneutics of African Philosophy*: *Horizons and Discourse.* London, Routledge.

21 Sanya **Osha** (2018) *op cit*

22 **Diop** Cheikh Anta (1974) *The African Origin of Civilization: Myth or Reality.* Chicago. Lawrence Hill Books

23 **Obenga** T (1992) *Ancient Egypt and Black Africa.* London. Karnack

24 **Heron** J (1994) *Feeling and Personhood.* Abingdon. Routledge

25 Sanya **Osha** (2018) *op cit*

26 **Ford** C (2000) *Hero with an African Face: Mythic Wisdom of Traditional Africa.* New York. Bantam

27 **Rima**, I. (2001). *The Development of Economic Analysis.* London: Routledge

28 **Aquinas**, T (1981) *Summa Theologica.* Grand Rapids: Christian Classics

29 **Smith**, A. (2003). *The Wealth of Nations.* New York: Bantam Classics.

30 **Marx**, K. (1992). *Capital.* New York: Penguin Classics.

31 **Marx**, K. & **Engels**, F. (2007). *Communist Manifesto.* Houston: Filiquarian.

32 **Friedman**, M. (2002). *Capitalism and Freedom.* Chicago: Chicago University Press.

33 **Moore** J (2015) *Capitalism in the Web of Life.* London. Verso

34 **Hoffmeyer** J (2008) *Biosemiotics: An Examination into the Signs of Life and the Life of Signs.* Scranton. Scranton University Press

35 Jakob **von Uexkull** (2010) *A Foray into the Worlds of Animals and Human: With a Theory of Meaning.* Minneapolis. University of Minnesota Press

36 **Ingold** T (2018) *Anthropology: Why It Matters.* Cambridge. Polity

37 **Williams** C (1993) *The Rebirth of African Civilization.* Chicago.

38 **Mawere** M and **Nhemachena** A (2017) *Death of a Discipline: Reflections on the History, State and Future of Social Anthropology in Zimbabwe.* Mankon. Bamenda. Langaa Research and Publishing CIG.

39 **Peters** T and **Waterman** R (2015) *In Search of Excellence. Lessons from America's Best Run Companies. Second Edition.* New York. Profile Books

40 **Khurana** R (2007) *From Higher Aims to Hired Hands: The Social Transformation of the American Business Schools and the Unfulfilled Promise of Management as a Profession.* New Jersey. Princeton University Press

41 **Purdy** J (2015) *After Nature: A Politics for the Anthropocene.* Cambidge. Mass, Harvard University Press

42 **McDonald** D (2017) *The Golden Passport: Harvard Business School, Limits of Capitalism and the Moral Failure of the MBA Elite.* Harper Business

43 **Hargreaves** J and **Dauman** J (1975) *Business Survival and Social Change.* London. Associated Business Programs

44 **Lessem** R and **Schieffer** A (2009) *Transformation Management: Towards the Integral Enterprise.* Abingdon. Routledge

45 **Lessem** R, **Mawere** M, **Matupire** P **and Zongololo** S (2019) *Integral Kumusha: Aligning Policonomy with Nature, Culture, Technology and Enterprise.* Mazvingo. Africa Talent Publishers

46 **Drucker** P (1977) *Management Tasks, Responsibilities and Practices.* London. Pan

47 **Koopman** A (1991) *Transcultural Management.* Chichester. Wiley-Blackwell

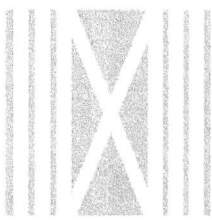

CHAPTER 7

Cird/A

Imvelo (the cosmic order) has three pillars of being: the Law, the Environment and the Person. *Umthetho wemvelo* regulates the individualisation of primordial substance into phenomena; it is the philosophy by which primordial substance defines itself to itself. The Law is the creative principle the demiurge which gives value to phenomena; it is definitive value and does not change.

Mfunislewa Bhengu (1), *AmaZulu: Ancient Egyptian Origin*

7.1. Introduction: Afrikological Imvelean Research

7.1.1. Social Innovation: Integral Knowledge Substance/Social Scientific Process

African Studies to ARICET; Afrocentricity to Afrikology

So much for the underlying, Afrikological knowledge *substance*, outlined in our previous chapter, whereby we drew, in trans-disciplinary guise, on a combination of, what we term *oikonomics* (see previous chapter), anthropology, biosemiotics, and management studies, taking on from where African Studies, including African Sciences and Humanities—philosophy and history, art and science, ecology and polity—have traditionally left off. "Afrikology" moreover, unlike "Afrocentricity", is locally grounded in the African "south", but thereafter emerges locally-globally, before assuming a newly global form, and then is ultimately applied globally-locally. All of such, moreover, requires an integral Communiversity, with its learning Community, transformation Journey, research Academy and socio-economic Laboratory.

Interestingly enough moreover, regarding the two African universities with which we are closely associated, on the one hand the Institute of African Studies at Ibadan University in Nigeria (Anselm) is Humanities based, on the other Manicaland State University in Zimbabwe (Samanyanga) is Sciences based. In working with them, respectively, the two of us, Anselm in Nigeria and Samanyanga in Zimbabwe, together with our institutional colleagues therein, are able to bring their complementary orientations to bear on CIRD/A as a whole.

At the same time, as we shall now see, the *substantive* integral knowledge cited above, and a social scientific *process* cited below, both need to be involved, if overall social innovation is to ensue. Together, then, they constitute Integral Research and Economic Development, hence emancipating economics, indeed in an Afrikological *Imvelean* (Zulu for cosmic order), or in the *ivhuyan* (meaning soil in Shona) from its hitherto capitalist-communist globalised stranglehold, so that it assumes *newly global* overtones: naturally, culturally, (social) technologically, and enterprise-wise.

FIGURE 7.1. CIRD/A NEWLY GLOBAL EMANCIPATION

NEWLY GLOBAL
Feminist
Indigenous Science, Nhakanomics
Afrikology, Health & Rejuvenation
Biosemiotics
Emancipatory Navigation

GLOBAL-LOCAL	**GLOBAL INTEGRITY**	**LOCAL-GLOBAL**
Participatory	Centre for Integral Research and	*Phenomenological*
Management	Development out of Africa	Anthropology
Effect Transformation	IUS	*Emergent Foundation*

LOCAL
Descriptive
Oikonomics
Grounding and Origination

(developed from *Integral Economics: Releasing the Genius of your Society*)

Drawing then on our (4) original *Integral Economics: Releasing the Genius of your Society*, initially conceived of a decade ago, we thereby generally build upon:

- community based *Self Sufficiency* (original Grounding in the South)
- culture based *Developmental Economy* (Emergent foundation in South-East)
- knowledge based *Social Economy* ("North-South" emancipatory Navigation)
- life based *Living Economy* ("South-Western" transformative Effect)

What then are the implications of such?

7.1.2. For Too Long We Have Pointed Ontologically and Economically West

For too long then the mono/cultural powers that be, economically at least—academics and practitioners, politicians and the business community—have, for us, in/authentically, pointed "east" or "west", with seemingly no place else to go. From the outset, these have been falsely conceived categories, indeed twice over. For firstly, in the last century, the so-called "east" was actually the "communist" world, as opposed to the capitalist "west". So east was not really "east", in terms of the Middle, Near and Far East, in Arab, Indian, Chinese or Japanese cultural terms.

Then, toward the end of the last century, another "emerging east" came to the ascendancy, first Japan and the Pacific Tigers (South Korea, Singapore, Taiwan, Hong Kong) and subsequently China and India. Yet these so-called far "eastern" countries have adopted more or less the same kind of economic system as our "western" one; give or take a few, most especially Japanese, variations (in the 1950s to 1980s before the Japanese miracle faded) a long already established "western" lines: protectionism versus free trade, state intervention versus laissez-faire.

In other words, by and large, "western" capitalism has ruled the roost, across both the Asian east and the Euro-American west, albeit there have been variations on such a theme, but all too few of them. Moreover, when we come to compare "north" and "south" in conventional terms, it is primarily in terms of the rich (north) versus the poor (south). So again, as we pointed out in our opening, centering chapter, there has been little economic, natural and cultural variety to draw upon. While at the end of the last century, there was some kind of distinction between Germanic and Scandinavian "northern" economic systems and the "western" Anglo-Saxons (UK and US), such differentiation has even become increasingly blurred. Our economic and enterprise imaginations have then been stunted, by TINA!

7.1.3. Knowledge Substance and Research Process: Towards Social Innovation

Via of course our "four worlds" (see chapter 1) we have encouraged movement, economically in practice as well as in theory, beyond one overarching "western" capitalist thesis, with its other virtually defunct communist antithesis. At the same time, epistemologically, research-wise, we have moved integrally beyond rationalism and empiricism to incorporate also interpretive/hermeneutic and phenomenological approaches to research and innovation. Overall as such we (5) offer a more clearly differentiated and integrated, altogether integral/imveyean economic and epistemological perspective, that now underlies CIRD/A (Centre for Integral Research and Development out of Africa). As such, we have now, decade subsequent to our original work on Integral Research and Economics:

1. *Substantively* differentiated and integrated diverse disciplinary perspectives from all our worlds, thereby building on *Oikonomics, Anthropology, Biosemiotics, and Management Studies.*
2. *Processally* and relationally built integrally on *local Grounding, local-global Emergence, newly global Navigation, global-local Effect,* recognising/releasing GENE-IUS (see Figure 7.1.), altogether now (in italics below) resulting in:

    *   Sciences, Humanities, All Round Polity (Center – *I/U/S*): *CIRDA*
    *   Nature and Community (South – Grounding): *Nhakanomics*
    *   Culture and Spirituality (East – Emergence): *Indigenous Science*
    *   Science and Technology (North – Navigating): *Afrikology*
    *   Finance and Enterprise (West – Effecting): *Healing and Rejuvenation*

Indeed, the above also represents an evolution (see chapter 6) from African Studies (African sciences, humanities, polity) to Afrikology, including also nature, culture, technology, enterprise, inter-institutionally, altogether embodied in a Communiversity. Intrinsic to such, moreover, is also, such work having been undertaken over four decades, building a meaningful link between the past, present and the future. While moreover we may have given the impression that "western" economics is all bad, that is not where we are coming from. The western strength of "management and enterprise" has shown remarkable results and released enormous energy all over the world.

However, as it has acted in increasing isolation, and as the allegedly sole "economic truth", it has lost its way, or, in other words, it has lost "southern" nature and community, "eastern" culture and spirituality, and, to some extent as well, "northern" science and technology, thereby departing ever more from the essence of science and humanity, as depicted in our earlier scientifically oriented chapter 4 (African Creation Energy) and philosophically oriented chapter 5 (Conversationalism and Creativity).

Altogether, we argue, that all four worlds need to be revisited and reconfigured in a newly global, now *Afrikological* way, drawing processally on now *imvelean* research, and substantively, in the Zimbabwean MSUAS case, if not also our Nigerian one, on four Research faculties, that is *Indigenous Science, Nhakanomics, Afrikology, Health and Rejuvenation,* alongside, and thereby mutually informing, learning communities, transformation journeys, and socio-economic laboratories.

TABLE 7.1 AFRIKOLOGY			
INTEGRAL COMMUNIVERSITY CD	IMVEYAN/ SOUTHERN RHYTHM: *PHD*	INTEGRAL ENTERPRISE: OD	INTEGRAL RESEARCH & ECONOMICS R AND D
Center: IUS Communiversity Religion/ Humanity/ Integral Polity	Integral Economics Releasing the Economic GENE-IUS of your Society	Societal Regeneration	Integrally based Moral Core/Humanity/ ACIRET *Imvelyan Research & Economic Transformation*
South: G Community Nature & Community	Descriptive Origination	Community Building	Community based Self-Sufficient Economy/ *Nhakanomics*
East: E Journey Culture & Spirituality	Phenomeno-logical Foundation	Conscious Evolution	Culture based Developmental Economy/ *Indigenous Science*
North: N Academy Science & Technology	Feminist Emancipation	Knowledge Creation	Knowledge based Social Economy/ *Afrikology*
West: E Laboratory Finance & Enterprise	Participatory Transformation	Sustainable Development	Life based Living Economy/ *Health & Rejuvenation*

7.2. Towards Social Innovation

7.2.1. Integral/Imvelean Rhythm

Integral Worlds

In moving from one "western" to four *integral* worlds, rhythmically and transformatively so to speak, initially in the first decade of the new millennium, we have built on a Four World archetype (see chapter 1) also now in trans-sectoral terms:

- Southern – *Grounding:* individual, communal and organisational "being" related to nature and community. We locate here the *environmental-animate* sector.
- Eastern – *Emergence:* individual, communal, organisational, societal "becoming" related to culture, spirituality and consciousness. We locate here the *civic* sector.
- Northern – *Navigation:* individual and organisational "knowing", focused on science and technology. In sectoral terms, the *public* sector is positioned here.
- Western – *Effecting:* individual and collective "doing", bearing upon finance, enterprise, and management, represented by the *private* sector.
- Centre – *Integrating/IUS:* linked with religion and humanity. The center, as its best, has the quality of holding the various elements together, as an all round *polity,* duly Synergising moral Inspiration with, for us, Universal truth.

To that extent, in overall Nhakanomic terms, to take just one example, the original *kumusha* (the term for "homestead" in the indigenous shona language in Zimbabwe) is grounded in the *animate* (nature and community), emerges *integrally* though the *civic* (culture and spirituality), navigates scientifically and *nhakanomically* via a *public* university e.g. MSUAS/CIRDA, effecting transformation *vakamusha*-wise through the *private* sector, altogether centred within an all round Afrikological polity, constructed out of primordial African grounds (see chapter 3). What then are these?

One, Two, Three and Four Dimensional African Ontology

As Griaule and Dieterlen (6) have previously pointed out (chapter 3), and American cosmologist Lloyd Scranton (7) has further evolved, the Dogon term *bummo* combines the Egyptian phoneme *bu* (meaning "place") with the Egyptian word *maa* (meaning "to perceive") and so takes it to imply "place perceived", our *grounding*. Dimensionally speaking, the concept of "place perceived" could reasonably refer to a *geometric point*, a figure that is understood to be one dimensional. The term *yala* then refers to the perspective of a geometric line, thereby a two-dimensional *emergent* construct. Similarly the Egyptian word *ahau* can refer to "a period of time", whereby the concept of measurable time coincides with that of measurable space. Following the same line of reasoning, we find that the Dogon term *tonu* refers to three-dimensional *navigational* space. We see this because the Dogon term *to* means both "arc" (implying the concept of "surrounding") and "to be the interior of", while *nu* refers to "waves or water", that can fill a three-dimensional space. The last of the four Dogon terms *toymu* means complete, that is our transformative *effect*.

7.2.2. Atuolu Omalu: Contemporary African Philosophy

Ethnophilosophy to Integrativity

In similar transformational, now African philosophical guise (see chapter 5), we now revisit the work of Jonathan Chimakonam (8), who has come up with a similar integral rhythm to ours, processally that is, underlying the development of African philosophy in the 20th century. Indeed because the development of such written philosophy is a recent, and as such prolific, development on the African continent—as opposed to the more longstanding, millennia/long historical development of Euro/American and Arab/Asian philosophy—Chimakonam is able to come up with such a composite distillation. In summary, for him, but now aligned with our integral, research-and-innovation, processal GENE-tic rhythm, as we see below, we have:

1. G: Early period: 1920s to 1960s: *Ethnophilosophy: Nhakanomics*
2. E: Middle period: 1960s to 1980s: *Traditional/Modern: Indigenous Science*
3. N: Later period: 1980s to 1990s: *Critical Reconstruction: Afrikology*
4. IUS: Contemporary Era: 1990s to Date: *Integrativity: Health and Rejuvenation*

Interestingly enough the Contemporary Era is more an integrating one (IUS) than effectively (E) transformative, in our terms, because, for Chimakonam though not for us, the economic and enterprise dimension, is largely missing from his African philosophy, as is the case for African Studies generally. We now review again his seminal work, in our all round Afrikological economic light.

"Southern" Origination: Ethno-Nationalist

DRAW LOCALLY ON NATURE AND COMMUNITY: NHAKANOMICS

First for Chimakonam comes the initial philosophical era (for us locally grounded) aimed at retrieving and reconstructing African identity from the raw material of African nature-and-culture. The schools that emerged and thrived therein were *ethnophilosophy and nationalist/ ideology.* In the former case *the lost African identity could be found in the seabed of indigenous African nature/culture* in which religion featured prominently.

In the latter nationalist case, were those who sought to retrieve and establish once again Africa's lost identity through economic and political ways, now bereft of nature if not also culture, including the work of such philosopher-statesmen as Ghana's Kwame Nkrumah – Consciencism (9), Tanzania's Julius Nyerere – Ujaama/Familyhood (10) and Senegal's Leopold Senghor – Negritude/African Socialism (11). These actors felt that the African could not be decolonized if he did not find his own system of living and social organisation. The question that guided their study therefore became *what system of economic and social engineering will project our real identity?*

In fact the economic (Senghor was the most strongly rooted in natural-cultural soil, though economically he parted from such) approach that each of the three philosopher-statesmen introduced was, at the end of the day, a flawed version of "socialism", rather than one that reached deeply into local social and economic, aligned with natural and cultural soils. Conversely the locally "southern" *Nhakanomics* (see below) that Taranhike has been developing in Zimbabwe, building locally-globally on *integral kumasha* (see Prologue) indeed reaches deeply into his African *nhaka*—legacy—hence *nhakanomics* (see below).

"South-Eastern" Foundation: Traditional-Universal

EVOLVE LOCAL-GLOBAL CULTURE AND SPIRIT: INDIGENOUS SCIENCE

Secondly thereafter, for Chimakonam, while the *Traditionalists sought to construct an African identity based on excavated African natural-cultural elements,* or in our case "Nhaka", *the Universalists sought to demolish such structures by associating it with a limiting ethnophilosophy.* The (for us emergent "local-global") schools then that thrived in this era included *Philosophical Sagacity* – Okura (12), *Professional Universalist* – Hountondji (11), *Afro-Hermeneutic* – Serequeberhan (13), and *Literary/Artistic* – Ngugi wa Thiong'o (14). However, none of the above ventured into economic terrain, and for such "southern-eastern" Afrikological economic overtones we turn then to the Arabic-and-Islamic cultural and spiritual influence, infiltrating the Middle and Near East.

This amalgam of art and philosophy, culture and spirituality, science and technology, tradition and modernity, in our "south-*eastern*" guise, taps into the deep-lying "soul force" of a nation, duly aligning such with *Indigenous Science*. This requires a degree of scientific insight, locally and globally, as we have seen, especially, with African Creation Energy (see chapter 4) linking the particular with the universal, which is absent in purely local, "southern" guise.

"South-North" Emancipate-Navigate: Reconstructionist
BASED ON NEWLY GLOBAL KNOWLEDGE AND VALUE: AFRIKOLOGY

The third period (or "newly global" emancipatory navigation), for Chimakonam, heralded the emergence of the Critical Reconstructionist and Afro-Eclecticist movements, inspired by a fertile interchange now between "north" and "south", if not also "east" and "west". The former desired a new episteme untainted by ethnophilosophy and later sought to reconcile different approaches. *There was a need to unify the goals of "southern" Particularists and "northern" Universalists, thereby giving rise to an authentic, for us "newly global" African philosophy*, alongside, for us, oikonomics, anthropology, biosemiotics, and management, as well as African sciences and humanities. While the particularists supply the raw material of "southern" culture, the universalists provide the "northern" analytical structures and conceptual frameworks.

While building on indigenous knowledge systems, therefore, it also combines such with the exogenous, whereby the two in combination has a wider, newly global economic meaning—thereby *Afrikological*—in the world, or indeed our worlds, at large.

"South-West" – Trans4mative Effect: Integrativity
WITH A VIEW TO GLOBAL-LOCAL PRAXIS: HEALTH AND REJUVENATION

The New Era or Contemporary Period of African philosophy began in the 1990s and took shape in the new millennium. The orientation of this period is conversational philosophy. For Nigerian philosopher Innocent Asouzu (15) who, going beyond previously botched attempts erected a new model of African philosophy, his theory of complementary reflection maintains that "*to be" simply means to be in complementary relationship. Every being, therefore, is a variable with capacity to join in mutual interaction. In this capacity every being is seen as a missing link* serving a missing link of reality in the network of realities. The complementarity on our African "south-western" case is between different kinds of capital assets, in conversation, as it were, with each other.

For fellow Calibar philosopher Godfrey Ozumba (16) (Ozumba, Asouzu and Chimakonam, until recently, were based at the University of Calibar's philosophy department) *"To be" therefore is to be in mutual, integrative relationship. Being is only being in a network of other beings.* Within the network of reality, every being is necessary. In our own integral, or in Bhengu's *imvelean* context, the "south" now is also in conversation with the all pervasive "west". This altogether coincides, ultimately, with Ozumba's integrativity, and, in our Amazulu terms, with *imvelo*, and of course our integral worlds, duly reflected in Health and Rejuvenation, though, as we have mentioned, even such an integrative approach to African philosophy is still only "with a view to praxis".

7.2.3. Giving Each World a Voice of their Own

Building on the Capacity of Each World

What we have aimed to accomplish then is to give each of the different worlds—in Chimakonam's terms each being part of a (for us economic) "conversation"—*a more distinctive voice of their own, especially in the Global South.* The purpose of such is manifold: firstly, we, particularly in Africa, avoid the trap of either being stuck with one economic and epistemological approach (neoliberal-empirical), or, alternatively, fluctuating between two both north-western approaches (neoliberal and Keynesian). Secondly, we make the particular strengths and contributions of each world (what we call overall GENE-IUS) evident; thirdly, we bring these different worlds into an equal and co-creative conversation (as per Chimakonam's conversational and integrative) with each other, driven by the ultimate purpose of, fourthly, developing integral economic and epistemological approaches that are authentic for a particular world, especially for those of us in the "south", if not also "east".

We now turn more specifically to our (17) own hitherto *Integral* Economics, with a view to releasing, generally, ontologically, and more specifically, economically, GENE-*IUS,* duly aligned with our transformative GENE-tic *process,* and thereby integral *rhythm,* research and innovation, following the above philosophical rhythm.

7.3. Releasing Economic Gene-ius

7.3.1. Overview of the GENE-IUS

The release of GENE-IUS (as originally intimated in our centering chapter) provides the transformational rhythm, or source of re-GENE-ration, which we have developed over many years of engaging with integral enterprise and economics, research and development, and ultimately embodied in Adodo's *Transformation Studies*. In other words, the GENE is the dynamically laden, *processal*, "gene-tic code" of the transformational work in which we are engaged, set alongside the stabilizing, *substantive* "four worlds". In other words, and in that guise, the "four worlds" provides our Grounding and origination, the GENE our emergent Foundation, and now Afrikological Economics becomes our newly global, emancipatory Navigation, prior to our global-local integral economics.

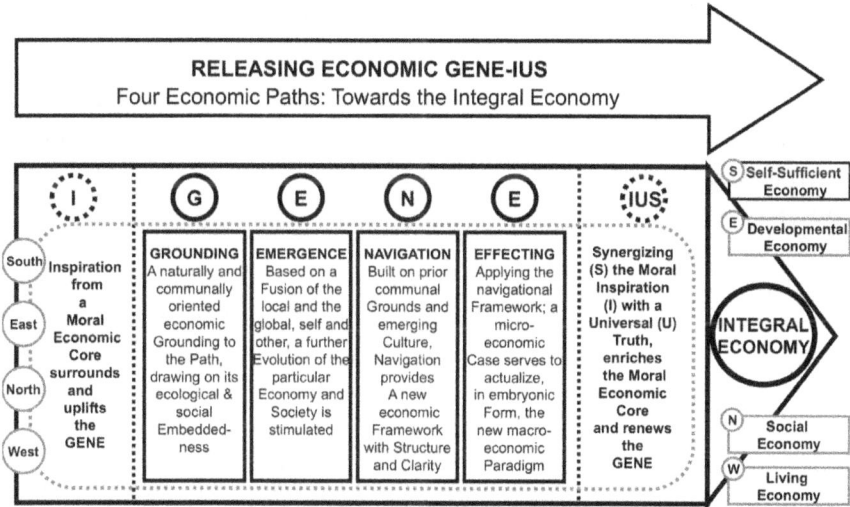

FIGURE 7.2: RELEASING ECONOMIC GENE-IUS VIA FOUR GENERIC ECONOMIC PATHS

Transformation, for us moreover, also—and paradoxically—links the inner I (moral Inspiration) and the outer U (Universal truth), through a Synergetic process (S), hence the GENE-IUS. That particular moral inspiration, for example in a "southern" African context, is provided by the homestead *kumusha* with the universal *oikos* set alongside, whereby *Nhakanomics* Synergizes the two. Of course, this is an idealized perspective, and in "the real world", this process of fully fledged re-GENE-ration seldom takes place. More often than not an economy fluctuates between a parochial "south" and a sub-optimal "west", rather than working its way through the south-east-north-west integral cycle, so that the proverbial "global-local" rides roughshod over an un-realized "newly global". The ultimate outcome would be:

1. to draw inspiration (I) from your societal moral core
2. by aligning this core with your own individual and collective grounding, emergence, navigation, effecting (GENE), and
3. releasing full GENE-IUS by synergizing (S) e.g. *Nhakanomics* with the locally derived moral inspiration (I) (*kumusha*), with a universal (U) truth (*oikos*).

7.3.2. Integral Between and Integral Within Worlds

The GENE-IUS then, to which we continually and dynamically allude, applies in two interconnected ways, that is *in between* and *within* worlds. In the first place, where it applies in between worlds, a continually self-renewing moral core (I-U-S), in a particular region of the world, provides the backdrop for the "southern" Grounding (Self-Sufficient Economy/Community Building Enterprise/*Nhakanomics*) of a society, which draws, in turn, on other worlds. These other worlds are comprised of "eastern" Emergence (Developmental Economy/Consciously Evolving Enterprise/*Indigenous Science*), "northern" Navigation (Social Economy/Knowledge Creating Enterprise/*Afrikology*), and "western" Effect (Living Economy/Sustainable Enterprise/*Health and Rejuvenation*).

Thereby and firstly, each society has to draw on the world as a whole, to become economically integral, albeit that it will give special emphasis to its own world. To that extent, each society has its centre, as well as its south (grounding), east (emergence), north (navigation) and west (effect), albeit that, for example in Africa, the "south" and "grounding" will be pre-eminent.

In the second case, economic GENE-IUS applies within worlds. To that extent, within each particular economic path, for example, that of Self-Sufficiency generally and "southern" Nhakanomics specifically (see below), there is a trajectory that extends from grounding to emergence, onto navigation and effect (g-e-n-e), altogether incorporating a continually self-renewing moral centre (i-u-s). That said, such an *imvelean* process, or rhythm, provides the overall, integral grounding and origination, as we shall see in each Afrikological case below, followed by the emergent oikonomic foundation, paving the way for our emancipatory navigation through CIRD-A.

We now, with a particular focus in this case on the relational "south" turn to our four specific—"southern" (nature and community), "south-eastern" (culture and spirituality), "south-north" (science and technology) Afro-European, and "south-western" (enterprise and wellness), versions—of generic *Afrikology*, building also on the more general technological and economic alternatives, of "southern" community based self-sufficiency, an "eastern" developmental economy, a "northern" semiotic economy, and "western" wellbeing economy.

In each case, moreover, and given our overall "southern" Afrikological orientation here, we build on prior *relational* process, from origination to transformation, as well as *oikonomic, anthropological, biosemiotics,* and *managerial* substance. Such a relational trajectory, of research to innovation, grounding to effect, proceeds then from *descriptive* method (origination) and *phenomenological* methodology (foundation) to *feminist* critique (emancipation) and *participatory* action research (transformation). As such, and unbeknown to most, social scientific research, unlike its natural sciences counterpart (see for example chapter 4), draws on a wide variety of "scientific" research processes, and we have only drawn here on the "southern" *relational* ones, as opposed to "eastern" *renewal* (narrative method to cooperative inquiry), "northern" *reason*, (grounded theory to socio-technical design) and "western" *realization* (experimental method to action research).

We start with the build up towards *nhakanomics,* closely aligned with "oikonomics". This is attuned to the *relational* rhythm of research to innovation—descriptive/phenomenological/feminist/participatory—as an altogether integral, social scientific, *relational* process.

7.4. Afrikology: Nhakanomics to Health and Rejuvenation

7.4.1. NHAKANOMICS – Community based Self Sufficiency: Grounded in Nature: Kumusha, Integral Kumusha, Nhakanomics, Vakamusha

Local Grounding in Kumusha: Passionate Homely Relational Involvement

In the course of re-Generating nature and community then, to begin with most specifically, and substantively *Oikonomically,* as American economic historian Ingrid Rima (18) has articulated, likened to our (19) African *kumusha*: "The modern word 'economics' has its origin in the ancient Greek word 'oikonomia', which means 'the art of household management' ... Aristotle undertook to examine what is probably the first economic issue to have been subjected to formal inquiry: what sort of wealth getting activity satisfies material needs as a desirable goal of human activity? For Aristotle in that respect, retail trade—as opposed to household trade—which is exchange for the purpose of making money, is unnatural. What is natural is the pursuit of 'autarky' or self-sufficiency."

We now re-present such, in GENE-tic, processal terms, starting with grounding and origination, and thereby rich *description,* socially, scientifically:

TABLE 7.2. LOCALLY RE-GENE-RATE NATURE AND COMMUNITY
KUMUSHA: Grounded Descriptive Origination
Engaging your total Self-and-Group in a State of Passionate Homely Involvement
You Illuminate such a process through Vital, richly comprehensive Kumusha Description
You reveal fully your Human and More-than-Human Individual/Collective Nature
Through Vivid Experience of Relational, resilient Depth, rather than Measurements

"Nhakanomics", ultimately then, grounded in *kumusha—shona* for "homestead", draws on "legacy" (*nhaka*). Ancient Greek thinkers moreover, like Aristotle, from their particular socio-political perspective, believed that a "good life" is the purpose of existence, and that it is best achieved within the city-state or "polis" (in the Zimbabwean case we substitute rural community for urban state), takes precedence over the individual. Grounding themselves as such, Shona villagers in Zimbabwe, for African anthropologist Artwell Nhcmcchana (20) tend to speak, on the one hand, about *chirungu*, which refers to European ways of life, including the spiritual/religious aspect of life, and on the other hand of *chivanhu*, which refers to the African way of life, as their communal grounding and origination, that we seek to regenerate.

All too often these terms have different valences to "modernity" and "tradition" as binaries which, in terms of "Euro-modernity", presume that one is present and the other is past. To that extent, as we have already intimated, our GENE cycle, starting with local Grounding as tabled above, is both cyclical and linear, spiralling and pin-pointed, while altogether as we shall see, regenerative. We now turn from local grounding in *kumusha*, via Zimbabwe's Nhemechana to local-global emergence, via Scotland's ecological anthropologist Tim Ingold's *being alive*, albeit still lodged in nature and community.

Local/Global Emergence – Integral Kumusha: Engaged Reciprocity

Renowned British anthropologist Tim Ingold (21) has spent decades with hunter-gatherers of the Norwegian Arctic, building as such, for us, on indigenous "southern" culture and spirituality, *the substantive spirit of being alive replaces the spirit of enterprise,* in the same way as, *kumusha* wise, "being relational" replaced "doing business", as an overall way of life (the essence of phenomenology as a social scientific research methodology). *Stripped of the veneer of stasis such organisms are revealed not as static objects, or stable relationships, but as hives of activity and interconnections, pulsing with the flows that keep them alive.*

TABLE 7.3. LOCALLY-GLOBALLY RE-GENE-RATE NATURE/COMMUNITY-AND-SOCIETY
INTEGRAL KUMUSHA: Emergent Phenomenological Foundation
Illuminate ever-emerging Natural, Cultural, Techno-Economic Integral Kumusha Scope
Immersed in immediately perceived Animate-Dynamic Relationships.
Wayfaring: Proceeding along an individual-collective path, you lay a trail: your nhaka.
Being Alive: drawing from multiple knowledge sources becoming Reciprocally Engaged

Such "aliveness" moreover, in our "southern" context, involves much more than being "enterprising", but rather, and interdependently, means being alive to the interaction between our nature, culture, technology and enterprise, to the now *integral kumusha* as such an overall way of "shona" life, also alongside worldly others. Through thereafter "newly global" Nhakanomics, we turn from the locally communal and local-globally communal-societal to the now newly global, communal-organisational, by way of, in this case, market-*and-community.*

Newly Global Navigation – Nhakanomics: Diversity – Interconnection

TABLE 7.4. NEWLY GLOBALLY RE-GENE-RATE NATURE, COMMUNITY AND ORGANISATION
NHAKANOMICS - Emancipatory *Feminism*
<u>Ukama</u> *(Relationships) evolve into Natural-and-Cultural Diversity: as per Biosemiotics*
<u>Utariri</u> *(stewardship) provides the macro-economic rationale for CARING: Community activation, Awaken consciousness, Instutitional Research, Embody Kumusha nation-wide*
Via <u>Nhimbe</u> (Teamwork) Feminist Communal Nhakanomics complements the individual
As Intenhaka (not entrepeneur) Interconnecting individual-collective <u>Upfama</u> (ownership)

From a now newly global, feminist and emancipatory perspective, we now draw on the work of American economic anthropologist Steve Gudeman (22). Also a Harvard Business School graduate, for Gudeman, the "south" (anthropology) leads and the "west" (management) follows, an *economy consists of two realms, that is community and market.*

In a specifically southern African context we have reframed such in terms of *Nhakanomics*. Humans are, biologically and anthropologically from the outset, communally motivated by social fulfilment, curiosity, and the pleasure of mastery, as well as commercially by instrumental purpose, competition and the accumulation of gains. Communally the economy is local and specific, constituted through natural and social relationships and contextually defined values. In its other guise (market–economic) it is impersonal, global, and abstracted from social context. For English literary critic and biosemiotician Wendy Wheeler (23), moreover, and as we saw in the previous chapter, in her work on *The Whole Creature: Complexity, Biosemiotics and the Evolution of Culture*:

Modern science developed as a study of quantities—of the measurable (what Galileo called the "primary" qualities of objects) features of objects (such as mass, position and velocity) in dynamical relationship with each other. The "secondary" qualities which were not quantitatively measurable (such as shape, colour and texture) were, as it were, set aside. Biology followed this route with its interest in genes. However, this can tell us nothing about organisms and their generative fields. It cannot tell us about conditions of creative flourishing. The complexity sciences, however, can enable us to have a sense of what a science of quality would be, that is a concept of life, and of individuals and societies and cultures, as processal, inter-related and emergent.

This leads us, finally in re-GENE-rating nature and community, from kumusha, integral kumusha, and nhakanomics practically onto our so-called Vakumusha.

Global/Local Effect – Vakamusha: Participation to Transformation

Rather than building up the economy at large, Daud and Kristina Taranhike (24), as businessman and woman, rural *intenhaka's* and public intellectuals in turn, have enriched their Zimbabwean rural home base in Buhera, located in the south-central area of the country, through their local community. One of their core businesses, Vaka Concrete, has then merged with their rural *kumusha* to become "Vakamusha". In many ways, based in rural Zimbabwe, they have taken on from where Albert Koopman (25)—see chapter 6—left off with Cashbuild, in his transcultural approach to management, in rural South Africa:

> Everything had to be focussed upon the common interest of creating wealth and fostering an understanding amongst workers that the

correct management of capital benefits the organization and community as a whole. This correct management, in turn, could only occur if the worker was democratically involved in contributing towards the overall success of the organization. I visualised that in this manner so-called capitalist exploitation (of southern community) would no longer exist.

In the same way, as the origins of *economics* and *ecology* lies in the ancient Greek term *oikos*, which means "home", so the Taranhike's, for example, started with their Southern African homestead, that, at a micro level, their *kumusha*, albeit with a difference. The difference lies in the fact that while Daud/Shumba (*shumba* is Daud's "lion" totem) and Kristina started out with nature and community, thereby close to home, they also sought to accommodate culture and spirituality, science and technology, as well as economy and enterprise, integrally together.

TABLE 7.5. GLOBALLY-LOCALLY RE-GENE-RATE NATURE/COMMUNITY/ ORGANISATION/SOCIETY

Participatory (PAR) Action Research: Transformative Effect: VAKAMUSHA

A problem is analyzed/solved by Family-and-Community, involving Active Participation

You are committed individual/organisational Participants, Facilitators, Learners in such

Creating Awareness of People's own natural, cultural, scientific, economic Resources

As a Vakamusha You Transform your community and economy from the Bottom-Up

---

As such their three businesses, Vaka Concrete, HPC Engineering and Lion Motorways have merged with their rural *kumusha*, in the first Vala case serving to co-evolve Vaka-musha. Thereby, both Daud/Shumba and Christina (26) have actively engaged, both with local nature and community, to build up their *kumusha*. Indeed, and in the process, they have become both facilitators and learners, of and development, individually and communally, economically and ecologically, in turn.

They have concertedly endeavoured, in the process, to enhance their community's awareness of their innate resources—physical, emotional, spiritual and intellectual—with a view to transforming their homesteads in *integral kumusha* guise, thereby aligning the natural and communal homestead with culture, technology, enterprise. At a macro level moreover, southern *nhakanomics* replaces "western" style neo-liberal economy.

We now turn, more wholeheartedly by way of social innovation, both substantively (anthropology to oikonomy) and processally (descriptive to participatory), from nature and community (community based economic self sufficiency via nhakanomics), to culture and spirituality (culture based developmental economy via indigenous science), once again with a view to now cultural and spiritual re-GENE-ration, whereby we turn "east", metaphorically if not literally, to a spiritual laden path, that is *Indigenous Science* (see chapter 4 on African Creation Energy) and *Soulidarity Economics*.

7.4.2. INDIGENOUS Science: Culture based Developmental Economy: Re-Gene-rate Culture/ Spirituality: Ubuntu, Metanoia, SOULIDARITY, Care

Local Grounding in Ubuntu/Unhu/Ivhu: Circular Rhythms and Patterns

We now turn from "south" to "south-east", following both indigenous spirituality and the religions of the book. Indeed, harking back to economic history, its next spiritual, emergent foundation, if you like for Rima (27), after its ancient, communal origination as "Oikonamia", in the Middle Ages:

> The Christian Schoolmen, for whom the cultural and spiritual dimension informed the economic and material, sought to lay down rules for Christian behavior and salvation. The prime mover of economic activity was comprised of custom and command, and was a reflection of the prevailing philosophical or theological standard for social and moral well-being. Tradition and law, the primacy of culture and spirituality as it were, explained virtually everything. Then everything fundamentally changed, as we entered the 17th century.

In other words, "western" economic evolved form the communal to the spiritual, and yet still in the "south-east" today, the holy Qur'an for example, for Pakistan-based Founder of Akhuwat, Amjad Saqib and his Anglo-Pakistani TCA compatriot Aneeqa Malik (28), is recognised as a book of profoundly spiritual *rhythms* and *patterns* both in its sound and construction as well as in its content and meaning. In similar guise, as we saw especially though African Creation Energy (see chapter 4), African science and technology has deep spiritual and mythological, metaphorically for us "eastern" roots, though all too seldom is such *indigenous science* recognised as such.

As such, we do not view history simply as a linear process but as a sequence of events which succeed one another, a series of patterns which occur over a period of time and which arise as the result of certain natural laws at work in society and within men. These patterns or rhythms in history are repeatedly illustrated, for example, in the Qur'an, by references to past civilizations which have all followed the same pattern of rise, decay, and collapse, and now, for them as for us, purposeful renewal.

TABLE 7.6. LOCALLY RE-GENE-RATE CULTURE AND SPIRITUALITY
Descriptive Grounding and Origination: UBUNTU
Rather than Measurements Rhythm and Patterns needs to be accounted for
Reveal fully your Culture/Spirituality through Brotherhood – Ubuntu – Unhu – Ivhu
Civilizations have followed the same pattern of rise, decay, and collapse, and now, prospectively, also purposeful renewal
Holy Matrimony between "I am Because you Are" as well as between Soil & Water

Thus, the pattern in the historical events that took place starting from Prophetic Hijrah from Makkah to Medina, following on from the soulful journey, on the night of ascension (*Mairaj*), thereafter, setting an exemplary tradition of caring and sharing/spiritual *Brotherhood* (*Mawakhat*) for the world to follow, forms the praxis of a *Circle of Soulidarity* (wisdom in solidarity) from a perennial perspective.

Interestingly enough, while this may be less apparent, say, in Zimbabwe than in Pakistan, the southern African version of "brotherhood", that is *Ubuntu,* is as evident in exogenous Christianity as it is in indigenous African religions. Indeed for its major, South African exponent, Bishop Tutu, cited in Mike Battle's (29) *Reconciliation: The Ubuntu Theology of Desmond Tutu,* for us also interlinking soil and water:

> Ubuntu means "humanity" and is related both to umuntu, which is the category of intelligent human forces that includes spirits, the human dead and the living, and to ntu which is God's being as meta-dynamic, rather then metaphysical. The proverbial Xhosa expression *ubuntu ungamntu ngabanya abantu* means that "each individual's humanity is ideally expressed in relationship with others", or "a person depends on

other people to be a person". First then, this theology builds up true, interdependent community. Second, it recognises persons as distinctive in their identities. Third, it combines the best of European and African cultures to produce a new and distinctive theology. And fourth it is strong enough to address—and even overthrow—apartheid.

Similarly for one of us, Anselm Adodo (30), now in overtly scientific context marrying up nature, power, quantum physics, and our own transformation journey:

> ... The first category is the *gravitational force*. The force is universal, that is every particle feels the force of gravity, according to its mass or energy ... our Communal Grounding ... the next category is *electromagnetic force*, which interacts with electrically charged particles like electrons ... The electromagnetic attraction between negatively charged particles and positively charged protons in the nucleus causes the electrons to orbit the nucleus of the atom ... our Emergent Transformation Journey ... The third category is called the *weak nuclear force*... exhibiting a property known as spontaneous symmetry breaking. This means that what appear to be a number of completely different particles at owe energies are in fact found to be all the same particle, only in different states ... our Navigatory Academy ... the fourth category is *the strong nuclear force*, which holds the quarks together in the proton and neutron, within the nucleus of the atom ... our Effecting Laboratory.

Local-Global Regeneration: Spiritual Dimensions/Social Design: Metanoia

It is in this transformational light, and for its founder in the UK, Aneeqa Malik, *I*ntegral *S*oulidarity *R*esearch *A*cademy (iSRA), is born—an archetypal reimagining of the Prophet's spiritual *Journey of Ascension* (raising our integral consciousness). iSRA, therefore, aims to act as an integrative R&D platform to invoke the "spiritus" of social dealing in matters of finance, economics & enterprise i.e. journeying through a Trans-migrational (trans-local) approach to Transformation.

In fact, and in a more "south-eastern" African context, *Ubuntu* has not been evolved in such an iSRA like way. Perhaps the closest we get to it is in the work of South African theologian John De Gruchy (31), alluding to the Hellenic/Christian notion of *Metanoia* (transformational change of heart):

> Truth serves the cause for reconciliation and justice only when it leads to a genuine "metanoia", that is a turning around, a breaking with an unjust past, and a moving towards a new future.

Like our "four worlds" then, there are, for him, four forms of truth and truth-telling:

- truth *healing* or *restorative* claims of a religious tradition (south);
- *dialogic* truth of existential commitment and action (east);
- *objective factual* scientific truth sought in the laboratory or observatory (north);
- *personal* or *narrative* truth of a value-judgment on morality or aesthetics (west).

Such a "turn around", epistemologically and economically, requires co-engagement with, and co-evolution between, all four worlds.

TABLE 7.7. LOCALLY-GLOBALLY RE-GENE-RATE CULTURE AND SPIRITUALITY:
Emergent *Phenomenological* Foundation: iSRA/METANOIA
Invoking a Two-Part Material and Spiritual Journey
Integral Soulidarity Research Academy (iSRA), is a reimagining of the Prophet's spiritual Journey of Ascension, for Christians in Metanoia, for African Creation Energy in Ptah
iSRA aims to act as an integrative platform to invoke the 'spiritus' of social dealing in matters of science and technology, ecomomics and enterprise
Journeying through a Trans-migrational (trans-local) approach to Transformation.

Finally, and again harking back to African Creation Energy we can see ways in which the ancient Egyptian God of technology, Ptah, can be resurrected in contemporary thermodynamic, electronic, even ethernet guise (see chapter 4).

Newly Global Navigation – Soulidarity: Flow of Barakah and the Orisha

For Arab linguists, Barakah is to do with increase and growth—above and beyond. It is thus, believed, if something has Barakah it grows, and it increases. The spirit of Soulidarity, as such, always emanating through an ever-present correlation; a soulful solidarity (Soulidarity) as a cyclical process between the vertical and the horizontal. This impulse, here in the twenty-first century, is necessitated with the rising needs of the new cultural, technological and environmental conditions that demand, not only a conscious shift, in the way we perceive our human conditionality, but also, to employ and reclaim our implicit primordial nature, reciprocating with this call of Soulidarity.

TABLE 7.8. NEWLY GLOBAL RE-GENE-RATION OF CULTURE AND SPIRITUALITY
Feminist Emancipatory Navigation: INDIGENOUS SCIENCE/SOULIDARITY
Soulidarity impulse – a primordial call of nature – for Barakah to flow through for universal (cosmic) as well as existential (species) evolution
Barakah is to do with increase and growth – if something has Barakah it grows
Guided by machine intelligence, having decoded some cosmic mysteries, are synergised with these trans-mutational impulses
Amongst the Yoruba people of Nigeria, this energy is called Ashe, which means "the power to make it happen", personified by the Yoruba "Orisha"

For Osiadan (32) as such, African Creation Energy (see chapter 4) is the energy, power and force that created African people and that African people use, in turn, to create. *Amongst the Yoruba people of Nigeria, this energy is called Ashe, which means "the power to make it happen", personified by the Yoruba "Orisha".* Amongst the Akan people in Ghana this energy is called *Tumi*, the web of energy and power that exists through space and all of creation, woven by the Akan deity of wisdom. Indeed the oldest creation stories, for cosmologist Lloyd Scranton (33) again, centre then on a surprisingly constant set of themes.

Firstly, *if we look at the themes that appear in the Dogon religion, we find that they can be grouped into two distinct storylines,* which Scranton calls *the surface story and the deep story.* In other words, the universe actually consists of two creations, one we can see and one that we cannot. Typically the unformed universe, for the Dogon, is described as an egg that contains all of the seeds, or signs of the world. In some cultures these signs are represented as the letters of the alphabet, but in others they are simply identified as the seeds of the world to come. *Implied throughout are a basic set of principles.* Both describe a set of emergent godlike entities created in pairs.

A second guiding principle is the pairing of male and female. The self-created god, in many societies is both male and female. We can see this pairing also reflected in the traditional organisation of Egypt into two lands, one called Upper Egypt and the other Lower Egypt. In modern Dogon culture, a plot of land is divided between those who farm and others who forge the tools and implements of farming. In contemporary guise this is more conventionally associated with the ancient Chinese cosmology of *yin* (feminine) and *yang* (masculine). *A third concept of great importance to the earliest religions is the idea of the cardinal points of the Earth—north, south, east and west.* Such can be seen, for example, in the Great Pyramid of Egypt, deliberately aligned with the four cardinal points.

iSRA, thus, aims to help us make sense of our role in evolutionary creativity, by engaging their heart faculty and not only their rational knowledge/ intelligence. Hereby, this call is for (wo)man to rise to the occasion of being a true caretaker of this world, something which Eastern philosopher Muhammad Iqbal (34), urged in his poetic expression of Khudi (Self). Furthermore, it inspires the concept of 'Khair' (of doing good) and the 'joy of giving'—for heavenly rewards—from an Islamic charitable perspective which forms the basis of our Soulidarity economic impulse.

Global-Local Effect – Ishq, Ilm, Amal, Ihsan: Participation/Transformation

Finally, and transformatively for Malik, she turns to the 4E's (Ethics, Epistemology, Erudition, Economics & Enterprise) of "Soulidarity Economics" juxtaposed with a Hikmah (perennial wisdom) praxis of Soulidarity of Ishq (love), Ilm (Erudition), Amal (Action) and Ihsan (Excellence). These constitute the core tenets of iSRA's CARE model, which in turn, aims to bridge the spiritual/ material divide in the socio-economic sectors primarily within the Islamic communities invoking a new realisation of a soulful communal solidarity.

At the same time the Qur'an is a book of principles, of truths, which, if they are implemented, will allow men to understand, and break free of the repetitious cycles of history. For the Dikenga people of Congo, their cosmogram involves: Red: unity of the finite and infinite (G); White: burnout of impurity the moon, female (E); Yellow: enlightenment, the sun, male (N); Black: change, dissolution individuation (E).

TABLE 7.9. GLOBALLY-LOCALLY RE-GENE-RATE CULTURE/SPIRITUALITY – TRANSFORMATIVE PARTICIPATORY ACTION RESEARCH: CARE
Problem Defined, analyzed and solved via Active Participation via the 4E's (Ethics, Epistemology, Erudition, Economics & Enterprise) of Indigenous Science and Economics
Juxtaposed with our Hikmah (perennial wisdom) Praxis of Soulidarity of; Ishq (love), Ilm (Erudition), Amal (Action) & Ihsan (Excellence)
iSRA's CARE model aims to bridge the spiritual / material divide in the socio-economic sectors primarily within the Islamic communities
The fourfold Dikenga cosmogram if the African Congo depicts Atomic cycles in Nature, depicting the flow of Energy as in Thermodynamics.

It is interesting finally to compare and contrast where Saquib and Malik are coming from, as above, in their Pakistani "Near Eastern", regenerative model of production, in spiritual-and-financial terms, and exchange, and leading management thinker in South Africa, Raul Khoza (34). For him, the enduring values of Ubuntu he identifies (seldom realised in practice) are:

- *servant leadership:* implying that African leaders derive their legitimacy and power from collaboration with, rather than command over their followers
- *cohabitation* referring to the proclivity to live with others in harmony, not only in terms of shared space, but also accommodating other people's ideas, and genuinely seeking to understand before proceeding to persuade them
- *emotional intelligence*, relating to sensitivity and introspection of leaders as they carry out their service role and employ arbitrage to reward their followers
- *social arbitrage* applies to the trade-offs made by leaders to satisfy conflicting demands and ensure that their leadership decisions reward every stakeholder with something
- *paradox* is often associated with leadership, but takes on new meaning from the servant leadership concept.

Indeed, we would argue that the reason the above is seldom realised in practice is because we do not build purposefully from origination to transformation, thereby progressively recognising and releasing GENE-IUS, and *ubuntu* is thereby stranded in "flatlands". We now turn from the cultural and spiritual "south-east", metaphorically speaking, to the scientific and technological "north-and-south", towards our knowledge based "social economy", and specifically to *Semiotic Economics* generally, and to *Afrikology*, more specifically.

7.4.3 AFRIKOLOGY: Towards a Knowledge based Social Economy: Re-geNe-rate Communication: Meanings, BIOSEMIOTICS, Ideation, Accounts

How Meanings are Made: Social Theory – Its Situation and Task

We start out in the "north-south" by revisiting Nabudere's (35) opening *rich description*, on the meaning of Afrikology:

> The word, "Afrikology" is not ethnic nor racial but a validation of a human knowledge of communal—including natural—living … It seeks to avoid any claim to an overarching epistemic superiority, but stands for plurality of epistemic directions.

Interestingly enough, and further to such, we find Brazilian American Roberto Unger (36), now based at Harvard Law School, undoubtedly thereby a brilliant child of the "north-south", declaring in his seminal work on *Social Theory: Its Situation and Task* that:

> Modern social thought was born in proclaiming that society is *made and imagined,* as a human artefact rather than the expression of an underlying natural order.

In other words, such 18th and 19th century social theory, esecially that of Adam Smith and Karl Marx also cited extensively by Rima (37) in her economic history was "meaningful". In fact Unger singles out the classical political economists especially in that light, notwithstanding all their faults, and argues that in the 19th to 21st century economics has gone rapidly downhill from there, becoming ever less *meaningful.* Then he (38) maintains:

> The materials for an alternative (economic) vision—methods, insights and interpreted observations—already lie at hand, though in underdeveloped, fragmentary and distorted form ... The disconnection then between images of society that lacked an institutional embodiment and practical experiences that lacked a ready-made interpretation, released the imagination of the possible and desirable forms of human association from its traditional bounds, making the third world countries a privileged terrain for institutional invention.

It is in that particular guise that we have integrally reworked Bhengu's (39), for us *imvelean,* for him *Amazulu,* "cosmic order", in "newly global" guise, thereby adding our oikomomic to his "law, environment and the person", recognising also that, for Unger, the "law" provides an overall, *inclusive* underpinning:

> *Imvelo* (the cosmic order) has three pillars of being: the Law, the Environment and the Person. *Umthetho wemvelo* regulates the individualisation of primordial substance into phenomena (see opening quotation to this chapter, *Umthetho* also meaning "cosmic law").

Alas, Unger goes on to say, the powers that be in the Third World, neither the intelligentsia or practitioners (we now being a humble exception), could see any new political and economic, institutional meaning in what was emerging out of their very particular natures, and cultures.

For Dr Tony Bradley (40) as such, a faculty member at Hope University in Liverpool, duly focused on societal enterprise, there are worlds of economic meaning that fall outside the narrow equations, econometrics and graphs of neoliberal economics. Semiotics, for him, is the study of how meanings (such as for us *imvelo)* are made, interpreted, communicated and utilised. But, so far as Bradley and ourselves can tell, this is not a discipline that has often been applied to alternative economic models.

TABLE 7.10. LOCALLY RE-GENE-RATE COMMUNICATION:

Descriptive Grounding and Origination: The Meaning of AFRIKOLOGY

The driving power that gives force and efficacy to all communication is Meaning

Semiotics is the study of how meanings are made, interpreted, communicated, utilised

Afrikology is a (bio)semiotic sub-set, albeit with an Integral orientation, purposefully drawing from the "south" (Africa), the "North" (Nordic Europe)

Semiotics is not a discipline that has often been applied to alternative economic models

---

How Meanings are Communicated through Signs and Symbolic Processes

As Bradley points out, Semiotics developed during the late 19th and 20th centuries as the study of meanings and how these are communicated through signs and symbolic processes, especially by Peirce (41) in America, and Saussure, (42) in Europe, and thereafter, as we saw in chapter 6, was applied to *Biosemiotics.*

TABLE 7.11. LOCALLY-GLOBALLY RE-GENE-RATE COMMUNICATIONS:

Emergent Phenomenological Foundation: BIOSEMIOTICS

How meanings are communicated through signs and symbolic processes

The discipline overlaps with socio-linguistics, philosophy of language and hermeneutics

The focus of semiotics is on the ways in which understanding is shaped and relates to objects, concepts and forms that they seek to represent

Its latest incarnation, related especially to more-than-human nature, is biosemiotics

---

This discipline overlaps with biology, socio-linguistics, the philosophy of language and hermeneutics. The specific focus of semiotics is on the ways in which understanding is shaped through the relationships of language, images and the media to the objects, concepts and forms that they seek to represent. Its latest incarnation, in fact, that of biosemiotics, as we saw in the previous chapter, indeed related to more-than-human nature life world (43), for example in our case to the meaning of shumba (lion totem), for Daud-Shumba Taranhike.

From Biosemiotics the Missing Naturally-Culturally Laden Dimension

The *sign relation*, as such, the key to Peircean semiotics, and to Hoffmeyeran biosemiotics, is our duly "feminist" emancipatory navigation, alluding to duly marginalised *Afrikology* in our "southern" socio-economic case. It is, overall and transformatively, the relation between the sign (representamum–naviga-tion), its subject matter (object–origination) and its meaning/interpretation/thought process–effect) that counts for Peirce as for us. At one end the object is subject matter then, in GENE-tic terms, is the sign's Grounding, in fact grounded in *Afrikology* in our case.

TABLE 7.12. NEWLY GLOBALLY RE-GENE-RATE COMMUNICATIONS

Feminist Emancipatory Navigation: SOCIAL ECONOMY

The sign relation is the key to Peircean semiotics and Hoffmeyer's Biosemiotics

Such triadic semiotics is the relation between the sign (navigation), its subject matter (origination) and its meaning/ interpretation/ thought process (transformation)

In Piercean semiotics, in GENE-tic terms, there is a missing emergent foundation (E), Biosemiotics, the emergence of awakening natural-cultural consciousness

Whereby meaning is ultimately expressed though semiotic accounts as opposed to financial measurements

---

Those in fact, according to Bradley, who have followed the logic of the in-tegral GEN*E*alogy (see above) will, in fact, have recognised this gap. Whilst the Peircean schema aligns perfectly with the GN*E* (object – original Grounding e.g. *Afrikology*; sign – emancipatory Navigation e.g. *Social Economy*; and in-terpretation – transformative *effect* e.g. *Semiotic Accounts)* in overall relation to the integral GEN*E*, there is a missing element (E) e.g. *Biosemiotics*. This reflects the all important Emergent foundation of awakening cultural/spiritual consciousness, or indeed culturally laden imagination. Interestingly enough Unger himself is largely oblivious to such.

As Bradley points out, the specific feature that is missing is a depiction of the *meaning-systems*, from which herein conscious Afrikological ideations emerge such as "southern" Nhakanomics or "eastern" Soulidarity economics or now "northern" Semiotic Economics. This can be understood, following the analytical psychology of Carl Gustav Jung (44), as missing the *archetypes of the collective unconscious*, that are invoked as structuring principles as our "integral realities". On this basis, Bradley indicates the need to uncover the *archetypes of signification* inherent in each economic system. For example, Bhengu's Amazulu-Egyptian "spirit of the heavens" is a perfect case in point. In "Southern-Northern"" guise, such an archetype might be best represented by Biosemiotics, interestingly enough Estonia (45) being the leading national light (Jakob von Uexkull being an Estonian-German biologist) as such:

> Jakob von Uexkull saw, long before anyone else, that a biology that would be true to its subject matter would have to direct its searchlight explicitly on the perceptual worlds of organisms, their Umwelts as he called them. The Umwelt is the subjective or phenomenal world of the animal. Thus while modern biology employs the objective term eco-logical niche, one might say that the Umwelt is the ecological niche as the animal itself apprehends it.

Not coincidentally, in "*southern*-northern" guise, animal totems rule the roost.

This isn't simply a question of meaning. It is an issue of the structures through which meanings become signs for economic, in our case *shumba/ku-musha* signification. These, frequently, lie beneath the surface of conscious-ness, as Unger has pointed out above, and Bhengu has illustrated, whereby we lack the imagination, and indeed cooperation (Mfuniselwa and Samanyanga-Gatsheni), to bring them to the surface, as they lie outside the observation of institutional processes and are, usually, invisible in respect of how signs (or institutions) come into being. They are, for Bradley, the slick subterranean surfaces across which objects glide, to generate signs, so that we, habitually, fail to notice these meaning-systems, for example underlying *Nhakanomics, Soulidarity Economics, Semiotic Economics,* if not also *Wellbeing Economics,* Afrikologically overall.

Biosemiotic Accounts: Beyond GNP

As such then, for Bradley, it is critical that we are able to identify actualized local models and examples of semiotic systems in place, as we are attempting to do Afrikologically and oikonomically here. He does not see much value in theory for its own sake. The urgency comes from the social fact that economics is a discipline that seeks to change the world but, dominated as it currently stands by a "north-western" consciousness, is in a state of disarray, precisely at a point when an integral, Afrikological approach is most needed.

It is vital then to signify the processes of semiotic economics in their full dynamic cycle, from grounding in communities (G) to effective innovations (E). But, in order to do so—through for Unger (46) our imagination, and cooperation, leading to an inclusive knowledge economy—we must emerge through the sub-structural meanings, "on the edge of semiotics". This involves, as Bradley indicates, the (Emergent) E in between Grounding and Navigation, if we are to more fully understand their natural and cultural as well as techno-logical and economic significance and interpretation, as alternative economic systems, straddling the fully integral paths (realities) and trajectories (rhythm), ulitimately giving rise to a "newly global" meaning.

A dominant facet of "western" economic neo-liberalism is that it is predi-cated on the ideology of growth in money systems, which fuels unsustainable patterns of production, consumption and investment, acting against, both, reciprocity and fairer distributive mechanisms. This indicates something that is, often, neglected, which is that the emergence of economics arises out of meaning-systems, spread across our four worlds, rather than algorithms based in iron "western" laws. In other words, as we have sought to show, here, it is the missing meaning giving realm in economics and semiotics that requires further elaboration, not simply in theory but, vitally, in terms of actualized practice.

This requires, specifically, then, as a form of "newly global" qualitative *accounting,* more meaningful then quantitatively based GNP, for example in our "south":

- identifying with the oikonomic object: *kumusha*
- uncovering an *imvelean* cultural archetype: *integral kumusha*
- newly addressing an Afrikological oiokomic sign: *nhakanomics*
- effecting material interpretations/innovations: *vakamusha*

In the final analysis, in fact, whereas the "southern" community and econ-omy is underpinned by our "southern" path to research and innovation, and "eastern" soulidarity economics by our path of renewal, this "northern" ap-proach to semiotic economics is underscored by the path of reason, and hence also semiotic accounting, as shown in Table 7.13, below.

TABLE 7.13. GLOBALLY-LOCALLY RE-GENE-RATE COMMUNICATION
Participatory Transformative Effect: Accounting for SEMIOTIC ACCOUNTS *(after Bradley's model of the Semiotic Economics process)*
Identify the Oikonomic Object
Uncover Cultural Archetypes
Specify the Sign to be Addressed
Effect Material Interpretations/Innovations

We now turn "west", from the knowledge based social economy, specifically for us represented by *semiotic economics* to a life based, living economy, a "west' that builds on the "rest", specifically embodied in *wellbeing economics*.

7.4.4. HEALTH & REJUVENATION: Living Economy: Re-geNe-rate Capital: Genuine Wealth, Impact Investment, Economic Wellbeing, 5 Capitals

Grounded in Weal-th as Wellbeing

For Canada's Mark Anielski (47, 48), a longstanding colleague and authority on the *Wellbeing Economy*, his so-called concept of Genuine Wealth is based on the etymological roots of the word wealth, which comes from the 13th Century Old English weal-th meaning "well-being conditions." In turn the word happiness, aligned with wellbeing, comes from the Greek Eudaimonia, richly described as well-being (*eu*) of the spirit or soul (*daimonia*), according originally to Aristotle.

In turn the word economy, as we saw at the beginning of this chapter, comes from the Greek *oikos* (household) *nomia* (stewardship or management), with which our African *kumusha* is also aligned. Mark has also worked intensively, in his home country Canada, with its indigenous peoples, enabling them to newly and economically reclaim their homesteads which had been hitherto colonized/appropriated. In fact, and further to such, marginalist and then neoliberal economics in the 19th, 20th and now 21st centuries, completely lost touch, for Rima (49) implicitly and for Unger (50) explicitly, with its roots.

Yet the original double-entry bookkeeping system, for Anielski, as we turn "south-west" to Renaissance Italy, was developed in the late 15th Century, by Franciscan monk and mathematician Luca Pacioli and his colleague, the renowned polymath Leonardo da Vinci, both Renaissance men. Luca was advising the Medici banking family of Florence as well as the guild-society merchants of Venice on how to be better their business operations by maintaining an inventory of the assets (in ledgers) organised into a 'balance sheet' where assets = liabilities + equity.

TABLE 7.14. LOCALLY RE-GENE-RATE CAPITAL AND VALUE:
Descriptive Origination of Wellbeing: GENUINE WEALTH

Genuine Wealth is based on the etymological roots of the word wealth which comes from the 13th Century Old English weal-th meaning 'well-being conditions'

The word happiness, duly aligned with such wellbeing, comes from the Greek Eudaimonia meaning well-being (eu) of the spirit or soul (daimonia)

The word economy comes from the Greek oikos (household) combined with nomia (stewardship or management)

Pacioli's orginal Accounting system was based on the Golden Mean, of debit-credits and the Fibonacci based Natural Progression (e.g. found in the patterns of a sunflower shell)

Pacioli's accounting system was based on the principle of the Golden Mean, of debit-credits, as well as the Fibonacci sequence, the numerical natural progression found throughout Nature (e.g. in the patterns seen in a sunflower or Nautilus shell). In Samanyanga's (51) own work in the 1970s on *Accounting for an Enterprise's Wellbeing*, he related such assets and liabilities to natural, social and psychological and to financial "double-entry" accounting, thereafter, as we saw in chapter 6, turned into "waste accounting", in natural and cultural, social and economic terms . What does that "golden mean" then *mean* today?

The Emergence of Impact Investment as a Phenomenon

Anielski then proposes a new era in capitalism that would make net positive well-being impacts the highest aspiration of any enterprise or organisation that has been given a social license to operate.

This will require a new means of calibration for assessing impacts across a wider spectrum of well-being domains. Such well-being returns on investment and on assets would complement existing financial performance measures used in the banking and investment world. Indeed, Anielski suggests that using a broader approach to accounting and reporting would strengthen the due-diligence of investment portfolio managers and would improve their capacity to choose companies in their investment portfolios that are resilient, sustainable and even flourishing. Today such is termed *Integral Impact Investment*.

"*Integral* Impact investment", now the focus of Robert Dellner's (52) activities, in his integrally based 3 I Partners, builds on *Impact Investment* in fact, which has become a new buzzword(s). This focus on ESG – *Environmental Social, Governance* impact has emerged, as a phenomenon in its own right, arising out of an original corporate social responsibility orientation, especially in the last decade, locally in the "west", and now globally in the "rest" of the world.

TABLE 7.15. LOCAL-GLOBAL RE-GENE-RATE CAPITAL AND VALUE:
Emergent Phenomenological Foundation: IMPACT INVESTMENT
Make net positive well-being impacts the highest aspiration of any enterprise or organisation that has been given a social licence to operate
Means of calibrating well-being returns on Investment would complement existing financial performance measures used in the banking and investment world
Strengthening investment managers' capacity to choose companies in their investment portfolios that are resilient, sustainable and flourishing
The focus should then be on asking the question: will this investment improve the well-being conditions of an enterprise, the community, society and nature?

The Emergence of Life Capital in Newly Global Feminist Guise

In the language of his life-capital paradigm, for Canadian radical philosopher John McMurtry (54), in his renowned work, in duly feminist guise, on *The Cancer of Capitalism*, transnational money sequencing is a direct and systematic assault on public life-support systems, wages, secure jobs and environmental protections. Thus from the Thatcher Reagan turn of 1979–80 on, a war-like campaign of one dispossession after another in the name of "market reforms" came from which people were never given a chance to recover because they now had to compete with the most exploited regions of the world with no unions, democracy, social programs or even civil rights in the global race to the bottom of wages, benefits, ecological and workplace protections.

Society's ill-being or well-being then is determined by sets of social circumstances which select for life rather than death, and for social life support systems rather than money-sequencing agglomerations. The continuous axing of the very roots of humanity has overlooked what native people have to teach global capitalism: grounding in the life-requirements of community and ecological life-host; instituted relationships to fellow creatures as life companions even in prey; and constitutional freedom from unaccountable money sequences overriding all else. As indigenous prophecy long ago counselled: "When all the trees have been cut down, when all the animals have disappeared, when all the waters have been polluted, you will discover that you cannot eat money".

The simplest framework of the general determinants of social health and disease, for McMurtry, has three parameters.

TABLE 7.16. NEWLY GLOBALLY RE-GENE-RATE CAPITAL AND VALUE:
Emancipatory Feminist Navigation: LIFE CAPITAL

Income Security: Continuity of Life Means to Members of Society: Deprivation of clean air and water or nourishing food or home always results in morbidity or disablement

Human Vocation – Contribution to Society: Each of its elements must contribute in some active way to the wellbeing of the interrelated whole

Sustaining the Life-Carrying Capacities of the Environmental Life-Host: the atmosphere, freshwater, oceans, top-soils, trees, animal habitats, species, mineral resources

Society's ill-being or well-being is determined by circumstances which select for life rather than death, for social life support systems rather than money-sequencing ones

---

Effect Global-Local Transformation Via Five Capital Assets

Anielski finally then, by way of our transformative effect, takes wellbeing economics further on, via his "Five Assets Capital Model".

Five Capital Assets Model

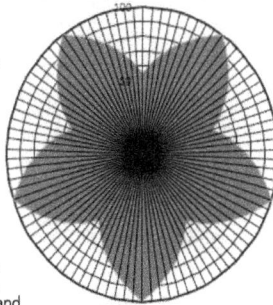

Financial Capital

Financial assets (Money, cash, stocks, bonds, derivatives), liabilities (debt) and equity.

Built Capital

Infrastructure, buildings, roads, houses, factories, machinery, equipment, and manufactured goods, and intellectual property (patents, copyright) that make up the material structure of society.

ASSET:
any tangible or intangible economic resource that is capable of being owned or controlled to produce value and that is held to have positive economic value.

Natural Capital

The land and natural resources, including soils, forests, water, air, and other species and life forms, and the services which the earth and its atmosphere provide, including ecological systems and life-support services.

Human Capital

Individual skills, education, knowledge , capabilities, and health (mental, physical, emotional and spiritual) of individuals that make up households, organizations and communities.

Social Capital

The web of interpersonal connections, relationships and networks, including trust, institutional arrangements, rules, and norms that facilitate human interactions. Also, the set of values, history, traditions and behaviours which link a specific group of people together.

FIGURE 7.3.   FIVE ASSETS CAPITAL MODEL

He proposes a new accounting system for measuring progress that integrates the five capital assets into an integral holistic system that tracks the physical and qualitative conditions of "well-being" of society or organisations. How would well-being metrics then work, how would they reduce risk and how can you gauge results? A well-being perspective and investment analytics, for Anielski then, would use the various well-being related forms of accounting for each of five classes of assets to both project and assess both progress, results and risks to the well-being of the five assets.

TABLE 7.17. GLOBALLY-LOCALLY RE-GENE-RATE CAPITAL AND VALUE: *Transformative Participatory Effect: FIVE CAPITALS ASSETS*
Natural capital: life forms and services the earth atmosphere provide, including ecological systems and life support services
Social capital: the web of interpersonal connections, relationships and networks, including the traditions and sets of values of a particular group
Human capital: individuals knowledge, skills, education, capabilities; health – mental, emotional, spiritual, physical – of people making up households, organisations, communities
Financial and Built Capital: financial assets, infrastructure and intellectual property, that make up the material structure of a society

For each asset class an assessment of trends in quantitative and qualitative well-being is made. Evaluation of the drivers of these trends and projections of future well-being conditions as well as Well-being Indices for each of the five assets is prepared to track progress. Furthermore, examination of the relationship between key human, social and natural capital asset well-being conditions and standard financial performance indicators is conducted to derive robust well-being ROI, ROA and ROE estimates. Each asset would be described in terms of how it is currently delivering well-being benefits as well as identified potential risk to assets attributed to current business practices and relationships the firm has with various stakeholders. These relational risks are important to manage to ensure long-range resiliency of the enterprise.

7.5. Conclusion: CIRD/A As a Whole

We have straddled the full spectrum of integral—now *Imvelean/ Afrikological* "newly global" worlds—now constituting CIRD/A, Centre for Integral Research and Development out of Africa. More specifically we have laid the *Nhakanomic* original "southern" Grounds; the *Indigenous Scientific* Emergent "south-eastern" foundation, the *Afrikological* emancipatory "north-south" Navigation; and finally the "south-western" transformative Effect, in terms of overall *Wellbeing/Health and Rejuvenation*. Moreover, in transforming economics into *oikonomics* we have drawn on not only economics' grounding, but also on emergent anthropology, biosemiotic navigation and transformative managerial effect.

CIRD-A then, whose first physical home will be at MSUAS (Manicaland State University for Applied Sciences) in the mystical and beautful Vumba mountains of Zimbabwe, will ultimately reach across, from "southern" to "east", to "north" and to "west" Africa, on the one hand, while reaching out "words-wide" on the other. Moreover, and in this MSUAS case, research faculty wise, Nhakanomics will be aligned with Agribusiness and Commerce; Indigenous Science with Engineering; Afrikology with Science and Technology; and Health and Rejuvenation with Applied Social Science. For Afrikology, as we will recall: *seeks to avoid any claim to an overarching epistemic superiority, but stands for plurality of epistemic directions.*

In Shona traditional philosophy, for Zimbabwean Professor of Literature Ruby Magoswongwe (55) the logic of being *munhu*/human being is labyrinthine with *Unhu*/ethics/morals/attitude to other people and life, rooted in belongingness with the land/*ivhu*/*dhaga*/soil. The essence of *munhu* is thus premised on both outward physical form and ethics, beliefs, values, and aesthetics as determined by society within its given geophysical land. At the same time, it is important to note that our CIRD/A is set alongside a Learning Community, Transformation Journey and Integral Laboratory. We now then turn, Laboratory-wise, to our specifically "southern", and generally integral, cases of economic re-GENE-ration, that is first to Sekem in Egypt and thereafter to our own (Anselm Adodo) Paxherbals in Nigeria.

7.6. References

1 **Nabudere** D (2011) *Afrikology: Philosophy and Wholeness: An Epistemology.* Pretoria. Africa Institute

2 **Bhengu** M (2014) *Amazulu: Ancient Egyptian Origin ; Spirits Beynd the Heavens.* Durban. Mepho Publishers

3 **Magosvongwe** R (2016) Shona Philsophy of Unhu/Hunhu and its Onamostics in Selected Fictional Narratives. *Journal of African Literature Association.* 10, 2, 158–175

4 **Lessem**, R & **Schieffer**, A (2010). *Integral Economics: Releasing the EconomicGenius of your Society.* Abingdon. Routledge

5 **Griaule M** and **Dieterlen** G (1986) *The Pale Fox.* Baltimore. African World Books

6 **Scranton** L (2002) *The Science of the Dogon: Decoding the African Mystery Tradition.* Vermont. Inner Traditions

7 **Chimakonam** J ed (2014) *Atuolu Omalu: Unanswered Questions in Contemporary African Philosophy.* Lanham. University Press of America

8 **Nkrumah** K (1996) *Consciencism: Philosophy and Ideology for De-Colonisation.* New York. Monthly Review Press

9 **Nyerere** J (1969) *Freedom and Unity. Essays on Socialism.* Dar es Salaam. Oxfod University Press

10 **Senghor** (1962) Nationhood and the African Road to Socialism. Paris. Presence Africaine

11 **Oduor** R et al (2018) *Odera Oruka in the 21ˢᵗ Century.* Vilnius. Lithuania. Council for Research in Values and Philosophy

12 **Serequeberhan** T (1994) *The Hermeneutics of African Philosophy – Horizon and Discourse.* Abingdon. Routledge

13 **Hountondji** P (2002) *The Struggle for Meaning.* Buckingham. Open University

14 Ngugi wa **Thiong'o** (2009) *Something Torn and New: An African Renaissance.* New York. Basic Civitas Publishing

15 **Asouzu** I (2007) *Ibuanyidanda: New Complementary Ontology.* Zurich. Lit Verlag

16 **Ozumba** G and **Chimakonam** J (2014) *Njikoka Amaka: The Philosophy of Integrative Humanism.* Calibar. Third Logic Option Publishing

17 **Lessem**, R & **Schieffer**, A (2010) *op cit*

18 **Rima**, I (2001). *The Development of Economic Analysis.* London: Routledge

19 **Lessem** R, **Mawere** M, **Matupire** P and **Zongolola** S (2019) *Integral Kumusha: Aligning Policonomy with Nature, Culure, Technology and Enteprise.* Mazvingo. Africa Talent Publishers

20 **Nhemachena** A (2017) Relationality and Resilience in a Not So Relational World: Knowledge, Chivanhu and (De)-coloniality in 21ˢᵗ Century Conflict-Torn Zimbabwe. Mankon. Bamenda. Langaa Research and Publishing

21 **Ingold** T (2011) *Being Alive: Essays on Movement, Knowledge and Description.* Abingdon. Routledge

22 **Gudeman** S (2001) *The Anthropology of Economy – Community, Market and Culture.* Chichester. Wiley-Blackwell

23 **Wheeler** W (2005) *The Whole Creature: Complexity, Biosemiotics and the Evolution of Culture*. London. Lawrence and Wishart

24 **Koopman** A (1991) *Transcultural Management*. Chichester. Wiley-Blackwell

25 **Lessem** R, **Mawere** M, **Matupire** P and **Zongololo** S (2019) *Integral Kumusha - Aligning Policonomy, Nature, Culture, Technology an Enterprise*. Mazvingo. Africa Talent Publishers

26 **Lessem** R, **Mawere** M, **Matupire** P and **Zongololo** S (2019) *op cit*

27 **Rima**, I (2001) *op cit*

28 **Saqib** A and **Malik** A (2018) *Integral Finance: The Case of Akhuwat as a Solidarity Economy*. Abingdon. Routledge

29 **Battle** M (2007) *Reconciliation: The Ubuntu Theology of Desmond Tutu*. Cleveland. Pilgrim Press

30 **Adodo** A (2020) *Nature Power: Natural Medecine in Tropical Africa*. Abingdon. Routledge

31 **De Gruchy** J (2000) *Reconciliation – Restoring Justice* Cape Town. SCM Press

32 **African Creation Energy** (2010) *The Science of Sciences and The Science in Sciences*. www.AfricanCreationEnergy.com

33 **Scranton** L (2017) *Seeking the Primordial: Exploring Root Concepts of Cosmic Creation*. New York. Self-Published

34 **Iqbal** M (2008) *The Reconstruction of Religious Thought in Islam*. New Delhi. Kitab Bhavan

35 **Khoza** R (2006) *Let Africa Lead: African Transformational Leadership for the 21st Century Business*. Johannesburg. Vezubuntu Press

36 **Nabudere** D (2011) *Afrikology: Philosophy and Wholeness: An Epistemology*. Pretoria. Africa Institute

37 **Unger** R (1987) *Social Theory: Its Situation and Task*. Cambridge. Cambridge University Press

38 **Rima** I (2001) *op cit*

39 **Unger** R (1987) *op cit*

40 **Bhengu** M (2014) *op cit*

41 **Bradley** T (2020) Semiotic Economics: the fourth way beyond neoliberalism, Chapter 7 in Bradley, T, Lessem R, Oshodi B and Malik A. *Islamic to Integral Finance*. Manchester. Beacon Academic

42 **Peirce**, C S 1904/1998, Vol 2 (Eds.). *The Essential Peirce - Peirce edition project*. Bloomington I.N.: Indiana University Press

43 **De Saussure** F (2013) *Course in General Linguistics*. London. Duckworth

44 **Hoffmeyer** J (2008) *Biosemiotics: An Examination into the Signs of Life and the Life of Signs*. Scranton. Scranton University Press

45 **Jung** C (1991) *The Archetypes and the Collective Unconscious*. Abingdon. Routledge

46 **von Uexkull** J (2010) *A Foray into the Worlds of Animals and Human: With a Theory of Meaning*. Minneapolis. University of Minnesota Press

47 **Unger** R (2018) The Knowledge Economy. London. Verso

48 **Anielski** M (2007) *The Economics of Happiness*. Gabriola Island. New Society Publishers

49 **Anielski** M (2017) *The Economy of Wellbeing. Commonsense Tools for Building Genuine Wealth and Happiness.* Gabriola Island. New Society Publishers

50 **Rima** I (2001) *op cit*

51 **Unger** R (1987) *op cit*

52 **Dellner** R (2020) *Integral Impact Investment.* Self-Published

53 **Lessem** R (1974) Accounting for an Enterprise's Wellbeing. *Omega Journal of International Management Science.* 2, 1, 77–95, February

54 **McMurtry** J (2013) *The Cancer of Capitalism: Crisis to Cure.* London. Pluto Press

55 **Magosvongwe** R (2016) *op cit*

PART FIVE

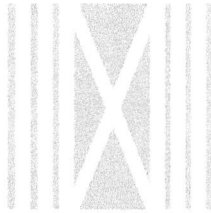

Global-Local
Transformative Effect

CHAPTER 8

Sekem: A Sustainable Community in the Desert

P. Maximilian Abou El Eisch-Boes

A new integral, sustainable enterprise design is desperately needed. A design of an enterprise, that is sustainably lodged in its society; an enterprise, that is not only focussing on its own economic progress, but also on its ecological, cultural, social and public impacts; an enterprise that is thereby ultimately contributing to the evolution of community and society as a whole. But we need to go even further. Even more important, a new educational approach is required, which embodies, teaches and evolves the new knowledge base that organizations and the people who run them, need.

Lessem and Schieffer (1) *Transformation Management: Toward the Integral Enterprise*

EFFECT TRANS4MATION: Social Innovation LABORATORY

- The Integral Enterprise develops organically over time and as a living organism goes through different dynamic maturation phases, from Pioneering to Association phase.
- Cultural, community/societal, economic and ecological life are the constituent spheres of life of an Integral Enterprise.
- The institutional ecosystem or structural world of an Integral Enterprise is highly differential giving a preliminary sense of order in the enterprise and serving different functions, for us community building, conscious evolution, knowledge creation and sustainable development.

- A clear long-term and inspirational vision for the community and society gives power through alignment and allows the Integral Enterprise to be purpose driven.
- Integrating all stakeholders along the value chain—from farmers to end-consumers—and entertaining a transparent dialogue on true costs and holistic value creation is the basis for an economic paradigm shift that can transform society.

8.1. Introduction: Transformation Journey

We now turn, subsequent to our integral "four world' centering, from local grounded origination (learning community—in ancient Egypt and Dogon country), and local-global foundation (transformation journey—via African Creation Energy and evolving African Philosophy), into newly global emancipation (CIRD/A) onto global-local transformational effect. In that guise, at the culmination of Trans4m's then (1) book *Transformation Management: Toward the Integral Enterprise*, Ronnie Lessem and Alexander Schieffer, co-founders of Trans4m (Geneva), concluded:

> From the very outset we have purposefully talked about transformation, not about change. We argued that mere change is not enough. We rather need to work towards a new organizational and societal form, within a specific cultural and communal context, where the formerly fragmented perspective of organization, self and society is altogether overcome. A merely economic perspective on organizations, and even on societies is still by and large the norm. All too often, for example, there is a tendency to use the terms economy and society even as equivalent terms, in which case we overlook the other equally important aspects of society, which are its environment (nature), its culture (civic sector), its public (political) sector and, of course, its economic (private) contexts. This general oversight is a clear expression of how imbalanced we have become, in defining ourselves, our organizations and societies in purely economic terms.
>
> In the beginning and throughout this book we have fundamentally challenged the prevailing monocultural (the west dominates), monodisciplinary (economics is key) and monosectoral (private sector leads) orientation of the current theory and practice of management, leadership and enterprise. It is high time that we develop a more integrated perspective, and we have shown here that it is not merely conceptual beauty that is driving us, but that there are farsighted organizations all over the world, that lead the way along such an integral path, and, by doing this, deliver extraordinary results.

This chapter focuses on one of two such major cases, this one in a North African context, namely the sustainable development initiative Sekem from Egypt. This initiative stands for a holistic approach to development that comprises elements from the societal, cultural, economic and ecological spheres of life, starting, as in the Pax Herbals case to follow, with nature. Sekem will not only be described from a functional perspective, shedding light on the different qualities of an Integral Enterprise (see *Transformation Management: Towards an Integral Enterprise,* above), but also reflect on the rhythm of social innovation, for us from Grounding to Effecting, and how Sekem releases individual, organisational and communal GENEius. Last but not least and applying Bernhard Lievegoed (2) and Friedrich Glasl's systemic evolutionary perspective on organisational development, the maturation process of Sekem as a living organism will be drawn upon in order to share with the reader the current climax of Sekem's vision-driven transformation journey that lays the ground for a new era of a globally emergent integral age.

8.2. Sekem – A Social Innovation for Sustainable Development

8.2.1. Historical Introduction of Sekem

In 1977, Dr. Ibrahim Abouleish started the Sekem Initiative on an untouched part of the Egyptian desert (70 hectares) 60 km northeast of Cairo. Using Biodynamic agricultural methods, desert land was revitalised and a striving agricultural business developed. But the vision of Ibrahim Abouleish (3) was far more than that:

> I carry a vision deep within myself: in the midst of sand and desert I see myself standing at a well drawing water. Carefully I plant trees, herbs and flowers and wet their roots with the precious drops. The cool well water attracts humans and animals to refresh and quicken themselves. Trees give shade, the land turns green, fragrant flowers bloom, insects, birds and butterflies show their devotion to God, the creator, as if they were citing the first Sura of the Koran. The humans, perceiving the hidden praise of God, care for and see all that is created as a reflection of paradise on earth. For me this idea of an oasis in the middle of a hostile environment is like an image of the resurrection at dawn after a long journey through the nightly desert. I saw it in front of me like a model before the actual work in Egypt started. And yet in reality I desired even more: I wanted the whole world to develop.

In 1990, Sekem encouraged the foundation of the Centre of Organic Agriculture in Egypt (COAE) as an independent certification body, working in accordance with Demeter guidelines and later the European Regulation for Organic Agriculture. Four years later, the Egyptian Biodynamic Association (EBDA) was founded as an independent non-governmental organisation to provide agricultural training and consultancy services in Egypt to more than 500 small scale farmers. Building on this ecological sphere is the basis for Sekem's value creation.

Between 1983 and 2008, Sekem established different companies in the sphere of economic life to produce seeds, plant and raise young fruits and vegetable plants (Mizan), as well as biological fertilisers and pest control (Predators) with the aim to reclaim and plant more than 2500 hectares in different parts of Egypt (Sekem for Land Reclamation), manage cattle and other farm animal produce (Libra), process and export herbs, seeds and spices (Lotus), launch product lines in the field of fresh vegetables, food and beverages, and herbal remedies for the local and international market (ATOS and ISIS), and manufacture organic cotton textiles, yarns and garments (Naturetex). With the added value from these products Sekem can finance its cultural and societal life.

An important base for its cultural life was founded in 1984 when the Sekem Development Foundation (SDF) was established that offers learning opportunities in the field of arts and science. In the following four years, the Sekem Kindergarten and the Mahad Adult Training Institute were opened and the Sekem School started with primary and secondary stages. Later up until the late 1990s, the SDF opened the Sekem Medical Centre, the Sekem Vocational Training Center (VTC), and a Literacy Program for disadvantaged children of the surrounding community. In 2000, the Sekem Academy for Applied Arts and Science was founded and started research in the fields of medicine, pharmacy, agriculture and arts. This work prepared the grounds for the inauguration and opening of the Heliopolis University for Sustainable Development in the year 2012—one year after the start of the Egyptian Revolution. The first three faculties were pharmacy, engineering and business and economics. In 2018, Heliopolis University (HU) opened the first faculty of organic agriculture in Egypt and the faculty of physical therapy.

All this development would not have been possible without a strong network of friends and partners in the societal sphere of life. Early in 1983, the German Sekem Friends Association was founded to support Sekem's cultural activities—other countries followed. From the business side, in 1996, together with its partners Sekem founded the International Association of Partnership for Ecology and Trade (IAP). Furthermore, in 2000, the Cooperative of Sekem Employees (CSE) was founded to foster employee relationships and basic human and labour rights. In 2003, Sekem received the Alternative Nobel Prize or Right Livelihood Award and Dr. Ibrahim Abouleish was selected as an "Outstanding Social Entrepreneur" by the Schwab Foundation. These events marked a breakthrough for Sekem to become internationally known and enter into a new phase of growth. In 2008, Sekem published its first Report on Sustainable Development to inform its stakeholders about its holistic impact.

In 2017, Sekem celebrated its 40 years of sustainable development and the 80th birthday of the founder Dr. Ibrahim Abouleish. In the same year, during the holy month of Ramadan, Ibrahim Abouleish passed away at the age of 80 leaving behind a legacy behind that many people consider as a "miracle in the desert". One year later, Sekem published its *Vision for 2057* as an outlook for the next 40 years and a roadmap for continuing the journey of social innovation and sustainable development.

A major event for Sekem's future happened recently in 2020, when the Sekem Future Council and Sekem Verwaltungsrat GmbH (to be turned into a charitable trust) were founded in Germany to form a legal vessel that holds the majority shares of Sekem in order to let Sekem be owned by itself and overseen by a council of people working and living in Sekem that keep its vision alive—independently of the dynamics inside the Abouleish family—which marks a major breakthrough of sustainable succession planning.

Now, after this general introduction, we will explore the different organs of Sekem as a living organism. In their book, Lievegoed and Glasl describe how organisations can be seen as such living systems that are able to self-develop, self-reflect, and self-organise through the interaction of people in the system. This view is consistent with Sekem's fourfold perspective on sustainable development: cultural, ecological, social and economic, which can be aligned with the thereby *integral* enterprise. Each of these presented subsystems of Sekem have their own dynamic when looking at it from an evolutionary perspective.

8.2.2. Sekem's Subsystems

The Cultural Subsystem of Sekem: Identity, Strategy and Programs

The identity of Sekem is grounded in the foundational impulse set by the founder Ibrahim Abouleish in 1977 when he decided to set a holistic development impulse for the cultural renewal of Egypt to confront the general environmental and social decay he faced. His vision was framed in a condensed form in order to guide the initiative and its people like a shining star constellation at the development horizon:

> Sustainable development towards a future where every human being can unfold his individual potential; where mankind lives together in social forms reflecting human dignity; and where all economic activity is conducted in accordance with ecological and ethical principles.

Derived from that vision and after Sekem's 40th anniversary and the passing away of Sekem founder Ibrahim Abouleish in 2017, the Sekem community further developed its vision, mission and goals for the coming 40 years. In total, 18 Sekem Vision Goals (SVG) have been formulated spanning over all four spheres of life (source). Below, a short overview of the thematic areas of the goals is presented:

Cultural Life	Ecologic Life
• SVG 1: Holistic Education and Potential Unfolding • SVG 2: Integral University Model • SVG 3: Holistic Research • SVG 4: Integrative Medicine • SVG 5: Living Arts and Culture	• SVG 6: 100% Organic Agriculture • SVG 7: Sustainable Water Management • SVG 8: 100% Renewable Energies • SVG 9: Rich and Resilient Biodiversity • SVG 10: Active Climate Change Mitigation • SVG 11: Zero Waste
Economic Life	Societal Life
• SVG 12: Circular Economy • SVG 13: Economy of Love • SVG 14: Ethical Finance • SVG 15: Sustainable Products and Services • SVG 16: Transport	• SVG 17: Organisational Development • SVG 18: Community Development

FIGURE 8.1. SEKEM VISION GOALS (SVGS) –
THEMATIC OVERVIEW (SOURCE: SEKEM INTERNAL)

By formulating its goals the Sekem leadership and community deliberately integrates the transformation of Egypt as a whole even if that seems to be a mission impossible from today's perspective. The reason is that societal transformation does not happen by building on the past but by also inviting the future.

With regards to its cultural subsystem the main challenge lies in understanding the complexity of the whole Sekem initiative. This is one reason why Sekem continuously invests in the development of consciousness of its people. What is very helpful to grasp the vision of Sekem are the weekly vision meetings where Sekem, SDF and HU co-workers and staff meet with Helmy Abouleish to discuss the vision or other related, contemporary issues. But of course, the bridge and implications for daily work life in all of the different institutions remain a challenge.

The Social Subsystem of Sekem: Organisational Structure, People and Functions

In its total composition the Sekem initiative is quite unique worldwide in the sense that it combines institutions from all four spheres of life under one umbrella, i.e. cultural, economic, societal, and ecological life.

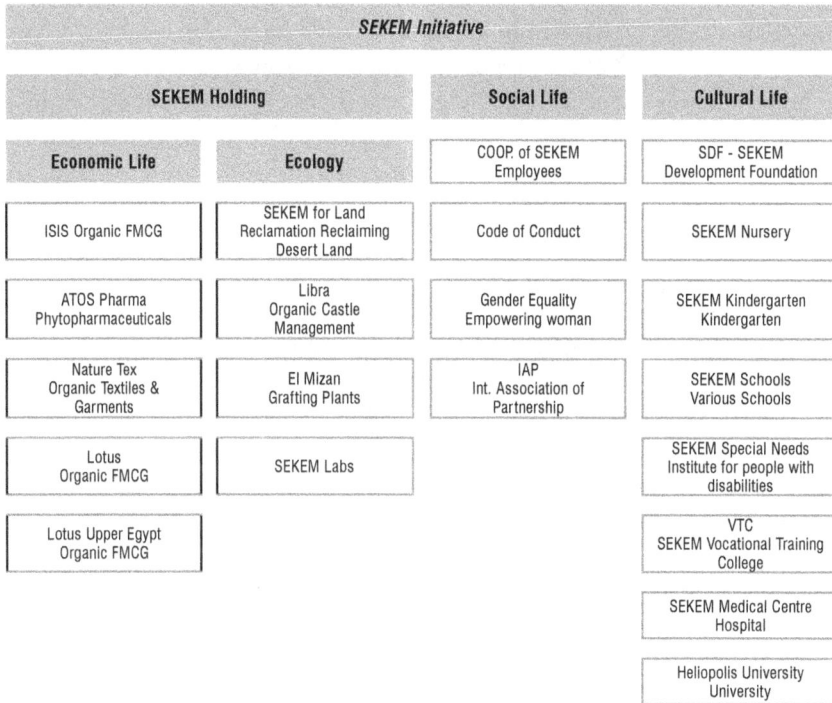

SEKEM Initiative			
SEKEM Holding		**Social Life**	**Cultural Life**
Economic Life	**Ecology**	COOP. of SEKEM Employees	SDF - SEKEM Development Foundation
ISIS Organic FMCG	SEKEM for Land Reclamation Reclaiming Desert Land	Code of Conduct	SEKEM Nursery
ATOS Pharma Phytopharmaceuticals	Libra Organic Castle Management	Gender Equality Empowering woman	SEKEM Kindergarten Kindergarten
Nature Tex Organic Textiles & Garments	El Mizan Grafting Plants	IAP Int. Association of Partnership	SEKEM Schools Various Schools
Lotus Organic FMCG	SEKEM Labs		SEKEM Special Needs Institute for people with disabilities
Lotus Upper Egypt Organic FMCG			VTC SEKEM Vocational Training College
			SEKEM Medical Centre Hospital
			Heliopolis University University

FIGURE 8.2. ORGANISATIONAL STRUCTURE OF SEKEM – INSTITUTIONAL DESIGN SOURCE

Sekem reaches out to large numbers of mainly rural people and their families, such as the supplying farmers, agricultural labourers, factory workers, administrative staff, specialists and people working in educational and academic life. Altogether, Sekem employs around 2000 people in its diverse institutions.

Knowledge and skills of the workforce vary according to their qualification. Most of the daily workers and employed agricultural labourers have a very basic educational level. Specialists have a formal education or even university degree but their level of knowledge and skills allows them rather to take responsibility on routine tasks with short time horizons. The educational level and problem solving capacity of the middle management varies and partially depends strongly on a hands-on management approach by top management. The senior management has adequate knowledge and skills and is often supported by monetary incentives but there is often more room to increase ownership and responsibility. Helmy Abouleish, as the top leader of Sekem, stresses the fact that he wants to see more entrepreneurial thinking and initiative by people who have higher management positions or that are a part of Sekem's Future Council. His affinity to the economic sphere and output orientation can be felt quite easily.

Sekem in general has within its subsidiaries all classical management functions according to Western standards with adaptations to the respective industry. Furthermore, Sekem Holding comes across with some major support functions, such as Communications, Sustainable Development, Finance and Quality Assurance to support the subsidiaries and implement cross-company projects. The main coordination mechanism inside the companies relies mainly on classical command-and-control mechanisms as well as management by objective techniques within the top-down hierarchy mixed.

With regard to Sekem's social subsystem one can highlight the complex organisational structure that comprises institutions from all four dimensions of sustainable development. It is striking that the majority of Sekem employees, as well as management functions are held by Egyptians, whereas "key protagonists" of the Sekem story, besides the Abouleish family, are the German-speaking core community who are mainly acting as catalysts in different roles that are not "visible" in the formal organisational charts. Recent organisational development efforts try to make these roles more explicit.

As mentioned before, the Sekem Future Council was established to build a vessel for committed community members that work and live at Sekem, regardless of age, nationality, religion or gender, to take responsibility for and keep the Sekem vision alive.

The Technical-Instrumental Subsystem of Sekem: Processes/Physical-Material Resources

Currently, Sekem, not unlike Pax Herbals, as we shall see in the next chapter, sources its supply from a pool of more than 120 contracted supplier entities, located throughout the Delta, the Nile valley and the Bahariya Oasis. Most supplier entities subcontract (formally or informally) a wider group of farmers, including sharecroppers (potentially as many as 500 farmers). Sekem provides their suppliers with inputs (such as compost or biodynamic preparations) and knowledge, offers pre-financing for their activities on a seasonal basis and a buying guarantee for the pre-financed harvest.

The dominant planning process for the diverse institutions under the Sekem umbrella is done via the annual financial budgeting that is finalized and approved in November of each year by the board of directors. Over the course of the year the budget is reviewed quarterly and eventually updated. This also shows the strong Western influence and dominance of the economic sphere even though the counter-balance comes in via the holistic Sekem Vision Goal portfolio that generates objectives and activities in all spheres of life.

One important issue with regard to Sekem's technical-instrumental sub-system is the risky and challenging financial situation and economic pressure that resulted from external economic shocks, such as severe local currency de-valuations and a long-time prevailing mismatch of short- to medium-term financing of long-term desert reclamation activities. The fact is that Sekem, like all other private and civic institutions in Egypt, over the course of the last decade, has been exposed to severe societal and economic crisis and challenges, from the last two waves of Egyptian revolution and the prevailing regional political instability, to the recent global pandemic of COVID-19. This keeps the prevailing climate of crisis management quite dominant and is one reason for the very powerful decision-making power of Helmy Abouleish across all Sekem institutions.

Despite the difficult recent times and with the help of strong partners Sekem managed to open the doors of Heliopolis University for Sustainable Development. It was like an expanding shining light in a period of darkness and contraction to invest in the future of young people and their potential un-folding. Furthermore, and despite severe debt imbalances, Sekem recently and successfully launched an incredible crowd-funding campaign that led to the reclamation of new desert land and the social and cultural development of one of Sekem's desert farms in Bahariya. In 2020, the first families moved to this farm to enliven the momentum of sustainable community development in the desert and show the replicability of Sekem's success story at its mother farm. It is again the momentum of engaging purposefully in a mission impossible that makes Sekem what it is today. It also reflects the power of African Creation Energy (see chapter 4) coming out of the visionary pioneer spirit that we will explore in the next part.

8.2.3. Sekem's Stages of Development

Sekem's Pioneering Phase

Dutch organisational psychologist Bernard Lievegoed, already referred to above, originally published his book on 'The Developing Organisation' in English three decades ago, introducing three organisational development phases (Pioneering, Differentiation and Integration). Later on, his concept was further developed by his colleague Friedrich Glasl (who added the Association phase). Lievegoed and Glasl's concept of the evolution of social systems is comparable to the growth, maturation, and development process of living organisms with their vitality, growth and structure building phases.

The strong vision, as one central element, is characteristic of the pioneering phase of an organisation. At the beginning, when Ibrahim chose a piece of desert land and started to reclaim the dead sand with compost for cultivating trees and crops, people did not believe in his vision. This vision is the anchor, the permanent source to which the Sekem impulse is connected to. But is it only his vision?

Ibrahim's role was marked by a very autocratic leadership style, which is normal for the pioneering phase. The risk lies in the fact that such a strong leadership, which is also perpetuated by his son Helmy also suppresses other voices that identify and contribute to the vision. Nevertheless, the autocratic leadership style is part of Sekem's success because by giving strong direction and exercising strong control Sekem could develop very quickly. As we will see, in the future it will be more and more important for Sekem's evolution to harvest all voices as relevant for managing continuous improvement and dealing with complex challenges.

It has to be acknowledged that strong leaders and direct communication with the leader, instead of relying on impersonal management systems, are typical for the local context also in light of Egypt's history. Not only in times of the pharaohs, but also during the millennia of diverse external powers that ruled Egypt, up to today's military regime and powerful president, a powerful leader seems to be an adequate response to the prevailing consciousness level of people.

Interestingly enough, moreover, the more nuanced approach to thereby allegedly matriarchal-partriarchal pharaonic leadership, as revealed in our chapter 2, on local grounding and origination in *Kemet*, has been lost to Egyptian, and indeed worlds-wide, posterity. At the same time, Africa's overall historical positioning, as home to such matriarchy, is equally lost, together with, explicitly, the African Creation Energy (our chapter 4) that goes with it. That said, of course, the "vital force" (our chapter 3) that is Africa's birth right, is embodied in the very being of Sekem (indigenous meaning: "vitality of the sun") and in the Abouleishs in and of themselves.

In the best case then, and aside from the above, and in light of the strong local patriarchal culture the leader is like a benevolent father figure that keeps the family together. Indeed, co-workers of Sekem describe this quality when they talk about Ibrahim Abouleish with his ability to really touch people's hearts while still being known for his strong and impulsive temperament. For most of the co-workers and community members Sekem is like a big family and this is also symbolised by the many circles where everybody is standing next to each other.

Summing up and taking a critical perspective on the situation one could say that Sekem has a very powerful leadership, as indeed a vital force, that is capable of initiating miracles in the Egyptian desert but the more complex the living organism Sekem gets the more difficult it will become for the single leader to find sustainable solutions and get out of a prevailing mode of crisis management, whereby the *vitality* will need to become more widely recognised and released, arguably in an all-round Afrikological guise. Like every phase this one also comes with its own challenges and it is the reason why Sekem started to further develop and differentiate itself.

Sekem's Second Phase of Differentiation

The logical answer to the problems of the pioneering phase is scientific management. This philosophy of corporate management was mainly founded by two successful engineers, US American Frederick. Taylor (4), and French Henri Fayol (5).

Mechanization and automation are central elements of this next phase of differentiation. In general Sekem's operations, especially the agricultural production processes are relatively labour intensive. The idea of mechanization is welcomed but some technology transfer projects show also the difficulties and limits to apply automation with the existing infrastructure and farm management capacity. On the industry side Sekem has significantly increased mechanization over the last decades as can be seen in the fact that Sekem produces more than 3.5 million tea bags per day.

Another element of the differentiation phase is standardization which comes with unification and exchangeability. This mainly came when Sekem adopted a diverse range of ISO standards, like a formal quality management system, driven by the requirements of international customers.

The principle of coordination counteracts the diverting forces of differentiation. All the manifold and diverse activities created by differentiation need to be pulled together. Coordination at Sekem is on the one hand reached by the unity of leadership, i.e. higher hierarchy levels direct lower ones inside one function. An exception comes through Abouleish family members or foreign core community members that are respected in a way that orders might come from outside the hierarchy system, which happens quite frequently. Due to their informal nature these situations bear potential for irritation. On the other hand coordination happens through a control span where at Sekem all managers have roughly 6–8 subordinates, which is a healthy level for keeping the overview. The exception comes through Helmy Abouleish who directly supervises and directs more than 20 people and keeps the control of many domains. This phenomenon is typical and stems from the fact that the pioneering leader with his overview is often in a better position to make adequate judgements.

Additionally, the bureaucratic organisation is not flexible enough to react swiftly to dynamic market or society changes. This is often compensated by a strong leadership impulse that overruns formal hierarchies. The risk is a decrease in motivation and personal productivity. One of the most obvious reasons for the loss of motivation is that people, who are not involved in decision making, lose ownership of the decision. The need for strong and charismatic leaders becomes apparent but the system produces less and less top-managers because the hierarchical silo system is creating too many specialists with no sense of overview—a vicious cycle that Sekem also has to deal with.

In the differentiation phase alignment happens through formalization of behaviour and relationships (see ISO management). The informal, and people-oriented pioneering style is continuing to live for a while to compensate for the negative sides of the differentiation phase. To some extent, according to Lievegoed, the informal organisation from the end of the pioneering phase that has been pushed to the underground is making the formal organisation possible. Still, personal relationships play a very important role in getting work done at Sekem. Today these informal non-structured communication flows bear the risk that only those who know "how it works" can be effective.

Given these problems of the differentiation phase and the challenges on the macro-economic and organisational level it is understandable that it is difficult to boldly enter another development phase, which would require an extra amount of focus and energy that may not have been a priority of recent years. But the transformational journey of Sekem is continuing and some clear signs of the next phase of maturation can already be seen.

Sekem's Third Phase of Integration

With the integration phase the focus lies on flourishing the cultural subsystem of the organisation, i.e. the vision, identity and strategy, etc. must not be exclusively owned by the top leaders but instead owned collectively by the employees. Through that the existing social subsystem (of the pioneering phase) and technical-instrumental subsystems (of the differentiation phase) can reach another level of synergy (which is the reason why it is called "Integration" phase). This can only be reached if an integrated entrepreneurship mentality of all employees is supported and awakened with an alignment towards the organisational goals, i.e. in the form of "intrapreneurship" (6). The collective process of setting up a roadmap towards the Sekem Vision Goals can be seen in such a light.

Grasping the complexity of a 40 years journey ahead is of course difficult given the different consciousness levels of Sekem's co-workers and community members. But the notion of "intrapreneurship" does not necessarily need to embrace high levels of complexity but rather awaken the initiative within people to take responsibility for something to overcome challenges. This is why human development is so important and taking initiative is taught in so many different artistic and creative ways when it comes to Sekem's Core Program—a central pillar of Sekem's cultural life to be described in more detail below.

But human development must not be limited to special time and spaces besides the normal work in order to unleash the potential of the integral phase. Profound human development must assure that the newly gained responsibilities are constantly carried into changing situations. It should be the aim that individuals and groups, to a certain extent, are responsible for parts of the planning.

Consequently, there shouldn't be "one-best-way" prescriptions but target commitments that leave room for own initiatives and more participation. That is not yet the case at Sekem because the top-management defines how things are done. In addition to that, there is not yet a human development department or circle in place that could support this process in the quality needed. Sekem has had many "human resource" or human development managers over the last decade—not one of them stayed. This can be seen as a misfit between the people filling the role and the leadership's understanding of how human development should work. Despite the above mentioned difficulties, Sekem's leadership still ensures that the unique human development efforts in the field of arts and cultural programs and meetings are delivered to the employees.

Another paradigm shift of the integral phase is a shift from a vertical towards a horizontal orientation. This means that employees rather focus on external or internal clients and suppliers and the process instead of the manager. A common interest must be developed to maintain an optimal work-flow within the limits of guidelines and principles and the general planning frame. Management development and job enrichment are a common practice that support human capacity building within the organisation. Continuous renewal of products, market, structures, process, etc. shape an organisation that is becoming a learning system. This is what Sekem claims to be: A big school of life.

All the mentioned elements of the Integration phase can only be achieved if there is a fundamental mentality shift from the current leaders and top management. To realise the integration of the cultural, technical-instrumental, and social subsystem a new organisational structure is required that differs significantly from those of the previous two phases. The pioneering phase was characterised by a flat, broad organisational structure. The differentiation phase built the deep, pyramid-like form with constituting and controlling leadership. The third phase anticipates the concept of what Lievegoed terms a "process organisation". The core idea is that all primary, supportive and leadership processes are directed towards satisfying customer needs.

Top management is not at the top of the pyramid anymore but is situated at the crossroad of all information and communication flows. The task of the top management is to create goals for the entire system and to integrate the process-flows via necessary tools and a swift information system. The leadership style towards middle and lower management shifts away from the previous mode of command-and-control towards stimulating people to ask questions, build judgements, and take initiatives.

Since 2015, Sekem has experimented with Holacracy (7) as a system for self-organisation. This implies a critical reflection on structures and governance systems and their ability to serve Sekem's purpose. New meeting formats are introduced to inform and synchronize people's work and a radical responsibility is put towards people to feel responsible for any sort of tension they feel. Furthermore, after a year of experimentation, Sekem's top management decided recently to use a digital platform for collaboration and project management to build up a trusted system across all Sekem institutions for transparency and accountability—a crucial foundation for this phase of development.

Through this development the affected people will develop capacities that are needed to cope with the new situations. The leaders that fit future situations will naturally emerge during the change process because they recognise that their engagement is honoured with more responsibility. This is exactly what happens with people living and working among the Sekem community.

To further cultivate that new culture, Sekem has created a special journey for Transformation Agents who aim to have a positive impact on society and support SEKEM to be a driving motor for sustainable development in Egypt and the world. This journey takes from 6–12 months and is designed around a specific rhythm mirroring the different qualities needed to initiate change and social innovation (as depicted also in the design of the Integral Enterprise described below).

Starting with a *Grounding* phase—see Schieffer and Lessem's (8) *Integral Development*—the Transformation Agent lands in SEKEM and gets to know the people and environment. It is important to identify the individual call from the agent as well as the collective call of Sekem and society that requires the support of the agent. In the *Emerging* phase the Transformation Agent understands deeper the local context and cultural realm in order to see the bigger picture and get inspiration for new solutions. Arts and the Sekem Core Program play an important role to widen consciousness and stimulate creativity. During this phase an innovation ecosystem of people is built around the agent to co-create solutions for the burning issues at hand and prepare him/her for the next phase.

In the *Navigation* phase, together with the innovation ecosystem, a solution is designed and necessary research is done for building new knowledge and to adapt solutions to the local context. The different research faculties of Heliopolis University play an important role in that time. Last but not least, the Transformation Agent has impact through the *Effecting* phase, i.e. implementing solutions together with SEKEM's different organisations. To support the Transformation Agent a double coaching system with a community coach and work lead is created to assure sufficient guidance and reflection time.

As the reader can feel the integral phase in essence can free evolutionary forces that will drive organisation and community development, which then naturally leads towards the next phase.

Sekem's Fourth Phase of Association

In light of the prevailing social and environmental crisis Egypt is facing a fourth development phase (9) comes into play that is already alive at Sekem. This phase is about the phenomenon that companies or organisations open up for macro-economic, macro-societal, and macro-cultural and ecological problems. Glasl describes this fourth phase as the Association phase because the openness to the diverse company environments implies new forms of cooperation, support, alliances etc. In fact, and Afrikologically for us, this may serve as a contemporary evolution of the ancient Egyptian (see Kemet, chapter 2) motion of *maat*, or dynamic balance, fused together with Sekem as a *vital force*.

In its Association phase Sekem directs its core function towards the associative integration of its environment so that it can cope with the diverse interests in a proactive, anticipating dialogue of partnership and take binding decisions to resolve social and ecological tensions. Information exchange and problem-solving with regard to the critical questions of the environment must become a core task of leadership, which is reflected on the core business of Sekem. Instead of the dominance of a single company, ways need to be found to deal constructively with the mutual dependencies of all related entities. Through this wide network groups are created that Glasl calls "company biotopes". As in nature where different living beings depend on and sustain each other, companies as independent organisms join each other to form loosely coupled social-ecological entities. In the context of Sekem it means if our farmers cannot strive and develop we cannot satisfy the needs of our customers in the future.

The intention for Sekem's Association phase lies in building trustful, long-term partnerships that foresee a continuous balance (i.e. *maat*) of interests, i.e. profit sharing, cross-ownership, that makes an integrated value chain possible. Under the Sekem umbrella already the biggest part of value creation is represented by a group of associative companies that help each other in times of problems, share resources, and also use the organic waste as further input for compost. The development challenge now lies in the need to shift away the functioning of this organisation, biotope, from being dependent on one leader to being carried by the social system and its people. This transition is a crucial task of the Sekem Future Council.

Summing up we can say that Sekem has already reached in some respects the Integral and Associative phase. The more we enter these two phases the more flourishing the Sekem organism will develop and become more and more a true Integral Enterprise. We will open this section then with Ibrahim's (my Egyptian grandfather) own words.

8.3. SEKEM as an Integral Enterprise

8.3.1. Grounding of Sekem in Nature and Community

> After arriving in Egypt I went to see the Ministry of Agriculture, and told them I was looking for a patch of desert, which I wanted to cultivate using organic methods. I was shown a patch in Belbeis, where the quality of ground was very bad and water supply difficult, but I knew I wanted it. If biodynamic farming could thrive in this wasteland, then it would be possible to transfer this model to easier environments. So I bought the land and moved over, leaving my family behind in Cairo. Most of the time I was alone, with only now and then a Bedouin with goats wandering over. They could not understand my idea, but they saw it develop before their eyes.

Starting with biodynamic agriculture methods in the midst of the Egyptian desert is a strong image that stands literally for a grounding in nature. The fact that the intention behind Ibrahim's vision was to set an impulse for the cultural renewal of back then war-shaken Egypt also highlights the aspect of community and human development at the core of Sekem. From a social innovation rhythm perspective it is important to realise that Sekem is by design and intention confronted with all major burning issues of Egypt—water scarcity, food security, education quality, climate change, and many more—and lives the narrative of struggle and pain from Egypt's rural population and farmers. Right from that harsh reality Sekem reaches out for claiming authorship for writing a new story for sustainable development that is born locally and starts with reclaiming land together with nature and not against it. This is also a fundamental principle reflected in the Islamic belief, which led Ibrahim Abouleish to be able to connect on a deep level with the local people and build up a relationship of trust.

> Allah says in Islam that the earth and the ground are only given to us to take care of. He alone owns the ground. It is the same with capital; we can only manage it for the good of the people. He says that whoever enters into trade works together with Allah and, following his principles, should give the proceeds to the poor. In the light of such I consider modern joint stock companies to be dysfunctional, as they act as if God's legacy was their own. The interest and the riches they receive are not their own achievement, because even intelligence and abilities are the gifts of Allah.

Another important element of *Grounding* comes with the strong connection that Sekem has—at least on a formal level—by the many company names relating to the ancient Egyptian pantheon. Furthermore, Ibrahim Abouleish embodied that Egyptianess that is so keen for us to be reclaimed and explicitly built upon:

> Dr. Ibrahim Abouleish pointed to the goddess Maat when he described the integration of all four spheres of life, which for him was expressed in the four leaves of the Sustainability Flower. In almost every lecture and speech that he gave he drew a picture of the ever unfolding four dimensions of life, and he always emphasised the importance of keeping everything in balance.
>
> Another illustration of this important link between ancient Egypt and Sekem's unfolding story is the Egyptian god Thoth, son of the creator god Ra and husband of the goddess Maat, who was credited by the ancient Egyptians as the inventor of writing and associated with wisdom. Later, the Greeks related Thoth to their god Hermes and one of Thoth's titles, The Thrice Great, was translated to the Greek τρισμέγιστος (trismégistos), making Hermes Trismegistus. Many Western esoteric traditions, such as Anthroposophy, were greatly influenced by the writings of Hermes Trismegistus and the knowledge field called after him, Hermetism. Here we can see (...) [how] the rich influence that Anthroposophy has on Sekem is ultimately rooted in ancient Egypt, i.e. a development impulse returning back to its origin.

After connecting to local nature and community, Islam and Ancient Egypt, we are ready to explore the global, the European/Western impulse, namely Anthroposophy, that Ibrahim Abouleish met early in his adulthood and which marks a central source of inspiration for him and Sekem.

8.3.2. Emerging of Sekem through Culture and Spirituality

> During my initial years in Austria I had absorbed much of European culture. Through this crosscultural exchange I could perceive my own roots, as well as Islam, from a totally different perspective. This kindled the first flame of my vision. (...) Somebody looking into my soul would have seen anything "Egyptian" left completely behind, so I could absorb everything new. Because of my childhood and adolescent grounding, though, in Egyptian culture, I could not leave such entirely behind. I now existed in two worlds, both of which were essentially different: the oriental, spiritual stream I was born into and the European, which I felt was my chosen course. But I was neither Egyptian nor European.

In essence, Ibrahim Abouleish embodied a synthesis of both cultures—the occident and the orient—and this fertile fusion of different streams marks the emergence of Sekem in its development path. The quality of emerging in light of giving birth to a social innovation is linked to creating new awareness and a balanced perspective on the burning issues from the grounding phase. Ibrahim Abouleish took his inspiration from Rudolf Steiner, especially biodynamic agriculture, that, like all anthroposophical disciplines, builds on a human centered worldview that has an evolutionary perspective on consciousness: Humankind as well as potentially every human being goes through a journey of (emerging) consciousness. This puts human potential unfolding at the core of our work at Sekem.

> People did not come here, of course, and fall in love with it straight away. It took time. Now they feel a sense of belonging. They are being taken care of, they eat together, they watch their children learn and play. This is a model for a society. It is sustainable and feeds itself. As Goethe wrote: "Neither time nor any power destroys forms, which develop in a living way." People become so caught up with the pace of city life that they forget to absorb the sounds, the smells and colours of the earth. Sekem has an orchestra and books to read. (...) Being an Islamic initiative, Sekem follows the principles of "learning by working and working by learning", and puts the social community at the centre of its actions.

As we can see today Sekem is a community for people of all walks of life. The fact that it was built literally on the borders of civil society, the desert, helped to make it become a microcosm of society combining all spheres of life. There was no infrastructure, no energy, no water, nothing. It took a strong visionary leader that kept the vision of this land close to his heart and started reclaiming and greening it, and people started coming. Over the decades, Sekem has grown organically and today stands as an institutional ecosystem for social innovation and cultural renewal—something we will explore in the next section.

8.3.3. Navigation of Sekem through an Institutional (Social) Innovation Ecosystem

The university, that is Heliopolis University for Sustainable Development, stands for the centre of new knowledge creation with currently five faculties: Business and Economics, Engineering, Organic Agriculture, Pharmacy and Physical Therapy. Students and faculty are simultaneously exposed to a humanistic core program, focusing on the inner development of the individual self in the context of group and community, and to initial specialists programs—on sustainable approaches to each of the faculty areas above. Learners and researchers, individually and collectively, are supposed to make a tangible outer contribution in their particular field, thereby engaging in the sustainable development of Egypt as a whole.

This is achieved through its enriched educational curricula as well as learning and research processes, that shall interactively link students to four interconnected areas, evolved out of the integral approach:

- Context: Engaging with relevant context
- Consciousness: Raising of human consciousness
- Content: Assimilating inspiring content
- Contribution: Making a significant contribution

The university as a whole becomes thereby fully embedded in society, dealing concretely with its most burning socio-economic issues and innovating viable sustainable futures. During recent years, several centres have formed inside the university to act as a transdisciplinary platform combining the knowledge and motivation of students and academic staff to deal with challenges of Egypt and the surrounding communities as well as Sekem's operations and network of farmers:

- The HU Carbon Footprint Center offers services to organisations to make carbon footprint reports and helps to offset emissions through local, accredited carbon sequestration activities in cooperation with Sekem.

- The HU Center for Education for Sustainable Development was born out of the effort to orient existing curricula from schools and universities of different disciplines toward relevant sustainable development related topics. Furthermore, it offers training to teachers, academic staff and students along the multidisciplinary dimensions of the core program.
- The HU Rural Development Center is engaged with a revival of the so-called 13 villages project that aims to develop and inspire the villages and people around Sekem in the rural governorate of Sherkeya towards themes of holistic education, zero waste management, renewable energy, organic agriculture, entrepreneurship etc.
- The HU Desert Research Center is born out of the needs and questions arising from Sekem's desert land reclamation activities on several remote desert farms, particularly the one in the Western desert near the oasis of Bahariya. There, Sekem is committed to reclaim more than 1000 hectares and plant one million trees in order to create a base for a living and striving community.

On an institutional level, Sekem has developed into a wider ecosystem for social innovation. Sekem as a whole can be seen as a laboratory for transformation on the individual, organisational and societal level. After a pioneering phase at the beginning and growth phase during the last decade Sekem wants to engage in deeply understanding and sharing the knowledge about itself and its integral nature and rhythm to become a model. Compiling a yearly, integrated report is one way to do so but by far not enough. Supporting Sekem's efforts towards a future oriented and transparent governance structure as well as framing a new paradigm for an economic system underlying the Sekem model is another outcome Sekem's leadership is working towards. Recently, Sekem launched a new standard named "Economy of Love" in order to make Sekem's approach to value creation more understandable to partners and final consumers.

8.3.4. Effecting via "Economy of Love"

Overall then, as such Sekem declares, here informed by Rudolf Steiner's (10) so-called cultural, socio-political and economic Threefold Commonwealth:

- We build our cultural, social and economic activities to invigorate each other.
- We intend to restore the earth through implementing and developing biodynamic agriculture.

- We want to provide products and services of the highest standards to meet the needs of the consumer.

The intertwined natural and economic realms of activity within Sekem's group of companies begin on a practical level, as we have seen, by healing the soil through the application of biodynamic farming methods. Through this method, it has raw material at its disposal and is able to develop and manufacture natural medicine and a wide range of other products. It always adheres to the highest possible quality standards, which conform to the true needs of its consumers. In partnership with its friends and colleagues in Europe and its local partners in trade, Sekem strives to market its products, moreover, employing what it calls the "economics of love". Again on its current website, Sekem claims:

> With the term "Economy of Love" Sekem expresses that it is not only about gaining the highest possible profit when cooperating with business partners, but more about social and respectful dealing with each other.

Furthermore, the team around Economy of Love that developed a tracing tool for making the holistic impact of products to society visible explains:

> To date, you can hardly find a transparent and sustainable value chain that fully recognises ecological and social standards. We believe that the mature client, the responsible client, actually doesn't want to "destroy the world". However, there is a lack of information on the environmental compatibility of all stages of the value chain. Furthermore, the client is not made aware of the social impact and the promotion of the individual development of all those involved in the production of a product. Therefore, a truly responsible decision is made impossible. We ensure that the consumer can enjoy a healthy high-quality product with a colorful cultural and eco-friendly background. Therefore we make every step, from field to shelf, visible. This will empower making a difference by a conscious product choice.

The inter-institutional ecology of Sekem and the different types of academies according to Lessem (11) are the driving force behind the continuous development and implementation of the above. Figure 8.3. depicts the ideal structure of such an inter-institutional ecology at Sekem.

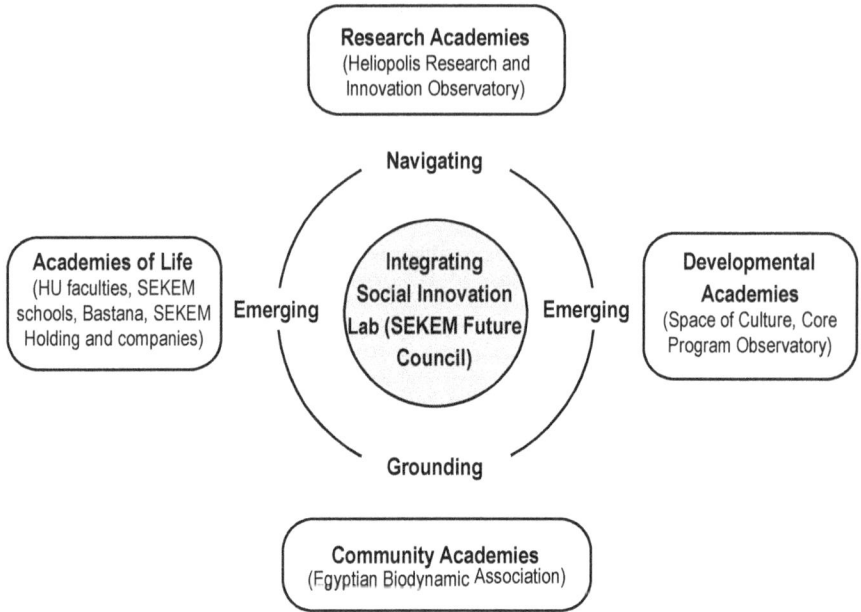

FIGURE 8.3. OVERVIEW OF SEKEM'S INTER-INSTITUTIONAL ECOLOGY
Source: Adapted by the author from Lessem (2017c)

Accordingly, Sekem's Social Innovation Laboratory as a whole consists of:

- A Community Academy (South) for institutionalized community activation is embodied by Sekem's supplying farmers, namely the Egyptian Biodynamic Association (EBDA).
- A Developmental Academy (East) for awakened integral consciousness applied to enterprise, economy and development, is represented by the Space of Culture at HU.
- A Research Academy (North) for innovation driven, institutionalized research, is formed by the HU faculties and the Core Program.
- An Academy of Life (West) for fully embodied integral development, is represented by the Sekem schools, Bastana (an informal environmental learning space for youth), as well as the educational programs at HU.
- The Sekem Future Council is an important entity to drive the overall integration of all the different academies (Centre). By doing so, the Future Council will reflect the quality of the GENE-rhythm, enabling Sekem's inter-institutional ecology to research, innovate and develop together.

Thereby, the Sekem Future Council can be seen as the locus of the liberation struggle from Sekem to fully arrive at its integral phase and become an Integral Enterprise.

8.4. Conclusion: Sekem as a Model for an Integral Enterprise that Develops Self and Community

When Trans4m, Ronnie Lessem and Alexander Schieffer, met Sekem's founder Ibrahim Abouleish for the first time, in 2007, in Egypt he talked about the enormous achievements of his enterprise and his people and he shared his frustration, that while many admire what Sekem has realised over the years, hardly anyone understands the processes the organisation went through to ultimately reach its current stage. His frustration was directed in two directions: on the one hand, he claimed that without understanding the deeper processes behind the transformational journey of Sekem, any attempt to create a second Sekem, will be a futile imitation, not an impactful origination. On the other hand, Abouleish feared that if the deeper meaning of the Sekem story is not understood within the organisation itself, then its own sustainability is endangered.

These ambiguous feelings of Abouleish underline what we have come to learn in our work: Each social innovator, in his or her attempt to create an Integral Enterprise needs to go his or her own, unique path. Such a unique path needs to release the particular gene-ius of the individual, community, culture and society in which any new enterprise is lodged.

If you are committed to engage in transforming your own organisation into an Integral Enterprise, you will need to identify and pursue your and your organisation's as well as your society's unique path. The pioneering work of an Ibrahim Abouleish from Sekem in Egypt, as such, is an extremely useful signpost. They help us to understand the core elements of the fundamentals of Transformation Management. But ultimately each agent of transformation needs to undertake the journey her- or himself. It is the journey of:

- rediscovering and assimilating the transformational flows of nature and community, thereby regrounding your enterprise in society,
- engaging with the transcultural forces of culture and consciousness, thereby enabling your self, enterprise and community to renew itself,
- creating new knowledge, thereby contributing to the transdisciplinary fields of science and technology, and ultimately,
- aligning self, organisation and society through transpersonal functions, to bring about Integral Innovation, through community building conscious evolution, knowledge creation and sustainable development.

With a view to such, in conclusion, Sekem is a unique example of ultimately global-local transformative effect, emerging out of local, desert grounds, emerging locally-globally across Africa and Europe, thereafter navigating "newly globally" through the "economics of love". Specifically then, and Afrikologically, taking on ubuntu-wise biodynamically leading, the now worldwide, thereby global, anthroposophical European movement, applied locally in Egypt. Indeed then, specifically, taking on from where Mfuniselwa Bhengu (12) has left off (see in chapter 6, his Amazulu: Ancient Egyptian Origin – Spirits Beyond the Heavens) Egyptian "maat" become African "ubuntu"—I am because you are—turning now into "economics of love".

In its essence then, Sekem is entering into a new phase of becoming a model for transformation, an Afrikological vehicle for change, lodged in Africa's North, reaching down to the South, and across to the East and West, reconnecting with ancient Egypt as the crossroads of civilizations. In other words, by allowing these worlds to have a closer look on how sustainable and holistic development can be framed and practically implemented it is even more important to purposefully reconnect to cultural roots and heritage. What remains then, as such an integral enterprise evolves locally, locally-globally, globally-locally, as well as "newly globally" in between, now follows, in Nigeria's local Pax Herbals, and thereby, as we shall see, "newly global" Pax Africana.

8.5. References

1 **Lessem** R and **Schieffer** A (2009) *Transformation Management: Toward the Integral Enterprise.* Abingdon. Routledge
2 **Lievegoed** B (1991) *The Developing Organization.* Chichester. Wiley-Blackwell
3 **Abouleish** I (2005) *Sekem: A Sustainable Community in the Egyptian Desert.* Edinburgh. Floris Publications
4 **Taylor** F (2014) *The Principles of Scientific Management.* Createspace Independent Publishing
5 **Fayol** H (2013) *General and Industrial Management.* Eastford. Connecticut. Martino Fine Books
6 **Lessem** R (1987) *Intrapreneurship.* Farnham. UK. Wildwood House.
7 **Robertson** B – *Holocracy: The Revolutionary Management System that Abolishes Hierarchy.* New York, Penguin
8 **Schieffer** A and **Lessem** R (2014) *Integral Development: Transforming the Potential of Individual, Organization and Society.* Abingdon. Routledge
9 **Glasl** F (1997) *The Enterprise of the Future.* Stroud. Hawthorn Press
10 **Steiner** R (1977) *Towards Social Renewal.* New York. Springer
11 **Lessem** R (2017) *Innovation Driven Institutionalized Research.* Abingdon. Routledge Focus
12 **Bhengu** M (2016) *Amazulu: Ancient Egyptian Origin – Spirits Beyond the Heavens.* Durban. Mepho Publishers

PART SIX

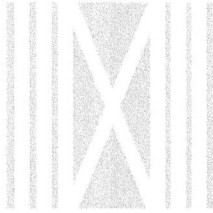

Science and Technology/ Afrikology

GLOBAL-LOCAL TRANSFORMATIVE EFFECT: PAXHERBALS

CHAPTER 9

Local/Local-Global/Newly Global/ Global-Local Paxherbals

So-called "bench laboratory science"—especially R and D—remains an elitist, university centred practice. It does not come home to the villages and the streets. The dilemma of knowledge production in Africa centres on how its structures, practices and concepts came to be informalised while inbound European ones were rendered formal. From the time that humans began making tools in stone, bone and wood, Africa hosted different forms of workshop.

C.C. Mavhunga. *What Do Science, Technology and Innovation Mean for Africa*

While in a clinic-oriented approach, emphasis is on scientific identification, conservation and use of medicinal plants, a community-oriented one applies simple herbal remedies to common illnesses: the need is to harmonise the two.

There is, conventionally, a rupture between the institutional design of an enterprise, and the underlying cultural philosophy within most societies. As a socioeconomic laboratory, this rupture has been surfaced, and healed, constructing a solidarity based economy.

Linking of social, economic and technological ideas is important not only in shaping the internal development of each cooperative but in beginning the development of a network of mutually supportive ones.

The idea of an industrial enterprise underpinned by cyclical processes, doing no harm to the biosphere, taking nothing from the earth that is not naturally and rapidly renewable, and producing no waste, prevails.

9.1. Introduction: Glocalizing Development in Africa: Renew Africa

In this chapter, following in the footsteps of Sekem in Egypt, restoring the earth, co-author Anselm Adodo now situates the Paxherbals enterprise and business administration as a practical model of integral business that encapsulates the principles of communitalism. Indeed, in 2020, as part of COVID-19 response, a new group comprising high net worth Africans at home and in the diaspora, came together, inspired by Adodo's theory of communitalism, to form a group called "Renew Africa", with a view to applying communitalism as theoretical foundation and perspective on African transformation. Members are medical doctors and health care professionals, academia, political strategists, social innovators, security experts, diplomats and members of the political class. The mission is to provide alternative theories and models to current challenges in Africa. Renew Africa, then, brings a new card to the table: going beyond criticism, lamentations and protests to providing contextualised, systematic and sustainable solutions and ideas and roadmaps for Africa, based on the principles of communitalism. The communitalism circle is a four-fold integral path, starting from local Nature/Community (Pax communis), emerging in awakened self/societal local-global consciousness (Pax Spiritus), Cocreating with other perspectives/traditions/ cultures through now newly global knowledge creation via a research academy (Pax Scientia), and finally, effecting global-local transformation through sustainable social-economic/enterprise based on Afrikological economic models (Pax Economia). Paxherbals, an integral enterprise founded by Adodo, represents a model of such an integral enterprise in Africa. For us, then, true development is a first a local-global movement. In fact, in a previous publication, Adodo describes it thus (1):

> For the African, the community is a place of creativity, healing and rela-
> tionship. Even though the community embraces both the visible and invis-
> ible, the natural and supernatural world, like the world of spirits, it should
> be noted that the point of interaction is always the visible community.
> The earth is where we live, relate, procreate and discover our creativity.
> As a person, I am born into a certain place, on a certain date, at a certain
> time, into a certain family. These facts play a key role in determining my
> destiny, my orientation and my sense of self. I am not just a vague entity. I
> belong to a place. No one becomes a global citizen at birth. Each person
> is a local entity, a local person.

9.2. Paxherbal: Pax Communis: Community Activation

9.2.1. Towards a Communiversity: Knowledge Creation in the Village

In 2018, the farmers in the local communities of Ewu, Edo State, had a challenge. They complained that cassava farming is no longer profitable. According to them, while many families in the village cultivate cassava—which they harvest and eat—only a few of these families are able to sell their harvest, most of which they end up selling as leftovers.

Ultimately, in Ewu, each family practises subsistence farming. The farmers spend a great deal of time and energy in the sun, clearing bushes, planting and then waiting for the cassava to grow and mature. Eventually, each farm is able to produce a few bags of cassava, and each bag is priced very cheaply in the local market. To generate a higher yield of cassava, the government distributes thousands of fertilisers. But the farmers insist the fertilisers don't provide the solution and only deplete the soil. They argue, instead, that organic farming is best.

The young local farmers arranged for a co-creative meeting with most elderly women in the community. These grandmothers and great-grandmothers are custodians of knowledge. "Once upon a time," one of the eldest women in the community said, "there were mushrooms growing all over the land, and we used to harvest them to cook. These mushrooms supplied us most of our nutrients. But these days, there are no more mushrooms. Rather, we have bread and fries. Bring back mushrooms to the village."

A month later, co-author Anselm Adodo, brought his theory of communitalism to bear in providing a solution to the problem. During a cooperatively conducted inquiry session with the local farmers, a consensus was reached to explore oyster mushroom farming. At first, the farmers believed that mushrooms only grow in the wild, and none of them, it seemed, knew mushrooms could be cultivated locally. But the way forward, it was soon discovered, is to blend local, indigenous knowledge with exogenous knowledge.

Communitalism is based on the need to forge synergies between different modes of knowledge creation. Communitalism acts, also, to bridge the gap between local and foreign insight. The fostering of inter and intra-communal connections built on knowledge creation is actualised in the *communiversity,* a calabash of wisdom into which knowledge flows to be shared by the community, and into which everybody has something to contribute.

In the following two months, a series of training sessions on mushroom cultivation for a select group of the local farmers were held. The two species cultivated during the session were *Pleurotus Ostreatus* and *Pleurotus Pulmonarius.* Despite the fact that several of the farmers selected did not attend—because they did not believe that mushrooms could be locally cultivated—those who attended were enthralled, surprised and excited. It was a eureka moment for the participants.

Since the initial training, hundreds of local farmers have applied to join the training sessions. Our goal is to provide small-scale farmers with the capacity to move from subsistence farming to secure livelihoods; from food sufficiency to food security; from agriculture to agribusiness. Whereas a 100-foot plot of land can only produce a few cassavas worth $100, the same plot of land can produce bags of mushrooms worth $350. Unlike cassava cultivation, mushroom farming is conducted indoors, and the waste from the mushroom soil is far more useful as fertilisers than the synthetic fertilisers the government provides.

9.2.2. Insights from Local Communities

Adodo, in this section, mentions some of the lessons learnt in the course of participative action research efforts. They are:

1. **Do not give the people what they do not ask for**. Development or community workers often present communities with ready-made answers to issues we have identified as problems, and we convince the people to accept our solutions. Convincing people is always easy. But the real impact is measured by how long those solutions last. What I've observed is that unless the people "own" the solutions, they will abandon it when you are gone.

2. **More money does not translate into better food**. We often think that the reason why poor people do not eat well is because they are poor. The reality on the ground is different. Higher incomes do not automatically translate into better diets, as the cost of food is, often, not the only reason people have less healthy diets. The most important factor in eating a healthy, balanced diet is not money but knowledge—of the right food, the right food combination and the right times to eat.

3. **People in the local communities know more than they can tell**. Local communities have vast deposits of implicit knowledge. This knowledge is a potential asset that can be explored and tapped into for the good of the society. But tapping into the knowledge reserve of communities requires an approach to education in the original sense of *educare*, the Latin word from which the English word "education" is derived. *Educare* means to draw out, to bring out what lies within.

We tend to see education as stuffing students with facts, figures and ideas. In this sense, institutions of learning become places separated from the community; laboratories where objective knowledge is generated and fed to students. Such an approach to education creates a dichotomy between teaching and learning, where the teacher is the one who knows it all, while the student is an empty vessel. The acquisition of Western knowledge has been and is still invaluable to all; but, on its own, Western knowledge has been incapable of responding adequately to the world's problems, especially in the face of massive and intensifying global and local disparities, the uncontrolled exploitation of pharmacological and other genetic resources, and the rapid depletion of the earth's natural resources. In that context, indigenous knowledge, cast in a contemporary guise, is important, hence our communiversity.

9.3. Paxherbals: Pax Spiritus: Awakening Consciousness: Regenerating Consciousness and Shared Humanity

9.3.1. Engaging with time

Paxherbals is in St .Benedict Monastery in Ewu, mid-western Nigeria. Life at the village of Ewu begins at 3:40 am daily, when the echoes of the huge metallic bell mounted on a wooden crossbar behind the Monastery church penetrates the morning mist to awaken the villages. All the young people in Ewu village born in the 1980s grew up accustomed to hearing this bell every morning, at precisely the same time. "O Lord open my lips, and my tongue shall declare your praise", so begins the Office of readings at Ewu Monastery. Meanwhile, farmers are preparing to go to the farm, and market women are putting their wares together, also preparing their children for school. For them is an engagement with time, Chronos, in the here and now. For the monks of Ewu however, it is a time for spiritual engagement, with Kairos, sacred time.

The vigil or Office of readings is a traditional monastic and ancient tradition of prayer where Christian monks wake up in the middle of the night to pray the psalms until dawn to usher in a new day. The practice of rising for prayer in the middle of the night is as old as the Christian Church and is a famous expression of religious piety and contemplation. Early Christian historians such as Pliny the younger, Tertullian and Cyprian (2) kept a record of this practice among the early Christians, especially among ascetics. Pliny the Younger reported that "Christians gathered on a certain day before light, sang hymns to Christ as to a god and shared a meal". The meal, of course, refers to the holy communion or eucharist. A report in the Acts of the Apostles in the Christian Bible (3) says: "About midnight Paul and Silas were praying and singing hymns to God, and the prisoners were listening to them."

Early Christian Historians and Theologians such as Clement of Alexandria (+215 AD), Tertullian of Carthage (+220 AD) and Hippolytus of Rome (+238

AD) all make mention of the night-time prayers, at midnight and at dawn, around 3 am. By the year 400 AD, these prayers were said in church buildings rather than private homes (4).

In the 3rd and 4th centuries, Christians kept vigil in preparation for solemn feasts. This usually began in the evening and continued until the early hours of the next day. The vigils involve singing of psalms, readings from the Bible, homilies, chants, intercessory prayers, all of which culminate in the celebration of the Eucharist. Over time, these evolved into the monastic celebration of "vigils", a term which featured prominently in the Rule of Benedict, who is regarded as the father of western monasticism (5).

9.3.2. The Benedictines: Between bonum commune communitatis and bonum commune hominis

The order of St. Benedict, also known as the Benedictines (in Latin: *Ordo Sancti Benedicti*) abbreviated as OSB, is a monastic religious order of monks and nuns within the Catholic church. It is one of the oldest religious orders of the church. The use of the term "order" to describe the Benedictines is somewhat inaccurate, as they do not strictly fit into the description of the order. Religious orders are often characterised by a hierarchical structure, built around a "motherhouse" or Generalate that has jurisdiction over other dependent religious communities. The Generalate is headed by a superior-General or provincial superior who can move members of the dependent communities around from one location to the other based on the pastoral needs of the institute.

The Benedictines do not have a superior general or motherhouse with universal authority. The concept of independent communities in the Benedictine tradition requires that the abbeys or independent houses and their members profess their "stability" to a particular abbey or monastic community, in a particular place, at a particular time. The three monastic vows are Stability, Conversion of life and Obedience. The vow of stability anchors the other vows and virtues in a context. Therefore, by virtue of his/her vow of stability, the Monk and nun cannot move—nor be moved by their Abbot or abbess—to another abbey or community, unless by a special arrangement. An "independent house" may occasionally make a new foundation which remains a "dependent house" (identified by the name "priory") until it is granted independence by Rome and itself becomes an abbey. The autonomy of each house does not prevent them being affiliated into congregations—whether national or based on some other joint characteristic—and these, in turn, form the supra-national Benedictine Confederations (which was set up in 1893 to represent the order's shared interests and deepen its values), which are in turn directly connected to the Roman Curia.

The thrust of the Benedictine Ideal is the constant need to find a balance between *bonum commune communitatis* (common good of the community) and *bonum commune hominis* (what is good for the individual). One can see how St. Benedict in his Rule for monks strived to promote a balance between these two seemingly opposing trends and urges the Abbot to apply wisdom in managing his monastery in such a way that there is a creative and dynamic balance between individual needs and communal needs. For Benedict, it is in prayer and meditation that the Monk finds the Grace to give up his selfish desire and ego to embrace an option for selfless service. In prayer, time is sanctified, and the Monk embraces a new understanding of time, which we call Kairos.

9.3.3. The sanctification of time

Monks and Nuns stay up late at night to pray and keep vigil. The night was the time the imagination ran riot, when the devil could play on the imagination of the Monks and tempt them through fear. The term "matutini", from which the word Matins is derived, really means morning, so the Vigils is the practice of prayer at night to usher in the dawn. The practice goes back to Apostolic times, with the goal of breaking up the night and sanctifying those hours, at least in private, and eventually in common, especially in monastic communities. For the early monks, night means darkness, a time to wait in patience until day breaks. The night is the time when the devil prowls about, looking for victims, and so great spiritual vigilance is needed to resist the tricks of the devil. The night was a symbol of mystery, fear, uncertainty, insecurity and anxiety. Unlike in the modern world where the night has practically been transformed into a day because of the availability of electricity, the case was different for the early monks. Today, even the association of night with darkness is weak. For the early monks, the night was dark, and the association of night with darkness was very real. The image of Christ as Light of the world, then was very real, powerful and tangible, both symbolically and literally. Christ is the light who dispels the darkness of the world (6, 7).

The monks of Saint Pachomius' (+ 346 AD) monastery initially seem to have performed the prayers of the night in private, but gradually, and certainly, by the time of Saint Basil (+379 AD), prayers at night were a community exercise. That was Saint Benedict's understanding of Vigils or Night Prayer as well. This custom has carried on to the present in the stricter observance monasteries of various Orders. After Vatican II, the night office came to be called "The Office of Readings", and could be prayed at any time of the day, partly in consideration of the weak and aged that cannot easily rise in the night for the traditional time of the pre-dawn vigil.

The content of the night vigil for monks has always consisted mostly of psalms, some lessons from Scripture or the patristic tradition and Collects, but the whole idea of an Office of Readings is a bit foreign to the ancient monastic ritual, which traditionally places more emphasis on the psalmody, usually 12 in number, as well as a set or Nocturn of Old Testament canticles of a psalm-like structure, on Sundays and Solemnities. The structure of the monastic vigils then gave more prominence to the recitation of psalms and canticles from the Bible, than to the patristic reading or commentaries assigned to the Office after the Vatican II reform of the liturgy. In fact, in the Benedictine tradition, the vigil or Office at night is rightly described as the "Office of Psalmody," but better still, the "Office of Vigils," implying as the word does, watching for the dawn. So important is the place of the psalms at this and all the offices that Saint Benedict's *Rule* says that if the brethren accidentally wake up late, which he highly frowns upon, the lessons and responses would be dropped, but not the psalms (RB 11.12–13, "How Vigils Should be done on Sundays"). "But if they should—God forbid! (*quod absit*)–happen to rise late, then some of the readings or responses should be shortened. All precautions should be taken that this does not happen." (8).

The idea is that Lauds should begin at daybreak. But if the brethren carry on with the usual length of the Vigil Office when they over-sleep, they may not be able to begin the morning prayer—Lauds—at daybreak.

9.3.4. The Monastery and the village: between Chronos and Kairos

This chapter began by connecting the prayer time at Benedictine monastery in Ewu, Edo State as Kairos, and the morning chores of the local community of Ewu villagers as Chronos. What then is Kairos and Chronos? The Christian tradition of payer and the monastic tradition of prayer distinguishes between Chronos and Kairos. The daily prayers give a meaning to life, the sanctification of life. This is done by dividing the day into different aspects to reflect the life of Jesus Christ (9).

The best way to differentiate between Chronos and kairos is to see time as either a flowing river which carries us away (Chronos), or a quiet lake which we swim in (kairos). We all experience time as both, all the time, in whatever we do. We experience Chronos when we are impatiently waiting for something to be over and done with, like when we attend a business meeting, fix our car or have a haircut. We experience kairos when we are so deeply engrossed in an activity that time seems to stand still. In Chronos, we are stressed—in kairos, we are refreshed.

Chronos measures time in terms of quantity: seconds, minutes, hours, days, years and decades. The English word Chronological takes inspiration from this word. Kairos measures time in terms of quality—in the best and significant moments of life. It does not measure Minutes, but it measures moments—the most beautiful, right, magical and opportune moments.

The anthropologists' concept of structured time is inspired by the Greek use of Chronos, while the concept of liminal time is inspired by the idea of Kairos. German-French anthropologist, Arnold Van Gennep, in his 1909 book, *Les rites de passage* (The Rites of Passage), (10) described rituals of passing from one stage of life to another. Van Gennep observed as he worked among different peoples of Africa and Oceania, that birth, puberty, marriage, and death, are specially commemorated in every culture. The actual ceremonies may differ, but their meaning is universal—a celebration of the transition from one phase of life to another.

In every society and civilization, both past and present, every change of place, of social situation, social and cultural and technological evolution and modification, in fact, all innovation is often accompanied by rites which always follow the same order and constitute the schema-type of the rites of passage. The concept of Liminality has come to the fore in recent years in social and political theory and extending beyond its original use as developed within anthropology. Liminality has come to denote spaces and moments in which the taken-for-granted order of the world ceases to exist, and novel forms emerge, often in unpredictable ways (11).

British cultural anthropologist, Victor Turner (12) examines rituals of the Ndembu in Zambia and develops his now-famous concept of "Communitas". He characterises it as an absolute inter-human relation beyond any form of structure. Turner demonstrates how the analysis of ritual behaviour and symbolism may be used as a key to understanding social structure and processes. He extends Van Gennep's notion of the "liminal phase" of rites of passage to a more general level and applies it to gain an understanding of a wide range of social phenomena. Once thought to be the "vestigial" organs of social conservatism, rituals are now seen as arenas in which social change may emerge and be absorbed into social practice.

9.3.5. A door to the Divine

In the 20th century, sociologist Arnold Van Gennep (13) and anthropologist Victor Turner (14) both proposed a model of ritual that consisted of separation from the ordinary physical and social context, and entry into an alternative state of experience characterised by the suspension of ordinary rules of behaviour, and the dissolution of standard measurements of space and time.

They referred to this state as "liminal", a word derived from the Latin word *limen*, referring to the threshold, the piece of wood or stone that serves as the foundation for a doorway. In their model, rituals take place in the space in-between spaces, where people have left one room (a symbol for a social identity or stage in life) but have not yet entered another room. The liminal space is free of the orderly structure that enforces a rigid sense of the passage of time. Those within it experience moments that have the feeling of eternity about them. Ritual participants within the liminal space are "off the clock" in many senses. Not only do they lose track of the passage of standardised units of time, but they are liberated from the responsibilities of the roles that are dictated by clocks.

The liminal experience thus provides an opportunity for transformation, in which ritual participants are temporarily uninhibited by the expectations that typically control them in more structured time. Yet, a rite of passage is not designed to provide for permanent liminal freedom. It is a bubble of liberated time within which important cultural work to create change in the psychology of ritual participants can be performed. A rite of passage thus moves an initiate out of structured time into transcendent liminal time, and then back into structured time, but in order to occupy a new social identity.

9.3.5. The African 'communitas'

Adodo, in his seminal work, *Integral Community Enterprise in Africa* (15), affirms the importance of story as a tool of inner exploration and meaning-seeking. Every society has its own story, its core images, its religion and spirituality, which bind all the members together as a people. What defines each person, according to Adodo, is not just one's tribe. The soil, the trees, the rivers, the mountains, the air and the animals who inhabit the environment define who we are. For Adodo, an African community is not just a place where human beings live. A community comprises the plants, animals, the ancestors and the spirit. In times of crisis of identity, each society naturally goes back to its core values, images to rediscover its sense of identity. In other words, nature and community is the home of humankind and is the foundation of all science, innovation and development. Above all, humans find their identity by reconnecting with nature. At the very core of every society is a sense of the sacred, a sense of a power "other", which goes beyond what the human reason can grasp. This "other" is what Otto (16), the German philosophical theologian, referred to as the "numinous". Whatever name is given to this "other" by each culture and religion, the image of the mysterious, almighty, divine power outside the self is common to all cultures and religions and forms the basis of how the people approach life.

9.4. PaxHerbal: Pax Scientia, Research Academy: Knowledge Creation

9.4.1 Action Research: Working with and for People

Although action research method in its modern western guise is attributed to American psychologist, Kurt Lewin, its origin goes far back in human intellectual history. Action research simply means what the term suggests: research-in-action, psychomotor research or researching and doing. Action research aims to move beyond the dichotomy between doing and thinking, between working and studying, to balance problem-solving with problem analysis. Action research challenges the tendency of conventional social science to arrogate to itself the ability to reflect on things and people and take this as the status quo for all cultures. It also challenges the dichotomy often created between action and research.

The dichotomy could be traced as far back as the Greek division between praxis (action) and theoria (research) (17). Greek thinking tended to treat praxis and theoria as two separates, even opposing ways of life, each occupying positions on a hierarchical social status. In fact, the two most prominent Greek philosophers, Plato and Aristotle, saw theoria as the superior way of life, reserved for the intellectually refined and cultured members of the society, the philosopher-kings, who are closer to the Divine than the rest of the people (18, 19). Theoria was said to involve contemplation on eternal principles, a detached focus on essential, intangible principles of the universe. Praxis, by contrast, is concerned with human affairs, and the temporal and mundane things of the world. The preoccupation of praxis was said to be such that it contributes nothing of significance for the universe as a whole (20).

This dichotomy, which was imported from Greek thought, introduced an unhealthy dualism into Christian thinking, an influence which persisted until the late Middle Ages. It contrasts with the traditional biblical Jewish way of thinking which conceived action and research as two sides of the same coin (21). The dichotomy later found expression in the monastic movements with its emphasis on "abandoning the world" and developing distaste for the things of the world. The things of the world included politics and the economy. The Monk became a symbol of *theoria*, one who is utterly detached from the world of praxis in order to focus on the superior life of contemplation on the eternal principles, on the Divine. So pervasive was the dichotomy that even within the monastic walls in the Middle Ages, a distinction was made between the "choir monks" and the lay monks or working monks. The choir monks were known as the special ones, usually ordained priests, whose main work was the celebration of the sacred liturgy: the daily celebration of Mass, sacred chants and praying for "the world". The working monks or lay monks were non-ordained and occupy a lower rank in importance. Their work required preoccupation with mundane things, that is, praxis rather than theoria (22).

It is a paradox that St. Benedict, whose Rule moulded western monasticism in the Middle Ages up until the present time, would have found this dichotomy strange and contrary to the spirit of his Rule. In fact, one of the major goals that St. Benedict, himself a non-ordained or lay-monk, set out to achieve in his Rule is the eradication of this dichotomy between theoria and praxis (23). For Benedict, "oratio", prayer, and "labora", work, are important and complementary aspects of the monastic life. Prayer is not work and work is not prayer. Rather, prayer is prayer and work is work, and both form an integral, co-creative whole (24). This integral combination of "oratio" and "labora" is one unique characteristic of St. Benedict Monastery, Ewu, Edo State, as reflected in a balanced interconnection of *Communis* (Community), *Spiritus* (Sanctuary), *Scientia* (University), and *Economia* (Laboratory). For St. Benedict, this healthy balance is the virtue of moderation.

In the 19th and 20th centuries, some thinkers such as Newton, Leibniz, Kant (25, 26, 27) contributed in changing the tendency to view theoria as superior to praxis. Modern philosophies such as positivism, historicism, life philosophy and existentialism rejected the view of praxis as inferior to theoria (28, 29). For Dewey (30), founder of American pragmatism, research or inquiry should not be seen as the human mind or intellect passively observing and analysing the world. Rather, an inquiry is a process of interaction between human beings and their environment in which each of them is affected in a symbiotic way. Dewey (31) argues that the Cartesian starting point where the researcher separates and detaches himself from the world in order to seek objectivity in raising philosophical questions is the wrong way to start a scientific inquiry. Scientific and philosophic enquiry, according to him, is always shaped by particular cultural contexts and should feed back into the society as part of ongoing dynamic interaction.

9.4.2. From Communitalism to communiversity

Adodo is of the view that Western theories such as Marxism, Capitalism, Socialism, Communism, while focusing on economics, technology and enterprise, failed to build their concepts on nature and culture, thus leading to unsustainable and imbalanced development. An integral approach, such as *Communitalism,* which takes account of the totality of the above, set within a particular society, building up from nature and community, and embracing culture, politics, economics, spirituality and enterprise, is a surer path to sustainable and integral development in Africa. What then is *Communitalism?* According to Adodo (32):

Communitalism, as opposed to capitalism or communism, is an integral approach to knowledge creation and development that is grounded in a particular enterprise-in-community, while ultimately effecting a whole society, emerging indigenously and exogenously as such. Such a communitalist perspective, built on the four Pax (4P's), addresses the four key dimensions of development, which are identified as follows: Pax Communis (community), Pax Spiritus (Sanctuary), Pax Scientia (university) and Pax Economia (Laboratory).

9.4.3. PAXHERBALS: From Nature Power to Oikonomia

Adodo's important book, *Nature Power (33)*, documents how common plants, weeds and shrubs are in fact reservoirs of life-saving medicinal properties. Nature Power seeks to interconnect community, Agriculture, Agronomy, ecology and enterprise, which altogether we refer to as "oikonomia". According to Adodo, Nature Power is inviting the world to come down to earth so as to regain our health. The earth is the primary source of our creativity, intelligence, and humanness. Before we set out to calculate, to create, to invent, to fabricate, the earth already was. Today, faced with globalisation, high-technology and a fast-paced modern lifestyle, we are often tempted to forget our link with the earth and therefore become DIS-EASED.

In the past, we heard about physicians who provided health CARE to the sick. Our health, our life, our future in fact depends on the quality of the earth: soil, water, sunshine, forests and air. The rich, the poor, the sick, the healthy, black people, white people, we all breathe the same air. At the end of the day what we put into the earth will come back to us, either to purify us or to poison us. The air we breathe is the same air inhaled by Jesus Christ, by the Blessed Virgin Mary, by Mohammed, and by the great scientists, philosophers and saints of the past.

Viewed from this perspective, according to Adodo, one can now see how right our Africa ancestors were when they asserted that only a thin line separates the physical from the spiritual, spirit from matter, life from death. *The wisdom of the ancients is there in the molecules of the air around us, waiting to be tapped when we are open enough to perceive them.* Millions of men and women from all parts of the world are coming together to remind us that it is our human greed and selfishness, rather than nuclear bombs, that constitutes the greatest threat to our human survival, to human health and peace. Humanity is sick, for Adodo, and needs to be administered the medicine of justice, fairness, concern for others and respect for our symbiotic cosmos. Adodo then turns specifically to the African universe, as a world of relationships.

9.4.4. The African Universe as a World of Relationships

The African universe is a world of relationships, of interactions between the living and the dead, between the natural and the supernatural. A community is not just a place where human beings dwell. *The African community comprises plants, animals, human beings, the spirit and the ancestors.* Trees are more than trees: the sky is more than we see. There is more to plants and animals than we see with our eyes. *Everything in the universe is a language of life and an expression of life. Therefore they are sacred and holy* (34).

Holiness, for Adodo, is a state of union with God, with oneself and with others. Others include your fellow human beings as well as plants, animals, and indeed the whole of creation. When you discover that you are not just anybody or just a spirit, but a complete and whole person, then you will discover the meaning of holiness. The holy person is the one who has discovered the balance between the physical, the psychological and the spiritual (35).

When there is an imbalance, there is a disease. For society says: be rich, have pleasure, obtain power, be famous, for these are the goals of life. The false conception of life, for Adodo, of all reality, is the root of all diseases. Having imbibed the mechanistic world view, which sees natural things as mere objects to be exploited and the human body as a mere object of pleasure, we eat what we like, drink anything that comes our way and live as we want. The result of this, for him, is dis-ease. We are no longer at ease. We have lost touch with our origins.

In the Yoruba language, there is a clear distinction between the spoken word and potent speech. The former is called *oro*, common words used in conversation. The latter is called *ofo*. The Hebrew equivalent is *dahbar*, while the Greek is *logos*. *Ofo* refers to words that have the power of becoming an event in life simply by being uttered. When an *ofo* is uttered it goes on to actualise itself. When sound is then organised into a rhythm, you have music. Music is a powerful tool. No one can resist the lure of music.

Music permeates your being, you are nothing but music. The body is a living entity and intelligent being with its own laws. The wisdom of the cosmos is reflected in the body, and the body is a musical composition. The different forms of sound, the human voice, sound of nature and the sound of music carry waves of energy which they impress on us. *It is only when we learn to be silent that we can hear the creative sound of creation restoring us to harmony, peace and contentment.*

We now turn to Adodo's 2003 book (36), *Healing Radiance of the Soul*. Adodo begins this second work of his by representing the four classes of natural forces, which we might align with our integral four worlds. The *force of gravity*, firstly, aligns with our "south", and our *grounding* as such. Like light and waves, material objects are subject to the law of energy and Mass. This means that all things are attracted, pulled or drawn to each other. Since gravitation has no mass, it carries a long-range force, which makes it very active over long distances.

Secondly, our "eastern" *electromagnetic force* results in the generation of a, for us, *emergent* force, through the action of electrically charged particles like electrons and quarks, resulting in the generation of a force stronger than gravity. This energy generation is caused by the mingling, or fusion, of some massless particles called photons, each one having both a positive and a negative charge.

Thirdly, we have our "northern" *weak nuclear force,* for us *navigation.* The photon plus three other particles combine to make up the weak nuclear force. The main characteristic of our "western" *strong nuclear force* is that it binds massless particles together, thereby having no colour of its own. To get a white quark, so to speak, the strong nuclear force combined red, blue and green quarks, *effectively* making up a proton or neutron, leading to a prolonged chain of reactions. Adodo then turns to the mystery of life, or more specifically the hidden life of plants.

9.4.5. Unlike Animals, Plants Manufacture the Essential Chemicals They Need to Survive

Plants then, for him, are more independent than animals when it comes to the essentials of life. *Unlike animals, plants manufacture the essential chemicals they need to survive. Making use of the essential cosmic elements of sunlight, air, and water, plants manufacture all they need to grow and reproduce.* Plants manufacture carbohydrates, proteins, fats, hormones, vitamins and enzymes. These chemicals are called primary compounds. Animals, including human beings, need these primary compounds to survive. Without plants to manufacture these compounds, animal and human life cannot be sustained. Each plant manufactures the precise amount of chemical it needs. Since animals depend on these chemicals, plants grow to make life possible.

Since moreover, for Adodo, plants are so important to animal and human existence, it is important that plants continue to grow and reproduce. In order to protect themselves against use and misuse, plants manufacture new sets of chemicals that can both positively or negatively affect or alter the biological state of animals and humans. These chemicals are called secondary compounds. There are as many as 100,000 of these. The compounds serve as a defence mechanism for the plants to help them fight against infections with bacteria, viruses and fungi.

When acacia leaves are attacked by an animal, for example, they re-grow leaves that have a higher concentration of toxic compounds which will harm the animal that is foolish enough to come back for more. Plants are able to send warning signals to other plants when they are being attacked. Flowering plants send out nice fragrances not to pamper or please our senses but to attract pollinators so that the cycle of life can continue. The amount of phytochemicals produced by each plant depends on the environment and soil condition. Some plants produce as many as 200 different phytochemicals. For example, the apple tree contains as much as 150 compounds, 60–70% of which are medicinal. *There is more concentration of useful compounds in the peels of fruits than in the fruits themselves.* The peel of a mango, for example, is richer in useful phytochemicals than the mango fruit itself, while the root of a pawpaw tree contains more active compounds than the trunk.

9.4.6. Every Plant has a Reason for Existing

There are more than 400,000 species of plants, according to Adodo, on this planet. Human beings in different continents use about 100,000 of these for medicinal purposes. Of these, only some 10,000 have been clinically analysed and thus recommended for human consumption.

The truth which science is discovering is that we have not yet begun to explore the deep mysteries of life. *Every day, every hour, new species of plant are created unnoticed to our human eyes.* To the untrained eye, plants remain what they are and there is nothing special about them. But the sensitive person knows there is more to them. Our universe, for Adodo, is composed of an energy field, an invincible power. This energy field vibrates at different frequencies. Plants grow and mature according to the energy field around them.

Every plant has a reason for existing. Plants grow for a particular purpose. Every plant is a manifestation of the energy field which is the universe. Some plants exist to give nourishment to the earth. Some exist to give support to other plants. Some grow to regulate the exchange of oxygen and carbon dioxide between human beings and plants. Some give information about events.

For one who has eyes to see and ears to hear, Adodo goes on to say, plants speak many languages. They are mirrors reflecting the intensity and nature of the energy field of the environment where they grow. There are some plants that signal the coming of a drought. Some sprout to signal the coming of rain or an epidemic. On getting to a new place, experienced herbalists and mystics know the prevalent sickness and mood simply by observing the kinds of plants growing nearby. The types of plants growing in a particular place often reflect the need or problem of the place. Shortly before any epidemic or disease, the plant that has the antidote begins to sprout. For every sickness, disease or lack there is always a medicinal plant growing nearby. It is left for human beings to open nature's book of wisdom and learn to use them.

9.4.7. Uncovering the Theory of Plant Signatures

In traditional African societies, and indeed in other parts of the world, people look at the colour and shape as well as the location of a plant to get an insight into its use and importance. This is called the theory of signatures. They believe that plants grow in a specific area because there is a need for them. Herbs that grow on mountains, for example, are believed to be good for the respiratory system. Herbs that grow in water are considered very medicinal, and specifically for treating infertility. Herbs that grow close to the soil are considered good for circulatory and digestive problems.

The challenge for today's African thinkers is to sift out the fetish and the superstitious from our inherited deposits of knowledge without throwing away the truth. May the silent echoes of the eternal wisdom, for Adodo then, continue to resound through us. This brings him, overall, to the art of healing, for us and for him, in an African context, underlying sustainable development.

9.4.8. The Art of Healing: That Single Creative Force That Sustains The Cosmos

African Traditional Religions generally believe in the presence of mysterious forces controlling activities in the world. These forces manifest in terms of spirits. Africans believe that it is through the manipulation of sound that they link up with this force and use it. Hence great emphasis is placed on speech, incantations, singing and music, including also dance. Modern science has also come to accept the existence of this force that sustains the universe. Even though science, for Adodo, uses different terms, it explains the same reality. What is the law of gravity, the electromagnetic force, the weak and strong nuclear forces, other than the effect of that single creative force that sustains the cosmos.

The universe, as we have seen, is vibrating at different intensities, creating an energy field. We too are vibrating and creating our energy fields. Each creature has its own energy field, making it clear that we are in a world that is alive with activities, charged with energies. Our energy fields, moreover, fluctuate according to our thought process, our psychological states and the influence of these thoughts on other people. Buildings, artworks, paintings, machines, literary work, poems were all thoughts or ideas that were eventually materialised.

The electromagnetic energy spectrum then radiates through nature: the seas, mountains, plants, earth and rocks. By living close to the land and nature, we receive this energy into our own energy fields and so are energised. However, as we build more highways, manufacture steel cars, build bridges and make electronic gadgets, we become prone to hitherto unknown diseases. As human beings become more complicated and adopt a so-called modern, sophisticated mode of life, so also our illnesses become more complicated.

Western man and woman, Adodo then goes on to say, has purchased materialism at the cost of their soul, pulling themselves away from the earth, from nature. Humankind seems to have lost its conscience. The result is intense anger and bitterness: leading to violence and war. The millions of immigrants from the plundered poor countries who sit at the gates of the rich nations without being given access to their opulence remind them that there will be no peace unless there is equity and justice in the world.

We are living therefore in a sick world, a world polluted by greed, injustice, materialism, racial prejudice and wickedness. Religion, which is meant to be an instrument of our reunion with the Divine also becomes an instrument of disunity and violence. Perhaps, he says, the time has come for us to drop the Bible and the Koran and look each other in the face. For right there in the eyes of the poor, the sick, the abandoned, the weak, the rich earning their wage from the honest work of their hands, there in their faces you will read the gospel of life, the Koran of the Just and Merciful Allah. What we have then is a lifeless religion, for religion without spirituality leads to death. Religion without spirituality leads to ignorance, bloody fanaticism, spiritual brainwashing and deceit. Religion without spirituality allows evil leaders to deceive and manipulate their subjects to their selfish advantage.

Science, in contrast, is only another word for knowledge. What knowledge? Knowledge of the deeper meaning of life. Knowledge of who we are, where we come from, and where we are going. Knowledge of the essence of religion, of spirituality. Knowledge of our inherent power to transform the world by love, not hatred; by gentleness, not violence. Knowledge of the true nature of power, that is nature power. It is only this knowledge which will bring permanent healing to our sick and wounded cosmos and set us free. Such knowledge is our African destiny.

9.5. Paxherbal: Pax Economica. Oikonomia, Eco-Economics Laboratory

The fourth pax dimension is pax economia. We begin by looking at another of Adodo's book, titled 'New Frontiers in African Medicine' (37), where he contextualises the notion of Pax within his paxherbal economic enterprise.

9.5.1. What is Pax?

The word *Pax* is a Latin word which means peace. Pax has over the years, become the motto of the Benedictine order. St. Benedict in his Rule for monks, encourages his monks to "listen" daily to the word of God. Listening is an art. It's something we learn to do. It is a skill. Listening requires that I lay aside my opinions and prejudices and *hear* what is being communicated to me. As you know, there are many means of communication. Speech is only one of them. In fact, only 30% of human communication is done through speech. The rest is done through gestures, body movements, facial expressions and our attitudes. It is important that we don't take these facts for granted.

For St. Benedict, listening to the Word of God brings peace to the soul. When we have peace, which is a gift from God, we see things in the right way and we are able to love God and love our neighbour. The cultivation of peace, then, is the aim of every monk. Peace does not just refer to the absence of war or strife. Peace is an attitude of the soul, whereby one accepts one's place in the world, and gives to God the honour and glory that belong to God. We are humans. God is God. Suffering came because we human beings wanted to become God. We do not want to accept that we are mere mortals. This leads to fear. Peace comes when we transcend our fears by accepting our place in the universe. Indeed, the root of all war and violence is fear. Fear is a sign of our unredeemed human nature; human beings in their weaknesses. The husband who hates his wife is afraid. The wife who detests her husband is afraid. The armed robber is afraid. The corrupt leader is afraid and hopes that he will attain peace by looting the treasury of the state he governs. When we have peace, we stop harming others. We begin to relate to others and people with honour and dignity. We stop exploiting and cheating others. This is what Pax is all about.

9.5.2. What sort of business?

What business, then, is Paxherbals up to? According to Adodo, Pax is into the business of life. We are into the business of promoting human dignity and human health. Salvation is holistic. It concerns all aspects of the human person: body, mind and soul. Paxherbals is into the business of redeeming the whole person. For Adodo, PAX Herbal Centre is not just a clinic. It is a centre of healing, of love, of service. Pax is not about mere eradication of suffering, or suppression of illnesses, or avoidance of pain. It is a fact of life that we all shall die one day, sooner or later. The mission of Paxherbals is to promote human health and human dignity, not just the eradication of pain, which in fact, is an essential aspect of being human.

> Pax centre is into the business of using our God-given natural resources to enrich ourselves. We want to re-write our history. We want to re-awaken the African Spirit. The African Spirit has been so suppressed and relegated that we are no longer even proud to call ourselves Africans. After all, Africa has been described as the "dark" continent. All that the world knows about Africa is civil war, poverty, famine, corruption. Other "spirits" have overshadowed the African Spirit: the American Spirit [propagated by CNN, Hollywood films, etc], The European Spirit [being propagated by BBC, western civilisation, etc]. Nowadays, the Indian Spirit, the Chinese Spirit, Japanese Spirit have been revived. These nations are now powers to reckon with in the world. Go to a typical city in the countries of the world, and you will see different restaurants: Chinese restaurants, Indian restaurants, Asian restaurants and McDonald's, the American fast-food giant. But you will have to search and search and search before you manage to find an African restaurant, located in a deserted, hidden corner somewhere in the city. We are not even proud of our traditional food and delicacy! (38).

For Adodo, Pax is into the business of re-awakening the African Spirit by first affirming belief in African inner resources and genius:

> Pax Herbal Centre is an apostolate of the Benedictine Monks of Ewu (our Spiritus). It's a community apostolate. The Benedictine order is one of the oldest religious orders in the Catholic Church. The Monks have always manifested a love for nature. We are Christians. We believe in Christ. We do not hide this fact. We are proud to be Christians. We are happy to be part of the Catholic church that has always aimed at the highest standards in every thing and never compromises when it comes to quality of life or vocation. However, we do not condemn or judge others who do not profess our faith. Only God can judge who is a true follower of his. We are free to relate to all irrespective of their religion. Here in our monastery (our Sanctuary) we do not find out the religion of our guests before accommodating them. We do not set out to want to convert others to our religion. We simply relate with them as our fellow brothers and sisters made in God's image. That is the spirit of Pax (39).

9.5.3. Paxherbals: from nature power to eco-enterprise, Oikonomia

The paxherbal business model and economic principles are not based on the work of Karl Marx or modern business literature. Rather, it goes far to the Rule of St. Benedict, written some 1500 years before Karl Marx:

If there are artisans in the monastery, they are to practise their craft with all humility, but only with the Abbot's permission. If one of them becomes puffed up by his skilfulness in his craft, and feels that he is conferring something on the monastery, he is to be removed from practising his craft and not allowed to resume it unless, after manifesting his humility, he is so ordered by the Abbot. Whenever products of these artisans are sold, those responsible for the sale must not dare to practise any fraud. Let them always remember Ananias and Sapphira, who incurred bodily death (Acts 5:1–11), lest they and all who perpetrate fraud in monastery affairs suffer spiritual death. The evil of avarice must have no part in establishing prices, which should, therefore, always be a little lower than people outside the monastery are able to set, so that in all things God may be glorified (1 Pet 4:11) (40).

Twenty-first–century business seems a far cry from a sixth-century reclusive model of enterprise. However, the life of St. Benedict himself is a revolt against the individualism and selfishness that characterised capitalist orientation. The principles of Benedict's life and work speak directly to the 21st century. That the Benedictine business tradition has persisted for over fourteen centuries is because it is grounded on sound ecological and spiritual vision. Benedict was born around the year 480 into a noble family. As a young man, he was sent to Rome to study. Shocked by the squalor and depravity of the city, he fled south, to the hills of Subiaco, to follow the hermit's life. He soon realised that the answer to his own problems and the problems of the world was to be found not in solitary escape but in laying the foundations of a society based on prayer (41).

The Roman Empire had crumbled by Benedict's time, and in the midst of collapsing institutions, moral decay, and social chaos, Benedict established religious communities based on gentle discipline, strict morality, and a well-ordered routine. Drawing on earlier monastic writings, Benedict crafted a rule that lays down the principles of Christian community life. The Rule of St. Benedict is a classic of Christian spirituality, which has inspired and sustained generations of monks and nuns for some 1500 years.

The Rule is not so much a spiritual treatise as a manual for community living. Apart from detailed instructions on daily liturgical prayer, much of the Rule is devoted to practical instructions on every aspect of daily living, from cooking, kitchen servers, respect for seniors, correcting faults and mutual respect. It outlines how the monks must constantly listen, respect, and forgive one another and the attitude they should have toward material things. The individual monks are not allowed personal property. However, the Benedictine community may hold wealth and property in common, and this property is to be treated with care, restraint, and reverence. For St. Benedict, the vessels of the kitchen must be treated with the same reverence as the vessels of the altar.

9.5.4. Business with a human face

It would seem that business and enterprise today has only one law: to make a profit, at all cost, in as short a time as possible. This attitude has had a devastating effect on our ecosystem, leading to the extinction of plant species, animals and worsening global warming. The Roman Catholic Pontiff, Pope Francis asked a very vital question in his 2015 encyclical (42): "What kind of world do we want to leave to those who come after us, to children who are now growing up?" Some 1500 years before Pope Francis's encyclical, the Benedictines were engaged in various kinds of business ventures that take the environment into consideration. One could still see models of such eco-friendly enterprises, or Oikonomia, in monasteries across the world. A sustainable eco-enterprise (our economia) must be grounded on a spiritual vision, eco-spirituality, eco-vision, which we call Sanctuary.

Paxherbals, located in Ewu village, Nigeria, shares in the spiritual vision and principles of this integral, holistic approach to enterprise. While paxherbals focuses on nature, agriculture, ethnobotany, traditional indigenous medical practice, other Benedictine monasteries across the four worlds are engaged in other forms of enterprises. The St. Joseph Abbey in Southern Louisiana, USA, established in 1889, built a flourishing casket making industry, and are today regarded as the best producers of caskets in America. Another monastery in Spencer, Massachusetts, has an award-winning brewery that produces high-quality beer, which is branded as Spencer beer.

The world-famous "Benedictine Liquor", was based on a 1510 recipe created by a Benedictine monk, Bernardo Vincelli, at the Abbey of Fecamp in Normandy, France. Monks created brewing as we know it, with the first large scale breweries in Europe and many advances to brewing techniques and technology. There were thousands of brewing monasteries, but then suddenly they disappeared because of the turmoil and devastation brought by the French Revolution, during the First World War. The world's oldest functional brewery, dating back to 1040, is in Weihenstephan Abbey, a Benedictine Monastery in Germany. Some of the best cheese, jam, crafts in the world are produced by monks within the confines of their monasteries (43).

St. Benedict had a highly entrepreneurial and decentralised vision of the enterprise. His Rule was revolutionary in its insistence that each organisation founded on its principles be financially self-sustaining, dependent on neither the Church nor the government, and in its assertion that labour was a noble enterprise that benefits the soul. Organisations adhering to his Rule must generate revenue enough to cover their operational costs and fund their charitable efforts. Moreover, the Rule of St. Benedict's lack of central planning regarding product selection and production has enabled monasteries over the centuries to adapt remarkably well to changing market conditions, expanding, diversifying, or reorganising as necessary. Long before the term "niche market" was coined, Benedictines were producing high-quality, niche-marketed speciality goods, from cheese, jams, honey to calligraphy pens, footwear, medicinal elixirs, computer software and biogas technology.

The Benedictine way of life has survived because the monks have been immensely adaptable. They have always understood the relevance of Benedict's principles and have been ready to apply those principles wherever they've happened to live. From the first monks who set up communes to the great monastic powerhouses of the Middle Ages to the Cistercians colonising and cultivating land nobody else wanted, the Benedictines have been smart and shrewd operators for the kingdom. Paxherbals, in Ewu, Edo State, Nigeria, continues in that same spirit, now fully indigenised in Africa.

9.6. Conclusion: PAXHERBALS: When the virus came: towards integral healing of self, society and the earth

With the advent of the novel coronavirus, code-named COVID-19, scientists at Paxherbals went to work and arrived at a combination of five major herbs, each of which has been used from time immemorial across the globe to control or treat one infection/disease or the other or merely used as spice.

The combination of herbs contains, various ingredients, including 6-paradol, gingerol, kolaflavanone, kolanone, curcumene, á- and â-turmerone and notable vitamins and minerals, such as Copper, Zinc, Calcium, Iron and Magnesium.

The blend of phyto-medicinal constituents of the drug exhibits potent anti-infective, immune-modulatory, anti-inflammatory effects. The constituents synergistically inhibit autoimmune diseases by regulating inflammatory cytokines and triggering the immune system to combat and overwhelm any invader. It is in this sense that the herb combination acts as an oral vaccine against the novel coronavirus.

The anti-inflammatory property of the herbal drug is particularly significant, given the high incidence of blot clots found in the late stages of treatment in many patients, who contracted COVID-19. This herbal drug is expected to prevent such clots from forming in the first place. What is even more interesting about the drug is the lack of side effects. Of course, none is expected since the herbs have been in use from time immemorial. The herbal drug has been packaged in 290mg capsules, encapsulated in gelatin shells. The capsule is characterised by a green-yellow colour blend, has a slightly bitter taste and pungent smell. The recommended dosage is two capsules taken with a glass of water twice daily.

The drug's use is not limited to the treatment of patients with COVID-19 alone. It is also useful in the treatment and management of compromised immunity and symptoms caused by viral infections. Moreover, it is a powerful anti-oxidant. During a pandemic, such as the one posed by COVID-19, the drug's full "vaccine" effect lies in its continuous use as a prophylaxis.

The drug, which, having passed through preclinical trials was as safe for public use as an "immune booster" by Nigeria's regulatory agency, the National Agency for Food and Drug Administration and Control (NAFDAC). In the meantime, those who have taken part in the preliminary human trials, including COVID-19 patients, have shown a very positive response and satisfaction with the drug.

The public reaction to the discovery by Paxherbals was a mix of excitement, admiration, skepticism, political intrigues and capitalist self-interest, depending on where one was coming from. For the general populace, it was a commendable effort and a clear message of self-determination. The Paxherbal COVID-19 discovery brought into national consciousness once again the discussion of African indigenous knowledge systems, health politics, global biopiracy, North/West monopoly of means of knowledge production and control and Africa's inadequate educational system, and the need to address them urgently. In providing solutions to their problems, Africa must tap into her inner and outer, building on nature, culture and spirituality, in addition to technology and science.

The world is heading back to the south: to nature and culture—to its roots. The planet and its people are living in times of major change. Our very survival is dependent on raising the collective consciousness of humanity, on shifting from conflict and war to love and compassion. In order to do this, we need to unite the old with the new, north with south, indigenous with exogenous. We need to look at the past to learn lessons that will help us to face the future with stronger hope, not to be stuck in the past. The richness of the ages must be drawn together to create a synergy that utilises the accumulated knowledge of ancient tradition, religion and science, while also embracing modern exogenous knowledge. As we evolve, rather than dismiss that which went before, respect must be cultivated for traditions that have stood the test of time. The ability to form a creative synergy, *Afrikologically* so to speak, between doing and being, thinking and doing, science and spirituality, business and ecology, nature and culture, is the hallmark of the integral enterprise.

9.7. References

1 **Morwenna**, L (2008) *The Early Church*. New York: I B Tauris & Co Ltd.
2 **The Jerusalem Bible** (1974) London: Darton, Longman and Todd.
3 **Lössl**, J (2009) *The Early Church: History and Memory*. Edinburgh: T& T Clark
4 **Bradshaw**, P (2008) *Daily Prayer in the Early Church: A Study of the Origin and Early Development of the Divine Office*. Oregon: Wipf and Stock.
5 **Glazier**, M (2003*) Who is Jesus? An Introduction to Christology*. New York: Michael Glazier Books.
6 **Akin**, D (2015) *Christology: The Study of Christ*. New York: Rainer Publishing (March 11, 2015)
7 *ibid.*
8 **The Rule of St Benedict** (2008) London: Penguin Classics.
9 **Dix**, Dom G (2015) *The Shape of the Liturgy*. Edinburgh: T&T Clark.
10 **Gennep**, A (2019) *The Rites of Passage*. Chicago: University of Chicago Press.
11 **Thomassen**, B (2018) *Liminality and the Modern*. London: Routledge.
12 **Turner**, V (1995) *The Ritual Process: Structure and Anti-Structure*. London: Aldine Transaction.
13 **Van Gennep**, A (op.cit)
14 **Turner**, V (op. cit).
15 **Adodo**, A (2017) *Integral Community Enterprise in Africa. Communitalism as an Alternative to Capitalism*. London: Routledge.
16 **Otto**, R (1958) *The Idea of the Holy*. London: Oxford University Press.
17 **Barnes**, J (2002) *Early Greek Philosophy*. London: Penguin
18 **Waterfield**, R (1996) *The first Philosophers: The Presocratics and Sophists*. Oxford, UK: Oxford University Press.
19 **Barnes**, J (2002) *Aristotle: A very Short Introduction*. London: Oxford University Press.
20 **Chevalier**, J & **Buckles**, D (2013) *Participatory Action Research: Theory and Methods for Engaged Inquiry*. London: Routledge.
21 **Emery**, K (1996) *Monastic, Scholastic and Mystical Theologies from the Later Middle Ages*. Rugby, UK: Variorum.
22 **Fals**, B & **Rahman**, M (1991) *Action and Knowledge*. Lanham, Maryland: Rowman & Littlefield.
23 **Natou**, T, **Bonazzi**, M & **Benatouil**, T (eds.) (2012) *Theoria, Praxis, and the Contemplative Life After Plato and Aristotle*. Leiden, Netherlands: Brill Academic Publishers.
24 **Clark**, J (2011) *The Benedictines in the Middle Ages*. London: Boydel Press
25 **Janniak**, A (2015) *Newton*. New Jersey: Wiley-Blackwell.
26 **Jolley**, N (2005) *Leibniz*. London: Penguin.
27 **Kant**, E (2005) *Critique of Pure Reason*. London: Penguin.
28 **Lefevre**, W (2013) *Between Leibniz, Newton, and Kant: Philosophy And Science in the Eighteenth Century*. Mineola, USA: Springer.
29 **Scruton**, R (2001) *A short History of Modern Philosophy: From Descartes to Wittgenstein*. London: Routledge.

30 **Dewey**, J (2012) *Human Nature and Conduct*. Boston, MA: Digi reads

31 **Dewey**, J (1998) *Experience and Nature*. Mineola: Dover Press.

32 **Lessem**, R, **Adodo**, A, **Bradley**, T (2019) *The Idea of the Communiversity*. Manchester: Beacon Academic Press.

33 **Adodo**, A (2013) *Nature Power. Natural Medicine in Tropical Africa*. London: AuthorHouse. pg.1

34 **Adodo**, op.cit

35 **Adodo**, op.cit

36 **Adodo**, A (2003) *The Healing Radiance of the Soul. A Guide to Holistic Healing*. Lagos: Agelex Prints.

37 **Adodo**, A (2005) *New Frontiers in African Medicine*. Lagos: Metropolitan Press

38 **Adodo** (2005) (op.cit.) p. 98

39 **Adodo**, (2005). (op.cit) p. 100

40 **The Rule of St Benedict** (2010) Nigerian reprint. Chap 57. P. 77–78. Umuoji: Jazuka press.

41 **Swan**, L (2007) *The Benedictine Tradition*. Minnesota: The Liturgical Press.

42 **Pope Francis** (2015) *Laudato Si – On Care for Our Common Home*. Indiana: Our Sunday Visitor, P. 53

43 **Staudt**, J (2018) *The Beer Option: Brewing A Catholic Culture, yesterday & today*. New York: Angelico press.

PART SEVEN

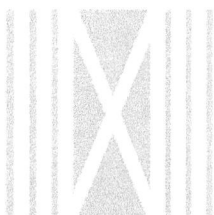

Re-Centering and Re-Gen**e**-Ration

Chapter 10

Deconstructing and Reconstructing
Knowledge and Value Out of Africa

> Our overall argument is that no society, hitherto, has pursued integral
> advantage, though some may have done so more than others. Indeed,
> we have been so blinded by the singularly economic logic of compara-
> tive advantage, that integral advantage has been severely inhibited.

Ronnie Lessem (1) *Integral Advantage: Emerging Economies
and Societies*

10.1. Introduction

10.1.1. Deconstructing and Reconstructing Southern African Management

We now come to the concluding chapter of this work, where we revisit and
renew our transformation journey in and around Africa, drawing on African
origins but reaching out to the world as a whole. Our overall intent, is to deconstruct and reconstruct knowledge and value, out of Africa, starting out in
the African "south" and venturing forth from there.

Some five years ago then, in South Africa where, until then and over
the course of the 1990s, one of us, Ronnie Lessem, had committed himself
most consistently to pursuing societal transformation, historically as part of
an African Management Program together with significant others (notably
Zimbabwean Rainmaker Lovemore Mbigi, Cashbuild's CEO Albert Koopman,
and Director of Wits Graduate Business School Nick Binedell), we, that is

then Trans4m, were asked to run a so-called transformation program for the University of Johannesburg (UJ), one of the country's largest academic establishments. Interestingly enough, as we saw in chapter 6, this was much further evolved, subsequently, through Anselm Adodo's Transformation Masters program, linked with Ibadan University Institute for African Studies in Nigeria.

For some two decades after the birth of the newly independent South Africa, universities still remained essentially, in our (2) view, colonized by the neo/liberal—not neo/associative as we shall see—"west". Interestingly enough, in the early 1990s, Ronnie as an Afro-*European,* now indeed wearing his European hat, had been asked by an Indian colleague Jagdish Parikh (3), renowned for his individually "transformative" work with corporations on *managing the self,* to do similar work for IMD (The Institute for Management Development) in Switzerland, following our prior *European Management Project* sponsored by Germany's Roland Berger Foundation. In this case, while IMD was seeking to climb on an "eastern" if not also "north-western" *transformational leadership* bandwagon, we immediately saw the opportunity, that is IMD's Director General, Chilean born Juan Rada, and Ronnie Lessem, to emancipate this "northern" European institution from alien "east-west" clutches.

10.1.2. Deconstructing and Reconstructing *European* Management Systems

The upshot was our (4) work on *European Management Systems,* philosophically and culturally, as well as economically and managerially encompassing the UK (west) and France (north), Germany (east) and Italy (south). Thereby, and in parallel, Ronnie (see chapter 6) introduced a first version of their *Integral* topography or societal rhythm, spanning *Images* (Core), *Ideologies* (Bedrock), *Institutions* (Subsoil or Branches) and *Inclinations* (Topsoil or Roots), in fact societally recasting Carl Jung's (5) model of the human psyche, applied to each respective European world.

In that context, he was grounding management and economics in European soils, something until then IMD had been failing to do, despite its glorious location in Lausanne, Switzerland, at the very heart of Europe, so colonized was it by the proverbial "north-west". Indeed, as a graduate of Harvard Business School myself, I knew very well where their standardized approach to management generally, and to their MBA specifically, had been coming from.

10.1.3. Comparative to Integral Advantage

Taking the prior South African request seriously, and as the management faculty with which we were working were developing a new masters program focused on *Emerging Markets,* very much in conventional guise, Ronnie proposed in 2014 that we use this new program as a platform for transformation. Thereby South Africa, as one of the emerging market BRICS, alongside Brazil, Russia, India and China, would be reconceived in our *integral* light, whereby an "emerging" technology and economy built purposefully on the nature and culture of each of the BRICS, rather then merely on comparative "economic" advantage.

Ironically, the book he then wrote on *Integral Advantage: Emerging Economies and Societies,* as intimated in the opening quote above, drawing on the nature and culture, as well as the technology and enterprise of each of the five countries, most especially on that fully integral topography of South Africa, ended up not at the University of Johannesburg but at the Nelson Mandela Foundation, supposedly by accident, but in all probability by deliberate intent.

That is how seriously the university took transformation! That is despite the fact that several of the faculty were aware of our (6) previous *South African Management* project in the 1990s, when we sought, indeed for the first time in that country, to uncover *African Management Principles, Concepts and Applications.* Interestingly enough, and analogously hitherto, in our previous IMD case in the 1990s, all of the management faculty staged a revolt when they heard they might be weaned away from their much beloved American cases.

So Ronnie's IMD colleague Frans Newbauer and he completed our *European Management Systems,* only because the institution's Chilean Director General, Juan Rada, retained his support for our work, in splendid isolation (Ronnie was relegated to a portocabin in IMDs driveway). This was all because I had maintained that, in Switzerland, they had more to learn from their own renowned psychologists, and social scientists, Carl Jung and Jean Piaget, in pursuit of individual, organisational and societal individuation, than from the highly fashionable Californian management gurus at the time, Peters and Waterman (7) *In Search of Excellence.*

Indeed, in both Africa and also European instances Ronnie made the case that, in our own *integral* terms, to be revealed in our (8) version of *Transformation Management: Toward the Integral Enterprise,* both Smith (capitalism) and Marx (communism), with their economic and technological pre-emphasis, had got it wrong. Neither the division of labour (Smith) nor economic determinism (Marx) offered, for us, integrally as such, a viable way forward for either the "south" or the "north". At the time, both in the mid nineties (IMD) and then two decades later, in 2015 (UJ) neither academic institution, as a whole, was ready to listen. Notwithstanding, or indeed because of such, the idea of an Integral *Topography* (1993) and thereafter an integral *Communiversity* (2019) were born.

10.1.4. Pursuing Integral Advantage: Societal Re-GENE-eration (SRG)

SRG: Releasing a Society's Genius

As such, Ronnie totally rejected the classical economic notion of "comparative advantage", because it focuses exclusively on *economic* advantage, in isolation of nature, culture and society, and what we term an all round "polity" (9) that serves to align each of such, altogether. It is that individual and societal all-roundedness that we will allude to, as *integral* advantage, bearing in mind that, on the one hand, *the west needs the east, the north needs the south, and they need each other, altogether;* and on the other hand *each and every society needs to build on its own local grounds, albeit that thereafter, in order to evolve, the local and the global need to interact.* That is what we mean by integral advantage.

Pursuing an Integral Rhythm

What, for us then, is qualitatively new, and thereby truly *emergent*, can only be found if we go beyond economics per se, and if you like the comparative *economic* advantage of each BRICS nation. In effect we need to uncover the *integral* advantage underlying each. In other words, we need to reveal the emerging nature, culture, society and economy of each "polity" as a whole, that is, for us, the source of its overall integrity.

So we argue that the fate of Greece or Slovenia (10) in Europe today, or indeed a Zimbabwe or South Africa (11), is determined, by and large, by the extent to which each can be enabled to pursue what we term its integral rhythm or topography (12), locally and naturally grounding, locally-globally and culturally emerging, newly globally and socially/scientifically navigating, and thereafter globally-locally economically effecting: altogether then serving to release its genius. That is no easy task, and currently there is no field of study, or agency in society, to integrally promote such. Hence the need for an integral Communiversity, to facilitate such.

Instead of the Part Dominating the Whole

For us then the pursuit of *integral advantage is not dependent on relative factor costs, and thereby economic specialization that follows, but on the overall uniqueness, and authenticity, of each society,* in itself and in relation to the wider world. Most if not all societies are inhibited, both internally and externally, from realizing such. Instead, one society tends to dominate over another, and prevent itself, or the other, from realizing itself as a whole. Alternatively one part of a particular society is dominant over others, whereby development, as a whole, is inhibited. As a result you might have poverty, autocracy, environmental decay, or another such malfunction, as such a part dominates the whole, both internally and/or externally. In short, the society, altogether, is disintegrating, to some degree or another.

Moreover, because all too often "western-northern" concepts and institutions—set apart from while dominating over the world as a whole—like free markets or liberal democracy have become so all pervasive, a particular society, be it Egypt or Ireland, is inhibited from *emerging*. Integral development, centered in middle-up-down-across guise, needs to arise initially and locally from the ground (core or roots) up: naturally and communally as such, and subsequently develop, culturally and spiritually (cultural bedrock and mainstem) and locally-globally so to speak, outgrowing its prior parochial self.

So, Libya or Lebanon, for example, disintegrate on the one hand, once supposedly released from its despotic shackles, because each is not enabled to emerge in such integral guise. Greece and Spain implode on the other hand, as each has done of late, because austerity may bite, and such austerity does nothing to help each uncover and release their overall, societally based integral advantage. Indeed, there is no integral agency—certainly neither for example IMF nor EU—to promote such. And we are by no means the first ones, societally, to be thinking that way.

Deep Brotherhood and the Group Soul

Firstly then for the Indian sage Sri Aurobindo (13), early last century each society, he claimed, develops into a sort of sub-soul or group-soul of our humanity and develops also a type of mind, thereby evolving governing ideas and tendencies that shape its life and institutions. The group-soul works out its tendencies through a diversity of opinions, wills, and diversity of lives. The vitality of its group-life as a national whole depends on such. A deeper brotherhood between nations, a yet unfound law of love is the only sure foundation possible for a perfect social evolution.

Senghor's Civilization of the Universal

Secondly, for the African poet-statesman Leopold Senghor (14), who was president of the Senegal in the 1970s, beyond the objective of material well-being, man aspires to fuller being, to that of his spiritual needs, especially in Black Africa and the developing nations. Africans hunger not so much for American or Russian surpluses, Senghor maintains, as after independence, dignity, science and culture: as after *love-in-union*. Such a love-in-union he identified as "the civilization of the universal" representing a symbiosis of different civilizations.

Co-Evolutionary Revisioning of Development

For geographer and environmentalist Richard Norgaard (15), based in California, and writing his work *Development Betrayed* in the 1980s, a co-evolutionary, as opposed to mechanical, competitive or even cooperative, theory, builds on the idea that species and other system components have a variety of traits that are context specific, and change over time, rather than being universal. For these reasons, co-evolutionary thinking is totally different from cause-and-effect thinking. In fact, co-evolutionary models of systems can be thought of as endogenously providing change from within, thereby developmental, rather than exogenously from without, as per development. Through this process, the world can be thought of as having become a patchwork quilt of loosely interconnected, co-evolving social, economic and ecological systems.

10.1.5. Towards a Neo-Associative Economics

Global Economy to Partnership in Economic Life

In the new millennium, in his book *Finance at the Threshold: Rethinking the Real and Financial Economies* the concomitant of a single global economy today, for Christopher Houghton Budd (16), a follower of Rudolf Steiner and founder of the Centre for Associative Economics in Britain, will be a choir of cultures, each able to sound its own note but able also to include the tones of others. Indeed such was very resonant with the overall, Afrikological approach we have adopted here, albeit for Budd starting out from the UK. He makes the case that ever since World War I, this potential has existed and that overlooking, or avoiding, such has been the cardinal feature of humanity's economic affairs ever since.

What as such, for him then, should be the next "big idea", Budd then asks, in money and finance in the 21st century? Such an idea of a commonwealth is that of a single global economy shared and mutually governed by a choir of the world's peoples. No one country or people or way of life should impose itself on any other, meaning that Anglo-Saxon dominance would need to give way to promoting economic partnership between peoples, but also that the people around the world would need to identify a future true to their own development, not merely a reaction to past domination.

Human beings everywhere need to give true expression to their deeper destinies and purposes. It could be added that in such a choir of cultures, for Houghton Budd, it will nevertheless be a feature of *the English contribution* that it *will appear in economic form. In particular, it will appear as shifting from possession of the global economy to partnership in economic life.*

Sekem as a Marriage Between the Occident and the Orient

In fact such partnership, or more specifically association, is the nub of the associative economics we are seeking to co-evolve, in particular natural and cultural contexts, also encompassing the "four-folding" approach spearheaded by Ibrahim Abouleish (17) and Sekem in Egypt (as we saw in chapter 8), as a marriage between the occident (anthroposophy) and the orient (Islam). Indeed we have been closely associated with Sekem for over a decade. It has been a source of ongoing inspiration, not only as a natural, cultural, social and economic alternative to "homo economics", but as a means of "re-imaginal rural", as an integral alternative to industrialised, urbanised, modernised, globalised development.

Beyond Sustainable Development

A decade ago, then, Alexander Schieffer and Ronnie Lessem (18) wrote our book on *Integral Economics: Releasing the Economic Genius of your Society.* Our *integral* orientation, as such, was towards a respectively "southern" (community based self sufficiency), "eastern" (culture based developmental economy), "northern" (knowledge based social economy), and "western" (life based living economy).

This book, in turn, built upon our (19) prior work on the *Transformation Management: Toward the Integral Enterprise,* which introduced the transform-ational GENE, underlying, in this current work, on deconstruction and reconstruction out of Africa, through local Grounding, local-global Emergence, newly global Navigation and global-local Effect, in both cyclical and linear (altogether spiraling) turn. The integral enterprise encompassed then, analogous to integral economics, "southern" community building (self-sufficiency), "eastern" conscious evolution (developmental economy), "northern" knowledge creation (social economy) and "western" sustainable development (living economy) respectively.

Where we were in fact mistaken, at the time of writing in 2010, now looking back with our current hindsight, is that we positioned Rudolf Steiner's *Associative Economics* in the "east", whereas we now see such a *neo-associative* economy, and indeed enterprise, in the "west-and-center", that is a *west that builds on the rest,* as indeed part of a nature based "living economy". Indeed as we intimated in *Transformation Management* as a prelude to our integral version of "western" sustainable development:

> In the last two decades (now three decades), there has been a new development spearheaded from the "west", in physics and biology as well as in management, towards what has been termed "self-organizing systems",

where the emphasis has been less upon free enterprise, than upon "living systems". In the process, "self-making" or indeed a "self-organizing universe" takes over from "self-help". The so-called "natural laws" of the "market mechanism" are now overtaken by the neo-associative laws of natural life.

All of such has a direct bearing on the "southern" primordial wisdom, of the Dogon, African peoples, if not also the ancient Egyptian approach to regeneration (see chapter 3), not to mention also Sekem, and the vitality (chapter 8) of the sun. In that reconstrcuted sense, we are saying, there is an altenative "west", which builds on the rest.

America's Global Responsibility

More specifically, for Israeli anthroposophist and kibbutznik, Jeremiah Ben Aharon (20), in his seminal work on *America's Global Responsibility:*

> This kind of economy brings forth the stems, branches, leaves, and fruits of political and cultural life as naturally as a fruit grows in its wholeness from healthy seed and fertile soil. Legislation, human rights, arts and culture, religion and science receive unmistakeable ecological and communal meaning in the new economy ... the American economy, grasped in this sense, bears in itself the sources of vital cultural and spiritual reality, because it is rooted in the native American talent to use generously the gifts of great Mother Nature. Life then is a perpetual process of becoming, evolution and transformation. This is the potentially unique contribution of the "west" to global culture.

10.1.6. Re-imagining Rural: Towards Pax Africana

Sekem: A Sustainable Community in the Egyptian Desert

We now turn back to Sekem itself, and ultimately to the overall theme of "re-imagining rural", by way of deconstructing industrialization and modernization, an reconstructing knowledge and value out of rural Africa. It is in fact nature, as we shall see by way of transformative *Effect* illustrated by Sekem as such an associative enterprise in Egypt, which has been an ongoing source of inspiration to us, which turns Steiner's (21) original "threefold"—cultural, political, economic—into a "fourfold", thereby also natural, and altogether *fourfold* integral, enterprise. In fact, Sekem's rural origins, in the Egyptian desert, were by no means unique to the integral enterprises with which we, at Trans4m, had been engaged in the new millennium.

Integral Community Enterprise in Africa: Communitalism versus Capitalism

More specifically moreover, one of us, Anselm Adodo (22), as we saw in chapter 9, founded Pax Herbals in rural Nigeria, born out of *nature power* generally, as an amalgam of clinical and community health, nature and economy, as thereby an *Integral Community Enterprise in Africa. Communitalism as an Alternative to Capitalism*. Pax Herbals, in association with Adodo's Benedictine Monastery, his Ewo community, and the Ibadan University Institute for Africa studies was also the birthplace of our (23) *Idea of the Communiversity,* duly constituting a 21st century *Pax Africana* out of four elements: Pax Communis, Pax Spritus, Pax Scientia and Pax Economica.

Nhakanomics: Harvesting Knowledge and Value for Regeneration

Moreover, and overall, the term *Re-Imagine Rural* emerged from Zimbabwe, via Dr Douglas Mbowene (24), who kindly gave the Preface to this volume. Douglas, and his company *Econet*, featured in our book *Nhakanomics: Harvesting Knowledge and Value for Regeneration through Social Innovation,* are heavily engaged in the rural areas, through their internet services. At the same time Mbowene, like our Zimbawean colleague Daud Shumba Taranhike, are developing their own *kumusha*s (indigenous term for homestead) in their rural areas, to become sources of such "nhakanomics", whereby *nhaka* signifies natural and cultural "legacy". And then finally, from the "southern" British Isles this time, came our most recent wake-up call, in Ireland no less, via the *Irish Agricultural Organisation Society,* which originated in the 1880s.

Ireland in the New Century: Irish Agricultural Organisation (Cooperative) Society

An economically "backward" Ireland, at the turn of the last century, was engaged in a battle for independence from the colonial power, Great Britain. That said, culturally and at the same time, it had gained worldwide repute, as the home of such renowned literary figures as the modernists WB Yeats, James Joyce and Samuel Beckett. By the new millennium, a century later, also following the notable "Good Friday Declaration" peace deal in Northern Ireland, Southern Ireland had gained its new economic reputation as the "Celtic Tiger". What was virtually unknown to the world was the way, early last century, it had been uniquely able to *re-imagine rural* in duly associative guise. The chief architects behind such were a Protestant aristocrat, Sir Horace Plunkett, and a Catholic artist and social activist, AE Russell.

For Horace Plunkett (25), who established the Irish Agricultural Organisation Society in 1884, as he put it in *Ireland in the New Century*:

> The English mind quite failed, until the very end of the 19th century, to grasp the real needs of the situation which had been created in Ireland. The industrial revolution found the Irish people fettered by an industrial past for which they themselves were not chiefly responsible. They needed exceptional treatment of a kind that was not conceded. They were, instead, still further handicapped, towards the middle of the century, by the adoption of Free Trade (for us modelled on an individualized "economic man"), which was imposed on them when they were not only unable to take advantage of its benefits, but were so communally situated as to suffer to the utmost of its inconveniences.

Such a misunderstanding was due not to heartlessness or contempt so much as to a lack of imagination. The English had as such "standardised" (for us universalised) their unacknowledged "particular English" qualities, and they could not get out of their minds the belief that divergence, in another race, from their standard of character, was synonymous with inferiority. Debarred from every other trade and industry then, historically, the entire Irish nation flung itself back to the land. Moreover a system of land tenure had been imposed by the English on Ireland devised for the purpose of perpetuating and accentuating every possible disability.

And what was the way forward? This is where Plunkett's artistic, and transformative "comrade in arms", so to speak, AE Russell (26), came in. Indeed, in Africa, the likes of a Leopold Senghor, for example, combined poet and statesman in one, albeit he found it difficult to hold that overall balance.

The Irish Farmer, for all his Economic Backwardness, has a Soul

For Russell the farmer's agriculture in Ireland then is largely traditional. It varied little in the 19th century from the 18th, and the beginning of the 20th century saw little change in spite of the establishment of a huge government department of agriculture. The farmer might be described almost as the primitive economic cave-man, the darkness of the cave unillumined by any ray of general principles. But farmer Patrick, so to speak, for all his economic backwardness, has a soul. The culture of the Gaelic poets and storytellers, while not often actually remembered, still lingers like a fragrance about his mind.

Farmer Patrick then, for Russell, must be led out of his economic cave: his low cunning in barter must be expanded into a knowledge of economic law— his fanatical concentration on his family begotten by isolation and the individualism of his life must be sublimated into national affections; his unconscious depths be sounded, his feeling for beauty be awakened by contact with some of the great literature of the world. His mind is virgin soil, and we may hope that like all virgin soil it will be immensely fruitful when cultivated. Discussing the business of his association with others, moreover, he becomes something of a practical economist. His horizon is no longer bound by the wave of blue hills beyond his village. The roar of the planet begins to sound in his ears.

Ireland has hitherto been to Patrick a legend, a being mentioned in romantic poetry, a little dark Rose, a mystic maiden, a vague but very simple creature of tears and aspirations and revolts. He now knows what a multitudinous being a nation is, and in contact with its complexities Patrick's politics take on a new gravity, thoughtfulness and intellectual character. Under the influence of these associations and the ideas pervading them our typical Irish farmer gets drawn out of his agricultural sleep of the ages, developing rapidly as a mummy brought out of the tomb and exposed to eternal forces which stimulate and bring to life.

Towards an Inclusive Knowledge Economy

Ultimately, as a bridge between culture and economy, the old and the new, for the Brazilian American polymath based at Harvard Law School, Roberto Mangabeira Unger (27) the Ricardian approach to comparative advantage, deals in the coin of static efficiency. This tells us nothing then about the adjacent possible, as for example for Plunkett and Russell in the rural Irish case.

The political divisions within mankind in fact, of which the existence of sovereign states is a merely special case, for Unger, offer expanding opportunities for diversity of experience, vision, organisation and action. The most compelling justification of their separate existence is that they can represent a form of moral specialization within humanity, embodying and developing distinct forms of life and consciousness. The existence of separate states—or of any other political division of humanity that might take its place—is a permanent inducement to diversity of economic arrangements as well as of other non-economic institutions and practices.

Re-imagining Rural: Societal Re-GENE-ration through Economic Association

More specifically, and more recently for Unger (28) then, as born out of his *inclusive* version of a *Knowledge Economy,* duly inspired by the modernist literary traditions, especially coming from Ireland, *imagination* and *cooperation* become the keynotes of such. Indeed for him the monolithic form of neo-liberal economy is a total anathema, given the myriad of alternatives that can be cooperatively imagined, which we term *neo-associative.* To bring these to life we now turn to our own integral approach to Societal Re-GENE-ration of a particular society, which underlies our proposed post-doctoral program: *Re-imagining Rural: Deconstructing and Reconstructing Knowledge and Value out of Africa.*

10.2. Deconstructing and Reconstructing Knowledge and Value

We now turn from such a transformational flow, rooted in nature, to our own interpretation of such, embedded more specifically in our GENE. To illustrate the proximity of both rhythms, formative to transformative and our GENE, we incorporated the GENE (grounding, emerging, navigating, effecting).

10.3. The Reconstructive GENE

10.3.1. GENE to GENE-I-U-S

gene/I-U-S

The GENE is set in motion by both an inner spark (centering), an initiation of an individual or a community, who either experience an internal impulse for growth, change or transformation which is calling for internal integration, and also an unfolding outer organisational or societal impulse. In any case, it is this initial tension between the particular I (moral Inspiration drawn from a particular world e.g. Nigeria/Yoruba) and the general (Universal truth drawn from all worlds south and east, north and west), duly Synergized (e.g. Afrikology as a whole) that initiates the transformation, or re-GENE-ration process, and which, by working its way through the four stages, cyclically and linearly—hence spiraling—helps to release the full gene-I-U-S of the living system.

GENE-ius

Local Grounding then, represents the first point of stabilization, in one society or another, for economy and society in turn. As the environment changes something has to give, creating the impetus for transformation and impulse comes from both the inside (indigenous) and the outside (exogenous). This is the dynamic, local-global Emergent process that follows the stabilizing grounding stage. There is dissolution of the old, for without an opening to change through the influence of an internal or external agency, there is simply no transformational flow. The axis needs to spin out of its original moorings in order for the transformation to emerge as a process.

After the first two G-E stages of grounding and emerging, the process now has to evolve to a stage where it forms itself as a "newly global" Navigating entity. Interestingly enough, and in the Irish case, this may be a "newly global" authentic *west*, born out of the old "western mystery stream". Without this process of explicit articulation the transformation process remains incomplete.

Finally, the fourth Effecting strand is the one that builds on the previous three stages, manifesting itself practically, globally-locally as such. Moreover, the four stages are alternatively stabilizing (grounding and navigation) and dynamic (emergence and effecting), one following the other rhythmically, in both cyclical and liner fashion.

FIGURE 10.1.
DECONSTRUCTION, RECONSTRUCTION, REGENERATION

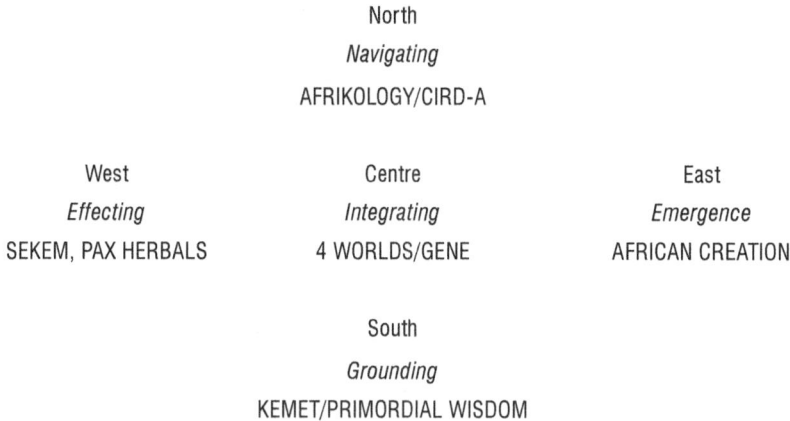

North

Navigating

AFRIKOLOGY/CIRD-A

West   Centre   East

Effecting   *Integrating*   *Emergence*

SEKEM, PAX HERBALS   4 WORLDS/GENE   AFRICAN CREATION

South

Grounding

KEMET/PRIMORDIAL WISDOM

We now follow each part of the integral rhythm of the GENE in turn.

10.3.2. The Transformational GENE

"Southern" Grounding: Local Identity: Kemet/Primordial Wisdom

The ultimate goal of societal re-GENE-ration is to evolve local identity—for yourself and community, organisation and society—towards a form of authentic global integrity. To begin with, you reach into the grounds of your individual and communal being, and that of your organisation or specific society, lodged to begin with in nature and community, be it as such for a Sekem (Kemet) or a Pax Herbals (Primordial Wisdom of Africa). As such:

- *Natural and communal* value provides the local *ground* for everything produced or offered
- Such value *gives a sense of purpose* to structures, systems and processes
- Value *enhances the identity* for those within and without a particular society
- Value *preserves the nature* of a community, organisation or society through overall consensus building

- At their best, *value-based* communities and societies are visionary centered, characterized by a powerful contribution to society, and vice versa; at their worst they are parochial, even corrupt.

"Eastern" Emergence: Local-Global Non-Entity: African Creation Energy/ Creativity and Conversationalism

Well-grounded, traditional leaders, enterprises, communities and societies, while strongly rooted in particular values, have a static, conserving quality to them. When confronted with modernizing forces, they tend to become either corrupted or subordinated. Rather than drawing upon the GENE, so as to deconstruct and reconstruct knowledge and value, they invariably get caught up in, or seek to catch up with, the "western-northern" mainstream.

As we loosen our socialized grip on our longstanding value grounds, or indigenous source, we need to open up to what is locally-globally emerging around us, and thereby renew the past, with a view to creating a future out of it; for example in the Sekem case the marriage of the occident and the orient, in the Pax Herbals case the fusion between community and clinical medicine, in altogether creative conservation, as an expression of African creative energy. Local-global "emergence", as a chrysalis in this case, whereby a locally grounded entity becomes an emergent local-global, thereby "non-entity", can be described as follows:

- Emergence stimulates the transformative journey, in which structures and systems develop and evolve cross-catalytically. It involves processes of destruction and creation, and an intermittent and discontinuous, but *flowing wholeness,* lodged within an interconnected, unbounded field.
- The emergent, *far-from-equilibrium* developments give rise to a new *dynamic balance*, weaving together, past and future, indigenous and exogenous, one philosophy with another; destroying static concepts of structures and systems, leading to a new order, born out of the renewed old one.
- Such emergent processes are therefore *destabilising;* they creatively "undo" the rigid structures of the conventional "west" and orderly systems of the "north", so that a subsequently *raised consciousness and renewed culture* arises.
- What emerges is not merely what happens between structures and systems; on the contrary, processes work around and through structures, making them *porous and permeable,* continually open to new possibilities.

- Without such conscious evolution, an organisation or society remains disconnected and abstract; processes *undo* predetermined notions of order and procedure.
- At their best, process-driven, emergent communities, individuals, organisations, societies, are dynamic, highly *innovative* entities; at their worst they are disorderly and chaotic.

"Northern" Navigation: "Newly Global" Entity: Afrikology/CIRD-A

Northern consolidation, combination, or conceptualisation involves the establishment of newly evolved communities, institutions, or indeed whole societies, evoked out of what has hitherto emerged. Characteristically systematically ordered and intricately patterned, as a newly forged synthesis between the local and the global, tradition and modernity, in our case as a newly global Academy, lodged in Africa, as per CIRD/A:

- Profound theories lead your organisation or society to become a *complex system or network,* rather than a simple structure, with interconnected patterns and relationships.
- Systems enhance the notion of order by connecting individual points into linear and *cross-linear relationships;* such systematic linkages serve to enhance predictability, order and control.
- Without such "newly global" social and economic systems, societal structures lacking coherence and authenticity; rather, born out of prior grounding and emergence, integral *systems give direction* to both structure and imagination.
- Such systems and frameworks use a higher order *synthesis* whereby local thesis and global antithesis are combined; problems and conflicts are addressed through attempts at realizing *consensus.*
- At their best, such rationally and systematically based entities *are ethical,* serving to 'do right', with a collective benefit to all; at the worst they become overly regimented.

We finally turn to a "west" that duly builds on the rest, not something that we see in the conventional "north-western" wisdom, whereby such a conventional worldview stands in isolation form the rest.

Western Effect: Achieving Global-Local Integrity: Sekem and Pax Herbals

To realise "western" efficiency and effectiveness certain culminating steps are necessary, to actualize the local/local-global/global/global-local integral rhythm.

Such analytically based order, integrally as such, needs to build associatively on all that has come before. The net result, each of which has proved to be both sustainable and transformative over several decades, is a Sekem in Egypt or a Pax Herbals in Nigeria, whereby:

- Structure building requires us to perceive any strategy, as an *assembly of parts*, like in a machine. It further requires making use of inductive logic, to build up your strategy.
- The structural world is highly differential—categories are created instinctively inside the structure giving a preliminary *sense of order* to the strategic activity.
- Clearly laid-out categories, including a *clear set of aims*, making focus easy, coupled with an easy internalization of knowledge.
- Structures are built on *convergent logic*: for every problem, there is one solution; every cause one effect; there is one way to do a particular thing well, thereby adding value.
- At their best, clearly structured activities lend themselves to effective *problem solving*, with clearly defined sections to each, neatly delegated functions, supervision and monitoring of all required tasks; at worst narrow and rigid.

10.4. Conclusion: Re-Imagining Rural

10.4.1. In Faltering BRICS Retrospect

In retrospect, now some 5 years since *Integral Advantage* was published, we note that only two of the BRICS—China and India—are still on the economic rise, though both somewhat problematically, because of their dictatorial political regimes, not to mention the ever growing inequality in each case. In the three other cases—Russia, Brazil, South Africa—economic development has stalled, Russia remains a dictatorship, and Brazil has a newly populist, unsavoury political regime. So the original BRICS so-called emergent case is altogether problematic, to say the least, indeed we would argue because they have not followed the integrally GENE-tic path laid out above.

Specifically, Brazil is cutting down the rainforests, and thereby its, and the worlds, natural heritage. Russia pays no heed whatsoever, culturally and spiritually, to its indigenous "cosmism" (29), having lurched from pseudo-communism to hyper-capitalism. India rides roughshod over its indigenous, if not also Muslim, peoples. China is now becoming something of a pariah state, worldwide, notwithstanding its growing economic power. South Africa has been patently unable, institutionally, politically and economically, to build on its Mandela legacy. So while there has been some degree of economic—albeit inegalitarian—emergence, especially in China and India, in our integral terms the BRICS have floundered, and it is for us now, in our one society or another, to promote such integral emergence, naturally and culturally, technologically, wherever we are.

Specifically, for us, then, and unlike the cases of Pax Herbals and Sekem, for example, building on prior African grounds, and emerging locally-globally, if not newly globally (e.g. Pax Africana in the Pax Herbals case), the BRICS have proceeded to industrialize, to modernize, and to urbanize, rather than to re-imagine rural, building technology and enterprise on prior on nature and culture, thereby deconstructing (industrialization) and reconstructing knowledge and value, whether out of Africa, Brazil, China, India or Russia.

10.4.2. Re-imagine Rural: Societal Reconstruction via a Communiversity

In the final analysis, with a view to *Re-imaging Rural,* worlds-wide, as an alternative, middle-up-down-across *neo-associative* approach to top down capitalism or communism, locally, locally-globally, *newly globally* and globally-locally, seek to overturn modernization, urbanization, industrialization and globalization. Arguably such a "neo-associative" approach is thereby trans-modern, serving to co-evolve pre-modern, modern and post-modern worlds.

The means to that end is communal, individual, inter-institutional, and societal, via a post-doctoral program aligned with an integral communiversity. As such, you as an individual continue on your *transformation journey,* post PhD/ PHD, from Call to Contribution, locally and globally. As such, you secondly co-engage locally and CARE-fully, with one, or more, *learning communities.* Thirdly, and critically, you build up your *socio-economic laboratory,* be it a Pax Herbals or a Sekem, each of which is rurally based, so it functions middle-up-down-across to develop a communally based (nor communist) neo-associative (not capitalist) economy in your society, thereby *re-imagining rural.* Finally, through—and also as yourselves individually and institutionally in association with—TCA (Trans4m Communiversity Associates) we *newly globally* together develop an integral *research Academy,* that serves both to *articulate* and to *calibrate* our societies and economies, worlds-wide.

Finally, and as such, each participating individual and institution becomes a constituent, *associated* member of the *Academy for Neo-Associative Economics,* whereby TCA, as such, builds newly globally, on what has come locally— via communal learning, and locally-globally—via your transformation journey, before, with a view to its wider global-local laboratory based application, to altogether *Re-imagining Rural.* The milestones for deconstruction and reconstruction of knowledge and value as such, would be, both cyclically and linearly, in thereby spiraling guise:

- Building our Local Learning Communities
- Consolidating on our Local-Global Transformation Journeys
- Establishing the Newly Global Research Academy
- Re-imagining Rural Globally-Locally via our Socio-economic Laboratories

10.5. References

1   **Lessem** R (2015) *Integral Advantage: Emerging Economies and Societies.* Abingdon. Routledge
2   **Lessem** R, **Adodo** A, and **Bradley** T (2019) *The Idea of the Communiversity.* Manchester, beacon Academic
3   **Parikh** J (1994) *Managing Your Self: Management by Detached Involvement.* Chichester. Wiley-Blackwell
4   **Lessem** R and **Neubauer** F (1993) *European Management Systems.* Maidenhead. McGraw Hill
5   **Stevens** A (1991) *On Jung.* London. Penguin
6   **Christie** P, **Lessem** R and **Mbigi** L (1990) *African Management: Principles, Concepts and Applications.* Johannesburg. Knowledge Resources
7   **Peters** T and **Waterman** R (1982) *In Search of Excellence.* New York. HarperCollins
8   **Lessem** R and **Schieffer** (2009) *Transformation Management: Toward the Integral Enterprise.* Abingdon. Routledge
9   **Lessem** R, **Abouleish** I, **Pogacnik** M and **Herman** L (2015) *Integral Polity: Aligning Nature and Culture, Society and Economy.* Abingdon. Routledge
10 **Piciga** D, **Schieffer** A and **Lessem** R (2016) *Integral Green Slovenia.* Abingdon. Routledge
11 **Mamukwa** E, **Lessem** R and **Schieffer** A (2015) *integral green Zimbabwe.* Abingdon. Routledge
12 **Lessem** R and **Schieffer** A (2010) *Integral Research and Innovation.* Abingdon. Routledge
13 Sri **Aurobindo** (1950) *The Human Cycle.* Wisconsin. Twin Lakes.
14 **Coetzee** P. and **Roux** A. (2000) *Philosophy from Africa.* Oxford. Oxford University Press
15 **Noorgaard** R (1994) *Development Betrayed: The End of Progress and Co-evolutionary re-visioning of the Future.* London, Routledge
16 **Houghton Budd** C (2011) *Finance at the Threshold: Rethinking the Real and Financial Economies.* Farnham. Gower Research
17 **Abouleish** I (2005) *Sekem: A Sustainable Community in the Egyyptian Desert.* Edinburgh. Floris Publications
18 **Lessem** R and **Schieffer** (2010) *Integral Economics: Releasing the Economic Genius of your Society.* Abingdon. Routledge

19 **Lessem R** and **Schieffer** A (2009) *op cit*

20 **Ben Aharon** J (2002) *America's Global Responsibility.* Herndon. Lindisfarne

21 **Steiner** R (1977) *Towards Social Renewal.* Forest Row. Rudolph Steiner Press

22 **Adodo** A (2017) *Integral Community Enterprise in Africa. Communitalism as an Alternative to Capitalism.* Abingdon. Routledge

23 **Lessem** R, **Adodo** A and **Bradley** T (2019) *The Idea of the Communiversity.* Manchester. Beacon Academic

24 **Lessem** R, **Mawere** M and **Taranhike** D (2019) *Nhakanomics: Harvesting Knowledge and Value for Regeneration through Social Innovation.* Mazvingo. Africa Talent Publishers.

25 **Plunkett** H (1904) *Ireland's in the New Century.* London. John Murray

26 **Russell** *AE.* (2016) *The National Being: Some Thoughts on Irish Polity.* Chichester. Palala Press

27 **Unger** R (2007) *Free Trade Re-imagined: The World Division of Labor and the Method of Economics.* Princeton. Princeton Univ. Press

28 **Unger** T (2019) *The Knowledge Economy.* London. Verso

29 **Young** G (2012) *The Russian Cosmists.* Buckingham. Open University

Index

A

B

C

D

U

ubuntu xii, xvii, 20, 131, 132, 137, 174–176, 180
USA v, xv, xvi, 5, 6, 8, 13, 16–18, 34, 40, 53, 105, 114, 127, 144–147, 182, 242, 244, 258

V

vakamusha 169, 172, 173
Van der Post, Laurens 3, 6, 8, 16, 27
VISA 18–19

W

World War I 256

Y

Yoruba 81, 90, 93, 178, 236, 262

Z

Zimbabwe v, xi, xii, 6–9, 11, 21, 27, 126, 150, 158, 162–164, 170–175, 191, 254, 259

www.ingramcontent.com/pod-product-compliance
Lightning Source LLC
Chambersburg PA
CBHW020339270326

41926CB00007B/246